Jungian Analysis, Depth Psychology, and Soul

Thomas Kirsch is one of the foremost architects of the contemporary Jungian scene and has influenced the evolution and organization of analytical psychology worldwide. His works on the history of Jungian analysis and his memoir of a "Jungian life" have been widely appreciated, and this book contains important examples of these interests. Gathered together in *Jungian Analysis, Depth Psychology, and Soul* are Kirsch's original and humane contributions to diverse areas, such as: training and the dynamics of analytical institutions; clinical themes in Jungian analysis and how these differ from what typically happens in psychoanalytic treatment; as well as a continuation of his remarkable work into the personalities and prejudices that characterize the profession of Jungian analysis.

As Andrew Samuels observes in his foreword, "In these chapters, we see Tom's humanity, generosity, and flexibility". Given the multifarious dynamics of the training community, Kirsch accepts that things can sometimes go wrong, and he is open about his experiences in this regard. For Kirsch, rather than a simple question of psychologically damaged people becoming analysts, the figure of the "Wounded Healer" is always present in depth psychology.

Kirsch is an exceptionally gifted communicator and several of these chapters stem from lectures and conference presentations. However, behind the appearance of informality emerges, not only a formidable intellect at work, but a warm and compassionate perspective on the human condition. *Jungian Analysis, Depth Psychology, and Soul* will be of vital interest to analysts, therapists, trainees, academics, and students working in the areas of Jungian analysis and Jungian studies around the world.

Thomas B. Kirsch is a Jungian analyst in private practice in Palo Alto, California, and the son of two first-generation Jungian analysts, James and Hilde Kirsch, who began their analytic work with C. G. Jung in 1929. He graduated from Yale Medical School (1961), did his residency in psychiatry in the Department of Psychiatry at Stanford University, and then spent two years with the National Institute of Mental Health in San Francisco. He completed his Jungian training at the C. G. Jung Institute of San Francisco (1968). He was president of the C. G. Jung Institute of San Francisco in 1976–8, served on the executive committee of the International Association for Analytical Psychology, 1977–95, and was IAAP president 1989–95. Dr. Kirsch was the co-editor of the Jungian Section of the *International Encyclopaedia of Psychoanalysis, Psychiatry, and Neurology* (1977), as well as editor of the Jungian section of the three-volume *International Dictionary of Psychoanalysis* edited by Alain de Mijolla, 2005. He is the author of *The Jungians: A Comparative and Historical Perspective* (Routledge 2000), consulting editor of *The Jung–Kirsch Letters* (Routledge 2011), the correspondence between his father, James Kirsch and C. J. Jung, as well as the author of many published chapters in books, articles in scientific journals, and book reviews. He co-edited with George Hogenson *The Red Book: Reflections on C. G. Jung's Liber Novus* (Routledge, 2013), and his memoir, *A Jungian Life*, was published in 2014. For more information on Dr. Kirsch, see his website at www.jungians.com.

World Library of Mental Health Series

The World Library of Mental Health celebrates the important contributions to mental health made by leading experts in their individual fields. Each author has compiled a career-long collection of what they consider to be their finest pieces: extracts from books, journals, articles, major theoretical and practical contributions, and salient research findings.

For the first time ever the work of each contributor is presented in a single volume so readers can follow the themes and progress of their work and identify the contributions made to, and the development of, the fields themselves.

Each book in the series features a specially written introduction by the contributor giving an overview of their career, contextualizing their selection within the development of the field, and showing how their own thinking developed over time.

Titles in this series:

The Price of Love – The Selected Works of Colin Murray Parkes
By Colin Murray Parkes

Attachments: Psychiatry, Psychotherapy, Psychoanalysis - The Selected Works of Jeremy Holmes
By Jeremy Holmes

Journeys in Psychoanalysis: The Selected Works of Elizabeth Spillius
By Elizabeth Spillius

Passions, Persons, Psychotherapy, Politics – The Selected Works of Andrew Samuels
By Andrew Samuels

Towards a Radical Redefinition of Psychology – The Selected Works of Miller Mair
Edited by David Winter and Nick Reed

Living Archetypes – The Selected Works of Anthony Stevens
By Anthony Stevens

Soul: Treatment and Recovery – The Selected Works of Murray Stein
By Murray Stein

A Developmentalist's Approach to Research, Theory, and Therapy – The Selected Works of Joseph Lichtenberg
By Joseph D. Lichtenberg

Existential Psychotherapy and Counselling after Postmodernism: The Selected Works of Del Loewenthal
By Del Loewenthal

Love the Wild Swan: The Selected Works of Judith Edwards
By Judith Edwards

Conscience and Critic: The Selected Works of Keith Tudor
By Keith Tudor

Jungian Analysis, Depth Psychology, and Soul: The Selected Works of Thomas B. Kirsch
By Thomas B. Kirsch

Jungian Analysis, Depth Psychology, and Soul

The Selected Works of
Thomas B. Kirsch

Thomas B. Kirsch

LONDON AND NEW YORK

First published 2018
by Routledge
2 Park Square, Milton Park, Abingdon, Oxon OX14 4RN

and by Routledge
711 Third Avenue, New York, NY 10017

Routledge is an imprint of the Taylor & Francis Group, an informa business

© 2018 Thomas B. Kirsch

The right of Thomas B. Kirsch to be identified as author of this work
has been asserted by him in accordance with sections 77 and 78 of the
Copyright, Designs and Patents Act 1988.

All rights reserved. No part of this book may be reprinted or reproduced
or utilised in any form or by any electronic, mechanical, or other
means, now known or hereafter invented, including photocopying and
recording, or in any information storage or retrieval system, without
permission in writing from the publishers.

Trademark notice: Product or corporate names may be trademarks
or registered trademarks, and are used only for identification and
explanation without intent to infringe.

British Library Cataloguing in Publication Data
A catalogue record for this book is available from the British Library

Library of Congress Cataloging in Publication Data
Names: Kirsch, Thomas, 1936- author.
Title: Jungian analysis, depth psychology, and soul / Thomas B. Kirsch.
Description: Abingdon, Oxon ; New York, NY : Routledge, 2017. |
Identifiers: LCCN 2017005901 (print) | LCCN 2017022851 (ebook) |
ISBN 9781315727073 (Master) | ISBN 9781134970087 (Epub) | ISBN
9781134970018 (Web PDF) | ISBN 9781134970155 (Mobi/Kindle) |
ISBN 9781138688698 (hardback)
Subjects: LCSH: Jungian psychology. | Psychoanalysis.
Classification: LCC BF173.J85 (ebook) | LCC BF173.J85 .K57 2017
(print) | DDC 150.19/54--dc23
LC record available at https://lccn.loc.gov/2017005901

ISBN: 978-1-138-68869-8 (hbk)
ISBN: 978-1-138-68870-4 (pbk)
ISBN: 978-1-315-53808-2 (ebk)

Typeset in Sabon
by HWA Text and Data Management, London

CONTENTS

Foreword by Andrew Samuels	*viii*
Acknowledgements	*xi*

1 The relationship of the REM state to analytical psychology   1

Jung's theory of dreams	*1*
REM research in relation to analytical psychology	*2*
Experimental approach	*4*
Summary	*5*

2 The practice of multiple analyses in analytical psychology   7

Clinical examples	*9*
On transference	*10*

3 Jungian analysis   13

Dialectic procedure	*13*
Transference	*14*
The final stage	*16*
The spiral	*16*
The aims of Jungian analysis	*17*
The endings	*18*
Distinct features	*18*

4 Analysis in training   20

5 Family matters: the descendants of Jung and Freud   29

6 Jungian diaspora   36

7 Toni Wolff–James Kirsch correspondence   40

8 History of analytical psychology   47

Switzerland	*50*
The United States	*54*
United Kingdom	*60*
Germany	*63*
IAAP	*65*
Analytical psychology in the rest of the world	*65*

vi   *Contents*

9   Thomas B. Kirsch interviews Edward Edinger, December 4, 1996   69

10 Cultural complexes in the history of Jung, Freud, and their followers   79

11 The role of personal therapy in the formation of a Jungian analyst   88

  Historical introduction   88
  Core concepts   89
  US and European training guidelines   90
  Current training issues   90
  The training analysis   91
  Limits of personal analysis   92

12 The legacy of C. G. Jung   94

  The Jung family and the Eidgenosse Technische Hochschul,
    (ETH) archive   100
  Philemon   101
  Conclusion   102

13 Joseph Lewis Henderson 1903–2007: a biography   104

  Origins and early years, 1903–1919   104
  Student days, 1919–1928   106
  Analysis and medical training, 1929–1938   107
  Transition from Europe to the United States, 1938–1954   110
  Maturity, 1954–1961   112
  Conclusion of work on initiation, 1961–1967   113
  Continuity, growth, and old age, 1967–2007   115

14 A visit to Hildemarie Streich   122

15 Reflections on the word "Jungian"   126

  Jungian communities   126
  Personal experiences   128
  Jung and the field of analytical psychology   130
  What is "Jungian"?   131
  Conclusion   132

16 C.G. Jung: fifty years after his death   133

17 Preface to *The Jung–Kirsch Letters*   139

18 Introduction to First Reflections: initial responses to C. G.
    Jung's *Red Book* (*Liber Novus*), based on essays presented
    in San Francisco, 4–6 June 2010   146

19	A lifelong reading of Jung	149
20	Jung's relationship with Jews and Judaism	161
	Index	*167*

FOREWORD

Andrew Samuels

I am delighted and honoured to have been asked to contribute a Foreword to Thomas Kirsch's *Selected Writings*. He is one of the core creators of the Jungian world as we find it today. His knowledge of the history, the issues, and the personalities is second to none. We Jungians know that Tom is kind, empathetic, related – and responsible for a raft of interesting publications never before gathered into one book. Maybe we overlooked how penetrating and controversial an observer of professional political process he is. At points in the book, he can be said to have taken no prisoners.

I entered the Jungian world in 1974, and I first met Tom at the Rome Congress of the International Association for Analytical Psychology (IAAP) in 1977. I asked him a question about his presentation and the consequent friendship stuck so that we easily talked about ourselves as "older brother" and "younger brother." Later, I served under him on the Executive Committee of the IAAP and was often employed as an emissary or even as a sort of fixer. He was a remarkable president who foresaw the global possibilities for analytical psychology.

It is not surprising that I have got to know his work pretty well. But I had never imagined it presented chronologically, and I think that this is a fortuitous feature of a collection that will appeal to analysts, candidates, academics, and students.

When reading these chapters, it is possible to see how the world of professional politics and history, and the world of psychological theorising interweave. That is, Tom has taken his roles as professional leader and chronicler of analytical psychology and turned them into platforms for serious theory making. This approach is exemplified in his book *The Jungians: A Comparative and Historical Perspective* (2000).

In this book, the several chapters on training effectively demonstrate this interweave. Always aware of the present moment in training, Tom's various contributions preserve the classical Jungian core but relate openly to the changes going on in psychotherapy internationally as it developed into a profession, often modeled (sadly) on medicine. The passages on the dynamics of training in Chapters 2, 4, and 11 should be required reading for trainees and candidates – maybe even before they start to attend the seminars and lectures. In these chapters, we see another feature of this book: Tom's humanity, generosity, and flexibility. He accepts that, given the multifarious dynamics of the training community, "shit happens," and he is open about what he has witnessed in this regard. For Tom, "the wounded healer" is always already present in anything to do with depth psychology. It is much more than a question of fucked-up analysts.

Tom's historical work on the growth and spread of analytical psychology brings a crucial international perspective to the book. Either "Tom was there" or he knew someone well who was there. The result is that we now have a history of our field of analytical psychology that addresses the questions surrounding its founders but does not at all stay on an anecdotal level. Indeed, when writing about the locales in which analytical psychology took root, Tom is remarkably sensitive to the cultural and even the sociopolitical situation that existed.

In this regard, Tom's style of writing reminds me of analysis itself. We now know that there is no "inner world" in a vacuum, sequestered from the society in which the participants in the process are situated. Moreover, you have to remember that the small details, the little character outlines, are in fact of the greatest importance. In a sense, analysis and psychotherapy involve a great deal of gossip, which is often what really matters in a profession like this one. You can see this at moments in Chapters 5, 6, and 8.

Tom's parents were both famous Jungian analysts, and this gave Tom access to things Jungian at a very young age. He grew up in the Jungian community. The personal disadvantages of this are obvious and can be taken for granted. But the advantages are considerable and often not as easily appreciated. For example, in Chapter 7, I, for one, learned things about Jung's close colleague and companion Toni Wolff as a person and as a professional that were brand new for me. This was solely because Tom had been able to examine the correspondence between his father and Wolff (Kirsch's father had been in analysis with both Jung and Wolff). What we read there about dream interpretation and also on the need for discretion in professional life will repay attention.

I think that many who write about their "ancestors" are, covertly, writing about the present and the future as well. Readers can check this out for themselves by reading Tom's memoir *A Jungian Life* (2014). When Tom writes about the Jungian "diaspora" in Chapter 6, he is, of course, chronicling the fate of those Jewish Jungian analysts who left Europe to avoid perishing in the Shoah. But the expansion of Jungian analysis into what used to be called "frontier zones," such as Russia, Latin America, and the Far East is also a kind of diaspora. So when you read about the analysts who spread Jungian analysis because of their very peril, it is worthwhile to consider how today's expansionist dynamics resemble some of those that were in play in the 1930s.

In many of the chapters, there are passages that demonstrate Tom's prowess as a clinical writer and some of them play a significant role in conveying to the non-Jungian clinical world several important things about how Jungians practice. For Tom, Jungian analysis and psychotherapy seem to occupy a middle position in today's spectrum of therapies. At one end of the spectrum, we see the tough therapies, the ones claiming to be based on science and on evidence. Tom is not averse to such modes of working, though it is not where his clinical heart is. He is a quintessentially relational practitioner, with a fine understanding of images and symbols as well as the therapy relationship. Yet – and this, I know, is important to Tom – at no point does he collapse his way of working into an ersatz psychoanalysis. It is different.

Thinking more about psychoanalysis (and maybe this is true about a wider range of today's therapies as well), there has been a "relational turn." Jung's standing as a pioneer of relational approaches is gradually being recognised. This is a serious strength. Like today's relational theorists, Jung asserted that analysis involved mutual transformation and was a "dialectical process." Analysis for Jung, just as it is for the relationals, is "an encounter, a discussion between two psychic wholes in which knowledge is used only as a tool" (1935, 7). Jung goes on to say that the analyst is a "fellow participant in the analysis." His focus was often on "the real relationship," making his point in unmistakeable terms: "In reality everything depends on the [person] and little on the method" (1931, 7). All of these themes are present in Tom's clinical writings.

Given that many of the chapters began life as lectures, I want to make reference to Tom's considerable communicative talents as a teacher and lecturer. Tom is a brilliant teacher who touches people's feelings very deeply. To my eye and ear the fact that the material reads as if it were being spoken is a huge strength. (The great Jungian analyst James Hillman once told me that to make one's writing sound as if it were spoken was a triumph!) I do realize that others might find the informality difficult to assimilate. But they should try! For this genre is one way of combining thought and emotion, intellect and soul.

London, January 2017

References

Jung, C. G. (1931) Commentary on "The Secret of the Golden Flower". In *Collected Works*, vol. 13. Princeton, NJ: Princeton University Press.

Jung, C. G. (1935) *Principles of Practical Psychotherapy*. In *Collected Works*, vol. 16. Princeton, NJ: Princeton University Press

Kirsch, T. (2000) *The Jungians: A Comparative and Historical Perspective*. London and New York: Routledge.

Kirsch, T. (2014) *A Jungian Life*. Carmel, CA: Fisher King Press.

ACKNOWLEDGEMENTS

I would like to begin the acknowledgements with my very dear friend, Andrew Samuels. As he said in his sensitive Foreword, he has known me and most of my work for over forty years. He has championed my writings, and this work would not have been possible without his complete backing.

I would like to thank LeeAnn Pickrell for her tireless work on editing the articles for this publication. During a time when I was seriously ill, she kept working on the articles without much help from me. Susannah Ferguson as the editor at Routledge made sure that the publication would be completed. The editing done by LeeAnn and Susannah was thorough and makes for a much better book.

Then I want to thank Tom Singer for his critical reading of many of the chapters. Tom is a perceptive editor, and his reading of many of the chapters for this publication was essential to the way the book has turned out.

Finally, I want to thank my wife, Jean Kirsch, for her overall interest and making sure that the book was as good as it could be.

Without the participation of these people, the book would never have come out. Thank you all for your efforts.

CHAPTER 1

THE RELATIONSHIP OF THE REM STATE TO ANALYTICAL PSYCHOLOGY

From the *American Journal of Psychiatry*, 124, no 10, April 1968[1]

A brief review of Jung's approach to dreams is presented. The author reviews four investigations of REM research that relate to analytical psychology: control of sleep by a dual mechanism; selective REM deprivation; effects of drugs on the time of dreaming; and the study of REM state in the earliest stage of postnatal life. This renewed interest may provide a new methodology for the study of dreams.

In the past ten years the study of dreams has ceased to be an exclusive realm of the clinical practitioner. Since 1957 the work of Dement, Kleitman, Aserinsky, and many others have confirmed the coincidence of the rapid eye movement (REM) state with visual imagery or dreams. This has led to the recognition of dreams as universally occurring cyclical phenomena, biologically rooted in man's genetic endowment. There have been attempts to relate the neurophysiological research to various psychological theories, mainly to psychoanalysis and Adler's theory (Altschuler, 1966; Fisher, 1965; Foulkes, 1964; Hawkins, 1966; Trosman, 1963; Ullman, 1962). It is the purpose of this paper to relate the REM research to Jung's analytical psychology.

Jung's theory of dreams

It is most difficult to summarize Jung's theory of dreams, since this would encompass a review of all his work. Therefore, I have selected those areas where a parallelism with the REM research exists. First, Jung considered the dream a natural and normal psychic phenomenon, which can act as a strongly positive and compensating force of considerable potential value. This assumption means that the dream transmits unconscious reactions or spontaneous impulses to consciousness. In every instance the dream presents contents that compensate the attitude of ego-consciousness. Thus, dreams are neither seen necessarily as a wish fulfilment, nor are they seen as being distorted, disguised, and governed by a "censor." It would follow that the dream is not necessarily the guardian of sleep, and that it may just as often awaken the dreamer. Dement (1966) has been critical of this aspect of psychoanalytic dream theory from the point of view of REM research.

Second, a discussion of Jung's theory of dreams must include a clarification of the meaning of archetypes. Jung states that the best way to experience the existence and reality of archetypal images is to remember our dreams. Dreams contain elements that are not individual and that cannot be derived only from the dreamer's personal experience. They are what Freud called "archaic remnants" and "seem to be aboriginal, innate, and inherited shapes of the human mind" (Jung, 1964, p. 57).

2 *The relationship of the REM state*

At another point Jung states:

> this immensely old psyche forms the basis of our mind, just as much as the structure of our body is based on the general anatomical pattern of the mammal ... The experienced investigator of the mind can similarly see the analogies between the dream pictures of modern man and the products of the primitive mind, its "collective images," and its mythological motifs.
>
> (Jung, 1964, p. 57)

Besides appearing as images, they are seen in typical patterns of behavior as marked as the impulse of birds to build nests or ants to form organized colonies. Further on Jung states, "Instincts are physiological urges and are perceived by the senses ... at the same time they also manifest themselves as fantasies and often reveal their presence only by symbolic images [archetypes]" (Jung, 1964, p. 58). Examples of typical motifs are: the motif of a departure; the motif of a passage or crossing a river; the motif of falling or of flying; etc.

Analytical psychology does not limit the number of archetypes, although certain ones are basic. Jung refers to this archetypal layer of the unconscious as the collective unconscious, a term that has given rise to much controversy. The collective unconscious needs to be differentiated from the personal unconscious. The personal unconscious contains those elements which have been individually acquired during a person's lifetime and which have been repressed. Personal associations of the dreamer are absolutely vital in dealing with material from this level, whereas a knowledge of symbolism is more important in working with archetypal elements. In a general way the personal unconscious would correspond to Freud's view of the unconscious. In an individual dream it is quite common for dream elements from both layers to be present.

It would follow from this discussion of archetypes that according to analytical psychology the child is born with these predetermined structural dominants. It is the essence of the child that it still lives in the mysterious world of mythical images and magical relatedness. The child lives in a state of participation from which it gradually emerges; thus the earliest dreams of childhood tend to have the quality of a myth. It then proceeds by way of the development of the ego and the separation of its personality from the identity with the collective images. The child's immersion in archetypal imagery has also been noted in the artistic productions of children (Fordham, 1944; Read, 1956). Children's drawings have shown this tendency to form a cross or fourfold division, which Jung called the "mandala." Mandala is a Sanskrit word meaning a circle or magic ring; its symbolism embraces all concentrically arranged figures, all circular or square circumferences having a center, and all radial or spherical arrangements.

In concluding this incomplete review of Jung's approach to dreams, it should be made clear that, at its most basic aspect, the dream as a reflection of the unconscious is seen as a psychophysical unity. Although Jung was most concerned with the symbolic imagery of dreams, he also acknowledged their biological side.

REM research in relation to analytical psychology

This next section will review those areas of REM research that relate to analytical psychology. This kind of evidence by analogy is open to disagreement, but there appear some basic parallelisms that deserve attention, if not acceptance.

One very important series of investigations has been that of Jouvet and his coworkers (1961). On the basis of his studies of the cat, he concluded that sleep is controlled by a dual mechanism and that two different neurophysiological systems are involved. The first system appears during stages 2, 3, and 4 and requires the presence of the neocortex. On the other hand, the second type of sleep is designated as rhombencephalic, hindbrain, or "archisleep." This corresponds to the stage 1 REM phase in the human. It is an active phenomenon and is triggered by a mechanism localized in the caudal pontile nucleus of the pontile reticular formation.

It is of interest to note the particular word "archisleep," which Jouvet uses to describe this state. This term designates that stage 1, paradoxical sleep, is triggered by a mechanism which is phylogenetically in the oldest part of the brain. Jung stated that the images of our dreams are a survival of archaic modes of thought, which include the archetypal ones. Thus, both from the electrophysiological studies and from analytical psychology, there is evidence of this ancient, archaic substratum in dreams of the adult human. Freud noted these "archaic vestiges" in the first five years of life, but he did not see them as operative in the adult.

A second parallel concerns Dement's work (1960) on selective REM deprivation. By awakening subjects every time there are objective indications of dreaming, it is possible to bring about a 70 percent reduction in total dream time. However, each succeeding night the subject makes an increasing number of attempts to dream. When the subject is allowed uninterrupted sleep, there is a marked increase in the amount of dreaming. During the period of "dream deprivation" mild to moderate behavioral disturbances have been noted. This type of study seems to indicate that following dream deprivation there is a compensatory reaction to increase the total REM time. On the psychological level Jung has referred to the function of dreams as being compensatory to the attitude of consciousness. He describes the relationship between the two as being analogous to many other examples of biological homeostasis. An illustration would be the case of a distinguished lady who has a whole series of dreams in which she meets a harlot in the gutter, completely intoxicated. This might be interpreted as her need to see an inferior aspect of herself, and the dream compensates (or overcompensates) her too high position.

A third kind of investigation concerns the effect of drugs on the time of dreaming. It has been shown that barbiturates, alcohol, phenothiazines, and dextroamphetamine sulfate are all dream depressors (Gresham et al., 1963; Oswald et al., 1963; Whitman et al., 1961). On the other hand, only two drugs which have had the effect of increasing the amount of REM have been studied. These are LSD-25 and y-hydroxybutyrate, both of these having hallucinogenic properties (Jouvet et al., 1961; Muzio et al., 1964). It is well known that LSD-25 is characterized by its ability to produce a variety of images and experiences, which are seen by the subject as nonego, transpersonal. It is just this type of experience which analytical psychology describes as exhibiting archetypal imagery.

A fourth area of interest comprises the study of the REM state in the earliest stage of postnatal life. It has been noted by Roffwarg et al. (1966) that the REM state is most prominent in the earliest stage of postnatal life in the human neonate. It occupies an average of 50 percent of sleep, and the proportion is still higher in premature infants emerging from an undifferentiated electroencephalographic state at about 31 weeks of gestational age. Between human birth and young adulthood the total reduction in sleep involves only a 25 percent reduction in non-REM sleep, and a 75 percent reduction in the REM state. In all the species which have been studied, similar results have been noted between the newborn and the adult animal. Dement has advanced the theory of a developmental function for the REM state – a

4 The relationship of the REM state

function providing the internal stimulation needed for the maturation of the central nervous system at a time when external stimulation is minimal.

It is also of interest that newborn kittens have the capacity to form images before they have opened their eyes. The whole optic and visual structure of the cortex is in a state of readiness at the time of birth (Wiesel and Hubel, 1965, 20). As has been mentioned, analytical psychology views the child as being very close to mythological fantasy and dreamlike thinking. The younger the child, the greater is its apparent immersion in the archetypal world. It is a basic notion of analytical psychology that the infant is at one time in its early existence completely immersed in the collective unconscious, primary process, or the world of dreams.

Experimental approach

The use of the new electrophysiological techniques should make it possible to test some of these aforementioned parallelisms. An institute for dream research has been opened at the Clinic and Research Center for Jungian Psychology, headed by Professor C. A. Meier (Meier, 1965). I would like to suggest some possible hypotheses with the attitude that these are only first approximations to a most difficult problem:

1   The quality of a dream is related to the phase of sleep. (Quality means the character and content of the dream.) It is predicted that dreams during the REM phase would have a significantly higher percentage of material about which the person has had no known experience in his outer life. It would be considered bizarre, would contain unknown persons, would take the dreamer into unknown places, and might have him in unknown situations. According to analytical psychology many of these dreams would be archetypal motifs. On the other hand, dreams reported from the non-REM states would be much closer to external reality or day residue. This prediction is based on the proposed association between "archisleep" and archetype.

2   The dream reported upon arousal during the REM state would be similar in imagery to the dream the person reports upon awakening in the morning. This hypothesis is based on the fact that the dream is considered to be a natural, spontaneous phenomenon. Thus, analytical psychology does not believe that the dream is a disguise for some other, more basic fact. Furthermore, it means that Jungian theory does not presuppose a "censor" or a process of secondary elaboration of the original image. The difference between the two reports would be based both on the function of memory and repression, rather than that the original dream image had been transformed by some other mechanism.

3   The dreams of young children, aged 4 to 7, would have a mythological character to a significantly greater extent than in adults. Also, one would expect to see mandala symbolism in their dreams. This kind of study needs to elaborate the criteria for differentiating the productions of children and adults. In general, do children's dreams have a different character and content than the dreams of adults? Again, one would predict that there would be a difference because of the child's greater immersion in the world of primitive motifs, magical relatedness, and animistic thoughts.

4   The dream reflects a compensation to the attitude of ego-consciousness. Attitude dimensions such as introversion–extroversion and masculinity-

femininity would be measured. These attitudes would be compared to the material that would emerge in dreams. The prediction is that the opposite attitudes would be reflected in the unconscious. Furthermore, for example, if the dreamer lives a rigidly moral life one might expect that his dreams would bring up the darker aspects of the dreamer's personality which he represses. This area becomes further complicated, however, because this brings us into dream interpretation.

5 The study of dream content should help clarify whether patients going to therapists of different theoretical orientations have particular kinds of dreams. It has long been folklore that patients have Freudian, Adlerian, Jungian, or existential dreams, depending upon their respective analyst. This technique gives us the ability to study dreams from anyone, and in a situation where the content is only minimally influenced by the experimenter. The prediction is that the dreams will show universal patterns which are consistent with analytical psychology dream theory.

6 Are there differences within a given REM period for an individual? At this point in our knowledge it is assumed that the entire REM phase is uniform. However, as technique is refined we may expect there to be differences within an, REM period. It would be predicted that the point where REM exists in its purest form would be the time when archetypal dream contents would be evoked. This would be analogous to the imagery of dreams, which has a mixture of both archetypal and personal contents.

Summary

There has been a greatly renewed interest in the study of dreams following the demonstration that dreaming occurs at the time of REM. This may provide a new methodology for the study of dreams. A very brief resume of Jung's approach to dreams has been presented, emphasizing those aspects which appear analogous to the REM state. There seems to be a parallelism covering the basic hypothesis, and there is the need for a reassessment of our psychological understanding of dreams based on the recent research.

Note

1 "The Relationship of the REM State to Analytical Psychology." *American Journal of Psychiatry* 124(10) (April 1968): 1459–63. Reprinted with permission from *American Journal of Psychiatry* (Copyright ©1968). American Psychiatric Association. All Rights Reserved.

References

Altschuler, K. Z. (1966) Comments on Recent Sleep Research Related to Psychoanalytic Theory. *Archives of General Psychiatry* 15: 235–9.
Dement, W. (1960) The Effect of Dream Deprivation. *Science* 131: 1705–7.
Dement, W. (1966) Psychophysiology of Sleep and Dreams. In S. Arieti (ed.), *American Handbook of Psychiatry*, vol. 3. New York: Basic Books, pp. 290–365.
Fisher, C. (1965) Psychoanalytic Implications of Recent Research on Sleep and Dreaming. *Journal of the American Psychoanalytical Association* 13: 197–303.
Fordham, M. (1944) *The Life of Childhood*. London: Routledge.

6 The relationship of the REM state

Foulkes, D. (1964) Theories of Dream Formation and Recent Studies of Sleep Consciousness. *Psychology Bulletin* 62: 236–47.

Gresham, S. C., Webb, W., and Williams, R. (1963) Alcohol and Caffeine: Effect on Inferred Visual Dreaming. *Science* 140: 1226–7.

Hawkins, D. R. (1966) A Review of Psychoanalytic Dream Theory in the Light of Recent Psychophysiological Studies of Sleep and Dreaming. I. Empirical Findings. II. Implications for Psychoanalytic Theory. *British Journal of Medical Psychology* 39: 85–104.

Jouvet, M. (1961) Telencephalic and Rhombencephalic Sleep in the Cat. In G. E. W. Wolstenholme and M. O'Connor (eds), *The Nature of Sleep*. London: J. & A. Churchill, pp. 188–206.

Jouvet, M., Cier, A., Mounier, D., and Valatx, J. L. (1961) Effets du 4-butyrolactone et 4-hydroxybutyrate de sodium sur l'EEG et le comportment du chat. *Compte-Rendus de la Société Biologique* (Paris) 155: 1313–16.

Jung, C. G. (1964) *Man and his Symbols*. London: Aldus Books.

Meier, C. A. (1965) Clinics and Research Center for Jungian Psychology. *Journal of Analytical Psychology* (Zurich) 10: 1–6.

Muzio, J., Roffwarg, H., and Kaufman, R. (1964) Alteration in the Young Adult Human Sleep EEG Configuration Resulting from d-LSD-25. Read at the annual meeting of the Association for the Psychophysiological Study of Sleep. Palo Alto, CA, March.

Oswald, I., Berger, R., Jaramillo, R., Keddie, K., Olley, P., and Plunkett, G. (1963) Melancholia and Barbiturates: A Controlled EEG, Body and Eye Movement Study of Sleep. *British Journal of Psychiatry* 109: 66–78.

Read, H. (1956) *Education Through Art*. New York: Pantheon.

Roffwarg, H. P., Muzio, J. N., and Dement, W. C. (1966) Ontogenetic Development of the Human Sleep-Dream Cycle. *Science* 152: 604–19.

Trosman, H. (1963) Dream Research and the Psychoanalytic Theory of Dreams. *Archives of General Psychiatry* 9: 9–18.

Ullman, M. (1962) Dreaming, Life-Style, and Physiology: A Comment on Adler's View of the Dream. *Journal of Individual Psychology* 18: 18–25.

Whitman, R. M., Pierce, C. M., Maas, J., and Baldridge, B. (1961) Drugs and Dreams: II. Imipramine and Prochlorperazine, *Comparative Psychiatry* 2: 219–26.

Wiesel, T. N., and Hubel, D. (1965) Extent of Recovery from the Effects of Visual Deprivation in Kittens. *Journal of Neurophysiology* 28: 1060–71.

CHAPTER 2

THE PRACTICE OF MULTIPLE ANALYSES IN ANALYTICAL PSYCHOLOGY

From *Contemporary Psychoanalysis* 12(2), April 1976[1]

The practice of multiple analyses, i.e., of seeing more than one analyst during an analysis, has long been an accepted pattern among Jungian analysts. This practice can further be broken down into (1) concurrent analyses or (2) serial analyses. The major focus of this paper will be on concurrent analyses.

Historically, this practice began with Jung who often sent his patients to a woman colleague. Jung preferred to deal with the impersonal symbolic contents of the unconscious and would have the personal aspects dealt with by a woman colleague (Wheelwright, 1975). Although multiple analyses has been a widely utilized practice, the literature on the subject is quite sparse (Hillman, 1962; Plaut, 1962; Fordham, 1962). Furthermore, it is a practice which has given rise to a diversity of opinion among Jungian Training Institutes. It is the purpose of this paper to elucidate the theoretical basis for simultaneous multiple analyses, and to discuss the pros and cons of its practice. To do so, some basic concepts of analytical psychology related to multiple analyses will need to be defined.

Basic to analytical psychology is a dialectical method of conducting psychotherapy. The therapist abandons all of his preconceptions and techniques and confines himself to a purely dialectical procedure, not unlike Sullivan's conception of the analyst as a participant observer. The analyst "is equally a part of the psychic process of treatment and, therefore, equally exposed to the transforming influences" (Jung, 1929, 72). This "reciprocal reaction of two psychic systems" (Jung, 1935, 4) represents a constant challenge to the analyst, which has to be met on the level of the patient. It leads to an approach to the patient that is highly individual, since it is impossible to assume superior *a priori* knowledge vis-a-vis the patient as a unique individual organism. Thus, each Jungian analysis is quite different from any other. Jung refers to the individual aspects of therapy as the "personal equation" which must exist if the therapeutic encounter is to work. Initially, Jung defined this personal equation as a difference in psychological type. But this personal equation clearly has its wider roots in every possible field of experience and mode of interpretation. The individuality of each analysis is fundamental to analytical psychology. Hence, one analyst only constellates one aspect of the unconscious, and therefore it may be of value to observe what gets constellated if the patient sees a second analyst. This difference in the analytical field is accentuated when the two analysts are of opposite sex and opposite psychological type. Their perceptions focus on different aspects of the unconscious of the patient, which ensures a more comprehensive analysis.

One of the advantages of multiple analyses is that it may activate the inner polarity existing in the human psyche between male and female components. Jung

8 *Multiple analyses in analytical psychology*

refers to the feminine in man as the anima and the masculine in woman as the animus. Both exist as *a priori* unconscious factors, frequently presenting viewpoints contrary to consciousness. Both anima and animus are often experienced in the form of projections upon the contrasexual object – man for a woman's animus and woman for a man's anima. The anima leads a man to search for what is strange and unknown in himself, usually through a relationship to a woman. The animus is the principle of discrimination and spirituality in the widest sense of the word, which is most often initially experienced in projection on a man. The withdrawal of anima and animus projections are seen as important initial goals of Jungian analysis, leading later to their assimilation for the enlargement of ego consciousness. Ideally, a Jungian analyst should be related to both the masculine and feminine in him- or herself. However, some aspects of the anima can only be seen for what they are when working with an actual woman in analysis rather than with a male analyst. Likewise, an animus projection for a woman may need the experience of an actual male so as to work through a particular aspect of the issue. The in-depth analysis of animus and anima projections is another important rationale for multiple analyses.

Jung's theory of psychological types, extremely relevant to multiple analyses, has to do with the direction of psychic energy. Extraversion is the flow of energy towards the outer world of people and objects, whereas introversion is the flow of energy towards the inner world. Each of us has a natural tendency to be one or the other and both are considered "normal" patterns. Alongside the introversion–extraversion dimension are Jung's *function* types representing the four principal ways of adapting to people, things and situations. Two of these function types are along the rational axis – *thinking* and *feeling*. Thinking deals with the ability to abstract and conceptualize, whereas feeling has to do with the rational function of judging, i.e., do I like someone or something, or don't I? On the other axis are the perceptual functions of *sensation* and *intuition*. Sensation has to do with the function of reality to the senses, whereas intuition is the world of possibilities and seeing around corners. Most of us have one or two developed functions, with the other two relatively unavailable. If one adds the introversion-extraversion scale, then there are eight distinct possible personality types. One of the aims of a Jungian analysis is to make the less adapted attitude and functions more available to consciousness.

The question of psychological type enters the analytic situation in a number of ways. One general pattern is for the analysand to choose an analyst of similar psychological type: i.e., a patient with introverted thinking as the superior function seeks out an introverted thinking type analyst. The two often experience an initial rapport which helps the analysis to "take." However, somewhere in the course of the work they may become too "comfortable" and thus might come to the joint decision that an analyst of the opposite type and function is indicated: i.e., an extroverted feeling one. A switch can be made at that time. Another analysand may be attracted initially to an analyst of a completely opposite type. At a later time the analysand may wish to work with someone more like him- or herself. Furthermore, at times of transition from one analyst to another, there is an attempt to have the analysand work with an analyst of the opposite sex from the previous analyst.

When the patient works with two analysts simultaneously, it is necessary for the two analysts to be in agreement with one another. If the two have different methods and or goals, the patient quickly picks this up and plays one against the other, much like a child with parents. This means that the two analysts must be quite clear in their feelings towards each other, as well as towards the patient. It does not require frequent communication between the two analysts, as long as the two processes are kept separate. In fact, a minimum of discussion between the two works better so that there is not undue contamination of the two analytical procedures, though the patient will need to discuss the same material with both therapists from time to time. The emotional climate can be different on these different occasions, discussing the same material with analysts of different sexes. The "constellation" in the analytical field is quite different. The discussion of the material with an introverted thinking type man can be quite objective and clear, whereas the same material discussed with an extraverted feeling woman can produce strong emotional reactions. Both can be valuable to the individual patient. When considering a second analyst, one attempts to choose a person of the opposite sex and, preferably, of opposite psychological type. In many instances the patient will discuss entirely different material with each therapist. In one typical situation, multiple analyses can help to separate the two parental images. An example of this would be a woman patient who discusses her difficulties in mothering or relating to other feminine problems with a female analyst, whereas she discusses her problems relating to men as well as her career issues with her male analyst. Some of the material clearly overlaps, but there are large psychological areas which naturally fall to one or the other analytic situation. These are generalizations about what happens in multiple analyses, which differ in each individual instance.

Clinical examples

A 19-year-old female college student first consulted me two years ago with severe depressive symptomatology. She required hospitalization initially and since that time has improved markedly. However, she has one obsessional thought which pervades much of her psychological life. It has to do with women who are housewives and mothers. She sees all such women as depressed, vacant, empty, and worthless. She fears that somehow she will end up that way. It arises from the fact that her own mother has never worked and has identified completely with the housewife–mother role. Over the years there has developed a deeply ambivalent mother-daughter relationship, wherein she consciously denies many of the attitudes and values of her mother. Over the years we have discussed the mother problem extensively, but it did not seem to change. Six months ago, I suggested that she might want to talk to a woman therapist about some of these feelings because it seemed as if we were not touching her feelings about homebound women. It was emphasized that she would continue to see me about other issues and that it did not have to be an either/ or situation. The female therapist whom I suggested was an introverted woman, opposite to myself, who would not intrude on the patient's psychological space. In fact, I was aware that my extraverted intuition had tended to overwhelm the patient at times. She has continued to see me twice weekly and the woman therapist once weekly.

Initially, the patient had a deep distrust of the woman therapist, but they have developed a therapeutic alliance. Both of us continue to work with the patient, sometimes on the same problem area and sometimes on different ones. I do not know how long it will go on in this fashion, but we shall continue it as long as it seems helpful. Recently the patient visited her parents and experienced her mother as real for the first time. I attribute this to her work with the female therapist. The other therapist and I have discussed the eventuality that the patient might want to see only one or the other of us.

My second clinical example is of a young male college student. He was seen by a female analyst when he was a senior in high school and then entered a college far

10   *Multiple analyses in analytical psychology*

away from home. He suffered from diffuse anxiety, inability to study, fear of the opposite sex, and a variety of other terrors. Early in the therapy, he stated that I did not help him with his problems as much as the previous female therapist had. During this time, he would occasionally telephone his previous analyst on the East Coast and complain about his life situation in Palo Alto. In a limited way, he was in multiple analyses through his phone contact with his previous therapist. This pattern continued for three years with his still feeling that I was not helping him. I realized that he needed a great deal of support and mothering which he was not obtaining from me. As this pattern persisted, I suggested that he might wish either to transfer to or see a female analyst concurrently. He decided to see a female analyst for six months while he continued his therapy with me. At the end of that period he decided to stop seeing the woman and continue working with me. I had hoped that his seeing a female therapist would help him resolve the transference to the previous therapist, but it did not. However, the work with the female analyst here did help to make the resistance more manageable.

On transference

The question that arises from the practice of multiple analyses is what happens to the transference? This is a most complex issue and one around which analytical psychologists are divided. Jung (1946, 164) has stated in one of his later works "that almost all cases requiring lengthy treatment gravitate round the phenomenon of transference, and that the success or failure of the treatment appears to be bound up with it in a very fundamental way." In psychoanalysis it is via the transference that unresolved infantile conflicts, unconscious emotions, relational problems, and the like are activated, released, and made conscious. Alongside the infantile component of the transference, Jung states that there is still another equally important quality. The analysand projects onto the analyst certain aspects of himself that have never been conscious. These latter contents are not repressed but represent unlived and unrealized potentialities in the unconscious. Among such prospective unconscious material the primordial archetypal images are of particular significance. Of special importance is the archetype of the *Self,* which is the central organizing principle in the unconscious. Symbols of the Self in dreams are represented by such varied images as the sun, the round object, the child, the superior man, the jewel, or an abstract symbol known as the mandala. As Henderson has stated it:

> We merely have to learn that there is a difference between personally motivated complexes on the one hand and the impersonal archetypal world of images on the other. This gives rise to two distinct goals for analysis of our patient's material. The first of these goals is determined by the ego and its needs following the personal line of development. The second is determined by the Self which seeks to integrate the ego's goal with an impersonal goal set up spontaneously by the objective psyche. In the state of transference one or both of these centers, the ego and the Self, are acutely activated to reach a goal of fulfillment through relationship with the analyst. The analyst is both the object of the patient's strongest personal need for understanding and at the same time he becomes identified with the symbol of a transcendent aim or goal.
>
> (Henderson, 1955, 78)

One example of this transpersonal aspect of the transference comes from a dream of a 60-year-old woman. The patient, an extremely conventional woman

Multiple analyses in analytical psychology 11

with Victorian values, was in the process of attempting to break out of her rigidly confined way of life. Severe headaches had led her to seek analysis. After three years of therapy she dreamt that she was bringing a young woman to see a well-known European woman psychiatrist. The patient's association to the young woman was that she was a conventional, nonpsychologically oriented person who was in need of therapy. The image of the European woman psychiatrist was unknown to her. The patient associated traditional values, mixed with a career and being out in the world, to this image. Furthermore, she felt that this woman had a great deal of wisdom and experience and could help the young girl. Since the image is of a psychiatrist, some of the energy must have to do with her relationship to me as her analyst. However, the image is of an unknown European woman psychiatrist, which has a broader meaning than purely her relationship to me. It has to do with the potential healer in herself, the archetypal psychotherapist, who resides deep in the unconscious of the patient. She needs to have the young nonpsychological woman in herself be in touch with the deep healing center as symbolized by the woman psychiatrist. Analytical psychologists would see this image as that of the "wise old woman" or of the Self. It is a subjective factor which represents a transpersonal potential in the patient.

Now within analytical psychology there are three main trends on viewing such material. Orthodox Jungians work almost exclusively with dreams and when the transference is interpreted the focus is on its archetypal aspect, particularly in relationship to the Self. This group tends to use multiple analyses the most because the focus is on the transpersonal aspects of the analysis. These inner symbolic contents can be transferred to another analyst more readily.

At the other extreme are those analytical psychologists who give the transference the central and all important place in their interpretive work. They do not use multiple analyses at all because they believe it would dilute the transference. They think that transference leakage and resistances will occur and the patient must work through the transference with one analyst.

There is a large central group which combines transference interpretation and dream interpretation, without regarding the latter only from the point of view of transference. For this group, in which I include myself, multiple analyses stands among many possible therapeutic methods.

Thus, Jungian Training Institutes vary in their use of multiple analyses, depending upon their view of the transference. Where it is used, multiple analyses are seen to give a more comprehensive experience of analysis and the transference relationship. Different unconscious contents are constellated, or at least constellated to a different degree, with either a man or a woman analyst. At the C. G. Jung Institute in Zurich multiple analyses, either consecutively or simultaneously, are frequent. Equally, the training program of the Institute in New York states, "The Board may request that a candidate have part of his analysis with male and part with a female training analyst in order to provide him with a broader basis of experience" (Adler, 1967). The Society of Analytical Psychology in London represented by Fordham and others does not favor multiple analyses, because of the danger of transference leakage and resistances. In San Francisco there is no set rule. Our experience has been that many candidates do see both a man and a woman analyst at some time during their training. Furthermore, if the candidate has seen only one analyst up until the time he begins control cases, the training committee often suggests a control analyst of the opposite sex and opposite psychological type. In our experience, this pattern works out extremely well if one is careful in the handling of the transference.

The method of multiple analyses has been used for more than forty years by analytical psychologists. The effects of these discussions on the transference has led

12 *Multiple analyses in analytical psychology*

analytical psychologists to be most careful about its practice. Initially, patients were transferred readily without enough consideration to the transference implications. In America, the tendency has been to utilize multiple analyses in a *serial* fashion rather than *simultaneously* in order to reduce transference complications. On the other hand, simultaneous analyses can be helpful in individual situations. The implications of this unorthodox practice are far-reaching and many aspects of its practice have only been hinted at in this paper.

Notes

1 "The Practice of Multiple Analyses in Analytical Psychology." *Contemporary Psychoanalysis* 12(2) (April 1976): 159–67, doi: 10.1080/00107530.1976.10745422. Reprinted by permission of the William Alanson White Institute of Psychiatry, Psychoanalysis & Psychology and the William Alanson White Psychoanalytic Society (www.wawhite.org).

References

Adler, G. (1967) Methods of Treatment in Analytical Psychology. In Benjamin B. Wolman (ed.), *Psychoanalytic Techniques*. New York: Basic Books, pp. 338–78.

Fordham, M. (1962) A Comment on James Hillman's Paper. *Journal of Analytical Psychology* 7: 24–6.

Henderson, J. L. (1955) Resolution of the Transference in the Light of Analytical Psychology. *Acta Psychotherapeutica* 3: 75–91.

Hillman, J. (1962) A Note on Multiple Analysis and Emotional Climate at Training Institutes. *Journal of Analytical Psychology* 7: 20–2.

Jung, C. G. (1929) *Problems of Modern Psychotherapy*. Collected Works, vol. 16. Princeton, NJ: Princeton University Press.

Jung, C. G. (1935) *Principles of Practical Psychotherapy*. Collected Works, vol. 16. Princeton, NJ: Princeton University Press.

Jung, C. G. (1946) *Psychology of the Transference*. Collected Works, vol. 16. Princeton, NJ: Princeton University Press.

Plaut, A. (1962) Some Observations on Hillman's Statement Regarding Training in Zurich. *Journal of Analytical Psychology* 7: 23–4.

Wheelwright, J. B. (1975) A Personal View of Jung. *Psychological Perspectives* 6: 64–73.

CHAPTER 3

JUNGIAN ANALYSIS

From the *International Encyclopedia of Psychiatry, Psychology, Psychoanalysis and Neurology,* edited by Benjamin B. Wolman, Aesculapius Publishers, 1977[1]

The task of writing on Jungian analysis is complicated by two problems. The first is that the specific technique of analytical psychology does not exclude the use of more generalized analytical methods. Second, Jungian analysis, like other forms of therapy, is continually undergoing change.

Dialectic procedure

In his earliest independent formulation, Jung stated that any depth-analytical procedure is an individual one between two people. The therapist must abandon all of his preconceptions and techniques, and confine himself to a purely dialectical procedure. By doing this, the therapist abandons the notion that he is an agent of treatment and becomes a fellow-participant in a process of individual development. This means that the doctor is in the analysis as much as the patient. He is an equal part in the psychic process of treatment, and is equally exposed to the transforming influences. Thus, the analyst must be continually watching his own unconscious as well as that of the patient.

The dialectic procedure has another source, namely, the multiple significance of symbolic content. Jung distinguished between the analytic-reductive and the synthetic-hermeneutic process of interpretation. The analytic-reductive view states that interest, or as Jung describes it, *libido,* streams back regressively to infantile reminiscences and is there fixated. This parallels the Freudian psychoanalytic view. The synthetic view asserts that certain parts of the personality that are capable of development are as yet in embryonic form, and there is a potential for growth and development. In the individual analytic situation, it is often difficult to know whether to interpret regressively in an analytic-reductive way, or to interpret the material in a synthetic-prospective attitude.

In the late 1920s and early 1930s Jung continued to differentiate his own views from those of Freud and Adler. He divided the process of any analysis into four stages. The first stage he called the *confession,* or *catharsis.* The person has unacceptable material in need of coming out and "confesses" to the therapist. The process of divulging has a therapeutic effect on the patient.

The second stage Jung called *elucidation,* or interpretation, in particular the interpretation of the *transference* and the infantile psyche. This exploration of the infantile psyche and transference would be close to classical psychoanalysis. The infantile roots of the neurosis and how they are acted out in the analysis would be explored.

The third stage of analysis he called *education,* that is, the adaptation to social demands, needs, and certain kinds of learning and educative process. In this phase

14 *Jungian analysis*

of the analysis the therapist behaves as a teacher who instructs the patient in new ways of adaptation. This third stage would be similar to the Adlerian phase.

In the final stage, called *transformation* or *individuation,* the patient discovers and develops his own unique pattern. This is the stage of Jungian analysis proper.

These stages are not meant to represent either consecutive or mutually exclusive stages of development, but different aspects of it which interpenetrate and vary according to the needs of the particular patient and therapeutic situations. In practice, all four stages are going on at the same time, and the analyst focuses on any one of them in the analysis. As we go on in analysis, more emphasis is placed on individual development and on the individuation process, and less time is spent going back into the infantile roots. Jungian analysis deals with childhood roots, existential encounter, adaptive processes, coping mechanisms, and whatever else emanates from the psyche of the patient. In Jung's writings one finds little discussion of the infantile parts of the psyche or the will to power. He felt that these areas had been adequately covered by Freud and Adler, so that he was free to deal with the more symbolic contents of the unconscious. Thus, Jung's writings tended to overemphasize symbolism and undervalue other aspects of the therapeutic process.

Jung did not assume that once the analyst has been adequately trained, his or her personal characteristics do not matter. Analysis is an individual experience between two people and their respective psyches, both conscious and unconscious. Jung refers to the individual aspects of therapy as the *personal equation,* which must exist if the therapy encounter is to work. Interpretations, insights, and archetypal symbolic interpretations are necessary, but without a genuine rapport between the two people, the analysis does not work. Initially, Jung defined this personal equation in terms of psychological types; he thought people of the same psychological type should work well together. Later he found this not necessarily to be true, and he widened his concept of personal equation to mean all of the personal characteristics of the two people involved. Analysis is a very individual matter, and *au fond* it is a mystery when it works. In his more mature writings on therapy, he became less interested in upholding rules and specific techniques and more interested in the individual encounter. However, one thing that has remained paramount in the training of the therapist has been his own individual analysis. The analyst must undergo a full analysis to become aware of his own unconscious; otherwise, he or she can be caught too easily in the unconscious complexes of the analysand.

The dialectical nature of the therapeutic relationship leads to the idea that the analyst is not an absolute authority. Hopefully, because of his experience in life and relationship to the unconscious, he can be of help to the analysand. The therapist needs to drop his preconceptions and not assume that he knows what is right for the patient. This can be very difficult if the patient and the analyst sees things from a different *Weltanschauung.* Each of us has an unconscious set of assumptions with which we approach a given situation. One looks for a signal from the unconscious, either the analyst's or the analysand's, to help break through the log jam. Sometimes one muddles through for quite a while before there is any resolution, and on occasion there is no answer. Basically, the resolution must develop within the analytical situation, rather than being imposed from outside.

Transference

So far, the analytic relationship has been discussed without the use of the word *transference.* Transference is a widely used term in analytical circles. In classical psychoanalysis, the term refers to those feelings and fantasies that the patient originally had toward various family members which are now "transferred" onto the person of the analyst. This tends to produce a certain regressive pull on the analysand as he relives certain childhood experiences and develops a full-blown *transference neurosis*. The aim of the analysis is to work through and develop insight into these feelings; thereby the patient is helped. Alongside the infantile aspect of this transference, Jung states that there is another equally important quality to the transference: the analysand projects onto the analyst those unrealized aspects of himself. Thus, the analyst may embody superhuman or mythological god-like qualities – that is, if it is a positive transference. The patient may also project negative, demonic, devouring qualities on the analyst. In the course of a working analysis, these attributes must be withdrawn from the analyst and returned to the psyche of the patient, as they represent his own unrealized potentialities.

At the same time that the transference takes place, there is a parallel phenomenon from analyst to patient called *countertransference*. The countertransference reactions are considered an integral part of the dialectical procedure. They may be destructive to the analytic process when the analyst's own unresolved complexes are evoked and get played out with the patient. Gerhard Adler referred to this phenomenon as *counterprojection*, as distinct from a countertransference (Adler, 1967).

At the same time that the transference and countertransference phenomena are going on, a real relationship develops between the two people; "real" means that it is based on conscious understanding rather than on unconscious assumptions and projections. The Jungian approach differs from the traditional psychoanalytic or other more conventional psychiatric therapies in that the Jungian analyst tries to be himself with his patients and expects a mutual exchange. This can be seen in the arrangement of the furniture, where most analysts use chairs rather than a couch. No reactions are hidden, and there exists a continual face-to-face contact. The couch may be used occasionally, but the chair arrangement is more customary, though the couch can be helpful in freeing emotions with certain kinds of regressed patients. As the analysis proceeds, hopefully the real part of the relationship between the two grows and the projected transference-countertransference aspects decrease. By the end of the formal analysis in the "ideal" sense, most of the unconscious aspects have been mutually analyzed, and a "symbolic friendship" forms. As a more equal give-and-take situation ensues, there remains a certain core of the transference-countertransference phenomenon (Henderson, 1955).

Jungian analysis encourages ongoing life with its varied experiences, which are grist for the mill in therapy, whereas the Freudian psychoanalytic approach tends to foster a postponement of major life changes until the infantile roots of the conflict are resolved. This is both an overgeneralization and an oversimplification, but on broad theoretical grounds it is a helpful distinction.

One of the criticisms commonly leveled at Jungian analysis is that its approach is too intellectual. The lore maintains that in order to be a Jungian analysand, one needs to be well versed in mythology and symbolism, for analysis then is the amplification of these symbols. This is understandable when one reads Jung, as his writing deals primarily with the symbols of the unconscious. One needs to remember that Jung was a true pioneer in exploring the unconscious, and he needed the symbolic amplification to affirm his hypothesis. Furthermore, as an introverted intuitive thinking type, he had a natural predilection for this kind of material. He was concerned with practical problems of psychotherapy in some of his writings, and one can see from his recently published letters that he dealt with these issues in his daily practice (Jung, 1973). However, amplification of symbols from a dream may be terribly important at one time, while at another time importance may rest

16 *Jungian analysis*

with simply telling a dream, or what is happening in the relationship between analyst and analysand, or with some other meaningful external experience.

The final stage

The question, "How long does the Jungian analysis take?" is impossible to answer, because the length of therapy depends on the individual's problem, whether the analysis "takes," the depth of the analysis, and a number of other factors. A slightly different question that might be posed is, "How long does one need the actual presence of the analyst?" Certain manifestations from the unconscious indicate that the formal aspect is coming to an end. A typical dream motif is one in which the analyst appears in the analysand's house. This suggests that the analysand is able to take care of matters in his own psychological house; he carries the image of the analyst more within himself, and he no longer needs ongoing therapy. This does not mean that the analysand will never again need or wish to go to the analyst's office, but this kind of dream image suggests a certain point of resolution. The end of the analysis does not mean that the person is problem free. It does imply that the patient is in touch with his or her own unconscious material, is able to grapple with it, and is firmly directed along the way to finding his or her own individual self. The aim of Jungian analysis is not to turn out a completely individuated person, but the development of an understanding that each of us is involved in a lifelong process of growth, development, conflict, tension of opposites, and change. Furthermore, the analyst encourages patients to come back for an occasional hour or brief period of analysis at times when there are new developments or recrudescence of old symptoms.

The spiral

Analysis implies creation and destruction, often occurring simultaneously. One commonly used symbol of analysis is that of a spiral around a central pole: one keeps going around the central pole, each time arriving at a slightly different level. Each view is slightly different and adds a new dimension to an already existing attitude. Another image is that of peeling an onion. Each time one peels off a layer, a new and different layer comes into view until one finally reaches the core of the onion or problem.

Another apt symbol for the process of analysis is seen in a familiar Greek wall decoration (Figure 3.1). Joseph Henderson (1968) has the following to say about its meaning:

> There is a rising crest of the wave which is reached at point *a*, after which the movement descends and recedes and reaches its own center *b*, after which the movement recovers its forward moving direction again, as it unwinds from *c* and proceeds to another rising wave crest. The retrogressive movement is relative to the progressive movement, and this figure corrects two sorts of errors that are commonly met in evaluating this pair of contrasts. Progression is not equal and opposite to regression; they form a cyclic unit which moves on the whole forward. Progression is not only positive and regression negative; they are relative as centrifugal movement gives way to centripetal movement. Progression leads the whole cycle forward and upward, regression returns to redefine the center of the whole cycle as if the movement were a self-concealed, self-restorative, creative act. The new forward movement emerges from the transforming center, the heart of the spiral.

Figure 3.1 Wall decoration from Tiryns (after M. and C. Quenell)

This is a most apt image for the description of the analytic process.

What percentage of the analyst's time is truly spent doing Jungian analysis? Most analysts tend to see patients up to the age and experience where they are themselves and thus, as they get older, their patients tend to be somewhat older. The older analyst is more likely to be dealing with people who are involved with the problems of the second half of life and the individuation process. However, as any deep analysis involves the whole person, both analyst and analysand, any area of life is dealt with in an individual Jungian way. For example, one may talk about infantile roots, a prospective image in a dream, questions concerning psychological type, or the relationship between the analyst and patient – all within the same analytical hour.

It is customary in Zurich, even today, for an analysand to see both a man and a woman analyst concurrently; preferably the two analysts also are of opposite psychological type. Seeing two analysts concurrently may cause a diffusion of the transference, but in specific situations and for a limited time it can be most helpful. The same material brought up to both a man and a woman can evoke markedly different responses, both of which are equally valid. Alternatively, the analysand may see a therapist of sex opposite to his regular therapist for a period of time to work out a particular problem. For instance, a female analysand may find it helpful to see a woman during and shortly after her first pregnancy, then return to her regular male analyst. However, one may go through the entire process with one analyst. Which route one takes depends, again, entirely upon the individual.

The aims of Jungian analysis

In *Psychology and Alchemy* Jung discusses the goals of analysis in a most succinct fashion:

> There is in the analytic process, that is to say the dialectical discussion, between the conscious mind and the unconscious, the development or advance toward some goal or end, the perplexing nature of which has engaged attention for many years. Psychological treatment may come to an end at any stage in the development without one always or necessarily having the feeling a goal has been reached. Typical and temporary terminations may occur: (1) After receiving a piece of good advice; (2) after making a more or less complete but

18 *Jungian analysis*

satisfactory confession; (3) after having recognized some hitherto unconscious but essential content whose realization gives new impetus to one's life and activities; (4) after a hard-won separation from the childhood psyche; (5) after having worked out a new and rational mode of adaptation to perhaps difficult or unusual circumstances and surroundings; (6) after the disappearance of painful neurotic symptoms; (7) after some positive turn of fortune, such as an examination, engagement, marriage, divorce, change of profession, and so on; (8) after having found one's way back to the church to which one previously belonged, or after a conversion; and finally, (9) after having begun to build up a practical philosophy of life (a "philosophy" in the classical sense of the word).

(Jung, 1968, para 3)

Jung stated that there are large numbers of patients for whom the outward termination of the work with the doctor is far from the end of the analytic process. There are many cases where greater changes occur after the end of the formal analysis when the people are involved in a dialectic between the ego and the unconscious.

The endings

There are nine possible endings. Ending one and two, advice or confession, correspond more to a crisis intervention model or a behavior modification approach. Three and four, infantile psyche and some unconscious content being raised to consciousness, are particularly linked with the Freudian view. Five, six, and seven, rational mode of adaptation, disappearance of symptoms, or a positive turn of events, are common to any type of psychotherapeutic procedure and would not be exclusive to a Jungian-oriented therapy. Eight, return to the church or creed, may be as true today as when Jung wrote this in the late 1930s. In spite of his criticism of organized religion, he also felt that it could be quite beneficial in certain instances. Nine, the practical philosophy of life, is in reality a description of the process of individuation.

Jung mentioned only once the removal of symptoms. Symptoms are extremely variable in their nature, for, in some cases, symptoms disappear early in treatment. Jungians usually do not focus on the symptom itself, but on a particular occasion they may directly attack the symptom. Jung refers to neuroses and symptoms as inauthentic suffering. Apparently, a symptom is a surface manifestation of a deeper unconscious conflict.

Distinct features

The Jungian analysand acknowledges the reality of his unconscious, and the analyst catalyzes an integration of its symbols into consciousness. There exists an everchanging relationship between the ego and the unconscious, and analysis helps the individual to maintain an appropriate connection between the two. If it becomes too close, one becomes inundated by the unconscious; if the connection is too distant, the individual is cut off from what is going on inside. In the ideal situation, various symbols from the unconscious become assimilated into ego-consciousness, and a new integration takes place which includes both ego-consciousness and the unconscious. The ego is no longer the center of the personality, and it is in touch with the archetypal dominants of the objective psyche, particularly the Self.

A second distinctive feature of Jungian analysis is the recognition and importance of psychological type. This implies a psychology of individual differences where several modes of apperception are seen as equally valid. Thus, an introvert will experience analysis and his world in a relatively inward fashion, while the extrovert will relate to analysis and his world more outside himself and will be more prone to experience the unconscious in projection. The important fact is that both modes are equally valid and yet quite different. When one adds the function differences of thinking, feeling, intuition, and sensation, this further individualizes the analytical experience.

The whole analytic process is a deeply personal one, and it requires a mutual trust between analysand and analyst.

Note

1 From B. B. Wolman, *International Encyclopedia of Psychiatry, Psychology, Psychoanalysis and Neurology*, © 1996 Gale, a part of Cengage Learning, Inc. Reproduced by permission. www.cengage.com/permissions.

References

Adler, G. (1967) Methods of Treatment in Analytical Psychology. In B. G. Woman (ed.), *Psychoanalytic Techniques*. New York: Basic Books, pp. 338–78.

Henderson, J. L. (1955) Resolution of the Transference in the Light of C. G. Jung's Psychology. *Acta Psychoterapeutica* 2: 75–91.

Henderson, J. L. (1968) Unity of Psyche: A Philosophy of Analysis. In *Second Bailey Island Conference*. New York: C. G. Jung Foundation, pp. 46–60.

Jung, C. G. (1968) *Psychology and Alchemy*. Collected Works, vol. 12. New York: Pantheon Books.

Jung, C. G. (1973) *Letters 1906–1950,* vol. 1. Princeton, NJ: Princeton University Press.

CHAPTER 4

ANALYSIS IN TRAINING

From *Jungian Analysis*, edited by Murray Stein, Open Court Press, 1995[1]

Jung was the first to recognize the necessity of the training analysis, and did so while still a Freudian psychoanalyst. Freud acknowledged the importance of this contribution when he stated, "I count it one of the valuable services of the Zurich school of analysis that they have emphasized this necessity and laid it down as a requisition that anyone who wishes to practice analysis of others should first submit to be analyzed himself by a competent person" (1912, 116).

Thus, the importance of the personal analysis for analytic training was central for both Freud and Jung from the beginning, before World War I. In Jung's later writings he continued to place the personal analysis of the analyst at the core of training, all the while recognizing its limitations: "anybody who intends to practice psychotherapy should first submit to a 'training analysis,' yet even the best preparation will not suffice to teach him everything about the unconscious. ... A complete 'emptying' of the unconscious is out of the question if only because its creative powers are continually producing new formations" (1946, 177).

In the field of analytical psychology, before the formation of training institutes, the way to become a Jungian analyst was through personal analysis with Jung and/ or one of his assistants. The first generation of analysts came to analysis primarily out of personal need, with little conscious thought of becoming analysts themselves. The early analysts were quite literally transformed into practitioners of their profession through their analyses. I would refer to this transformative aspect of the analysis itself as the individual calling to become an analyst.

Today's potential candidates have some notion of what it means to be an analyst before starting training. Usually they have been exposed to the analytic community through seminars, public lectures, workshops, and the like. They also have some idea, albeit a mixture of fact and fiction, of what the professional community is like. Today, in 1993, to become an analyst of the Jungian school carries with it a prestige that in former times did not exist, and aspiring candidates are well aware of this fact (see *U.S. News and World Report*, 7 December 1992). It is my hope that the individual sense of vocation will not get lost as it becomes "prestigious" to become a Jungian analyst, whereas barely a generation ago one had to overcome collective professional disapproval to want to become an analyst. A discussion of the applicants' structures of training, the selection, academic requirements, and the aims of training is presented elsewhere in this book [referring to David Tresan's chapter in *Analysis in Training*].

Jung's statements, quoted above, emphasize the importance of the personal analysis of anyone wishing to become an analyst, but they do not elucidate what a training analysis is, nor is a distinction made between it and other types of therapeutic analysis. In the English-language Jungian literature, only two articles specifically address themselves to the subject of training analysis (Fordham 1971) and Jungian analysis (Kirsch 1982). In the first edition of this volume, I defined the training analysis as the analysis of a person who is in analysis for the express purpose of becoming an analyst. The person generally has entered analysis because of some form of suffering but, at some point, has decided to become an analyst.

Prior to entering training, the potential candidate's analysis is qualitatively not different from other therapeutic analyses. The fact that the analysand is also a therapist leads to a certain mutuality of interests, but this is not so different from the analyst sharing common interests with other analysands. Once the analysand applies for candidacy, it has important implications for the analysis. What role does the analyst play in either encouraging or discouraging the analysand to apply for training? The task is somewhat easier when the analyst can in good conscience encourage the applicant. The analyst is an ally of the candidate, which has implications for the transference-countertransference. Sometimes an apprentice model is constellated, in which the candidate becomes a "disciple" of that particular analyst.

However, what happens if the analyst does not believe the analysand would make a good candidate? Should the analyst be the one to tell such analysands that they are not suitable to become analysts? When I definitely feel that the person would not be suitable, I have discouraged the analysand from making an application for training. Often, the analysand then realizes that being an analyst is not what he or she really wanted. When I do not have a definite sense one way or the other, I encourage them to apply and let an admissions committee evaluate them.

In addition to training analysis, the institutionalization of training has produced "training analysts," which implies that some analysts are better suited to train candidates than others. Some analysts are indeed better suited for training, because of their charisma, intelligence, maturity, lack of power complex, etc. However, this adds another level to the ever-increasing hierarchical structure of training, which is not good. Also, with the increasing size of institutes, the politics of who becomes a training analyst is sometimes arcane, and the "right" analysts are not necessarily given the stature of training analysts. Ideally, analysands or candidates should be free to choose their own analysts based upon the personal characteristics of the analysts, rather than being limited to certain preselected analysts, no matter how qualified they may be. The argument usually given against this freedom is that trainees will pick analysts who have the same defense structure and thus will not work out their issues. Strong arguments can be made for both points of view. In the end, every analysis is incomplete, and one keeps working out the issues in analysis and life. What happens in most analytic societies is that candidates tend to gravitate toward a few select analysts who see most of the trainees in a given institute, but the choice is hopefully based upon the psychological authority of these analysts rather than on their political power. It seems unfortunate when an analysand has to change analysts in order to conform to the institutional structures of a particular analytic group.

In the United States, there is a division between those institutes that do have a training analyst category and those that do not. San Francisco has felt strongly from the very beginning that there should not be a category of training analyst so the candidate has the widest possible options in the choice of a personal analyst. Many of the other larger American analytic groups do have the training analyst category. On the other hand, San Francisco does make a distinction in the area of control and supervisory analysis; in order to be eligible to do control work, the analyst must be a member in good standing for five years.

Regardless of whether the analyst is called a training analyst or not, the process of being in analysis is considered central in all Jungian training programs throughout the world. What this central process of analysis is varies tremendously from society to society. Over the past two decades there have been major changes in the field of analytical psychology that have influenced the practice of analysis. On one hand, through the object-relation theorists, such as Heinz Kohut, W. R. Bion, Thomas Ogden, and others, this kind of analysis has emphasized frequency of sessions – usually four times per week – the couch, the transference-countertransference, and more attention to the personal childhood aspects of the unconscious. The other main branch continues to stay close to Jung's original message, with less emphasis on frequency, use of face-to-face contact, symbolic interpretation of unconscious products, and less emphasis on the transference. No matter what their emphasis, almost all analysts of a Jungian persuasion have been heavily influenced by the object-relation theorists in psychoanalysis and the developmental school founded by Michael Fordham of London. All training institutes demand a certain minimum time in analysis prior to becoming a candidate – 150 to 200 hours – as it is only here that the future candidate can experience whether this is the right path or not. Also, certain basic complexes need to be worked on prior to training; otherwise, they are acted out in the training process. This happens enough under the best of circumstances. Some potential candidates have had long and deep analyses prior to their training, so one hopefully finds a variety among the candidates selected.

The International Association of Analytical Psychologists (IAAP) requires a minimum of a paltry 300 hours of analysis to complete training, but most American candidates have far more than that! How the different American institutes handle this requirement varies, but most of them require that a candidate be in analysis throughout the training period. This is a delicate subject, because training committees can be in the position to evaluate the analysis, and this represents an intrusion into the analytic process.

A related issue is what role the analyst has in the evaluation of the candidate. In the early days of the Jung Institute in Zurich the personal analyst was intimately involved in the evaluation process (Hillman 1962a, 8). This position was also held in New York and other centers, except San Francisco where there was a complete separation of the personal analysis from the rest of the training process. The San Francisco position held that if the training analyst were also involved in evaluation, this would overburden the already difficult work of analysis. If the training analyst had the power to pass judgment upon the candidate, it would seem likely that the candidate might withhold information, fearing that it could be used against him or her. Experience from psychoanalytic institutes where the training analyst had input on the evaluation had shown that candidates had withheld personal material in order to get through the training. After qualifying as a psychoanalyst, they would then submit to an unpressured therapeutic experience when they were no longer under the scrutiny of the analyst as evaluator.

In recent years almost all Jungian training institutes, including Zurich and New York, now separate the training analysis from the rest of the training process. The philosophy behind this is that, no matter what else happens, the candidate's analysis is private. The increased awareness about what happens when boundaries are transgressed, as well as the problem associated with dual relationships, has led all American institutes to delineate a clear demarcation between the personal training analysis and the rest of the training process. The early days of a mélange of analysis, seminars, and supervision by a small group of people who all talked to each other are gone forever (I hope!). All the larger institutes, and many of the smaller ones too, have well-placed safeguards against contamination of the analysis and the training process. The task of evaluating the candidate then falls to review committees that collect information from seminar leaders, control analysts, and the like. Also, many institutes require written case reports and in some cases a thesis so the candidate is evaluated in his or her development in a number of different ways.

Even if the analyst does not have an official voice in the evaluation of a candidate, the analysis of a candidate is different in many ways from an ordinary therapeutic analysis. Persons who enter analysis with the idea of becoming analysts have a definite aim or goal beyond their own therapy. They wish the analysis to serve the end of their becoming Jungian analysts, an ego aim. Such an aim is clearly different from that of a person who comes with no specific goal other than to get treatment for suffering. In the nontraining analysis, there is an endpoint at which the analyst and analysand separate, whereas in the training analysis there is continued connection in their shared professional world.

As a result, in the latter situation, unconscious material is constantly being influenced by the pressure of ego demands, such as seeking inclusion in the professional community and the training program. These ego demands may be quite similar to those of the analyst him- or herself. Some candidate's dreams may deal only with personal unconscious material, for example, and they may be concerned that their dreams do not include enough archetypal material; they doubt their "Jungian identity." Or candidates may strongly resist having their material interpreted in a Jungian way. This resistance may manifest itself in several ways. In order not to conform to collective expectations, they may not want to discuss dreams or other unconscious material. If they do present dreams, they may be resistant to their symbolic meaning, again, so as not to conform to the Jungian expectation.

What we are dealing with in the analysis is the archetype of initiation (Henderson, 1967; Micklem, 1980). The analysand as initiate may have a resistance to emerging unconscious material. The analyst as one of the elders may be seen as the wise old man or priestess in the initiation process. Furthermore, the analyst is a member of the group into which the candidate as initiate wishes to enter. There is a necessary ordeal and trial of strength that the analysand as initiate must undergo in order for the rite of passage to take place. It is an archetypal situation in which both the personal analyst and training institute carry the projection of the group of elders or communities.

Von Franz (1979) has discussed the vocation of analyst in the context of shamanic initiation. In primitive tribes, the shamanic initiate is the one who experiences a breakthrough of the collective unconscious and is able to master the experience, a feat many sick persons cannot achieve. Von Franz emphasizes that such an experience must occur in the analysis of a candidate as part of the training of an effective analyst. It is the perspective of initiation that differentiates the Jungian point of view from that of some Freudians. The latter often see resistance as only the product of the parental introjects, now projected onto the analyst and institute. For the Jungian, resistance includes not only those aspects, but also the dimension of shamanic initiation, which evokes the collective unconscious.

On the extraverted side, the persona of the analyst, as well as the sum of collective conscious attitudes that have developed toward the profession of analyst and toward the local training institute, may become critical concerns to a candidate. The candidate may question why the institute has a particular rule or a certain seminar topic and not another. These issues tend to surface within the training analysis, but in my experience they are often used as a form of resistance to some more personal issue for the candidate. Although one must deal with their content, it is important for the training analyst to recognize the resistance aspect and deal with it.

An even deeper issue involves the tension between individuality and collective responsibility. Training analysts must, on the one hand, honor the individual

24 *Analysis in training*

expression of the analysand; on the other, they have a collective responsibility to the Jungian community to affirm certain values basic to the practice of Jungian analysis. Candidates are in a profound search for their own identity and will often question the value of becoming analysts. Eventually, the candidate may cause the training analyst to question the value of analysis itself, with thoughts like these: after all, analysis can help so few people; some are not helped at all; analysis itself may be just a luxury. Training analysts must be secure enough in what they are doing to stand the "test."

More agonizing still for the candidate is that he or she, like all analysands, must eventually realize that there is no point of security outside the analysis itself to provide a sense of direction, and whether a personal transformation will take place cannot be known beforehand. All training institutes say that they honor the individuality of the candidate, but at the same time they emphasize certain collective values and attitudes about the meaning and importance of Jungian analysis. Beyond that, the different institutes embody certain styles and emphasize certain aspects of the analytic process, and individual candidates must come to terms with those nuances of emphasis with which they may not agree.

A further complexity in most training analyses is the fact that most candidates are in the first half of life when they enter training, even though Jungian psychology often emphasizes changes that take place in the second half of life. This creates a tension between the candidate's own experience in analysis and certain aspects of Jungian theory and practice. Moreover, the institute wonders how the candidates will develop as they mature. What one hopes for in the training analysis is that enough genuine dialogue with the unconscious will be experienced to foster a commitment to continue the process. This does not always turn out to be the case.

A large issue in any analytic relationship is the transference-countertransference. In a training analysis, this phenomenon has many complications not found in a normal therapeutic analysis. Training analysts are potential models for the candidates. Out of their analytic experience candidates initially find the model in which they will practice themselves. If there is a mainly positive transference, the trainees will introject the analyst and will begin their own practices by using a similar style. After all, who else's work has the candidate experienced at such close hand and so intimately? The problem is, though, that the training analyst's style may not work for a particular candidate. Differences in psychological type and personality may mean that the analyst's style cannot be imitated by the trainee. If, for instance, an introverted thinking type is attracted to an analyst whose typology is extraverted feeling, the experience may be good for the trainee but will serve poorly as a model for the trainee's own analytic practice. The training analysts, on the other hand, may have considerable difficulty in letting the candidates go in directions that are not consonant with their own dominant attitudes and orientations. It is hard for an analyst to judge whether differing attitudes derive from differing psychological typologies or from unresolved transference-countertransference issues.

Fordham (1971) has offered insight regarding the irreducible pathological core in any transference-countertransference situation. All analytical psychologists value the individuating factor, but the shadow of human nature surfaces when candidates' individuation contradicts their mentors' most sacred tenets. How the training analyst and candidate handle this complex impasse is extremely important, not only for them but for their institute. If genuine differences are not accepted, they can lead to splits within the training institute after the candidate becomes a qualified analyst. The training analyst therefore is both a role model and a person against whom the trainee can react.

Extra-analytic contacts, rivalry with "sibling" patients, and decisions about self-disclosure by the analyst are factors that frequently generate psychological issues in training analysis. Although the relationship to the analyst is initially restricted to the consulting room, this situation often changes when analysands become candidates. It is then probable that they will have contact with their training analysts outside of analytic hours. Candidates' experiences of seeing their analysts as seminar leaders are often initially fraught with difficulty. One typical reaction of the candidates is to feel exposed. They feel as if their analyses are continuing right there in the middle of the seminar, and that everyone else is noticing how vulnerable they are at that moment. They may feel as if their analysts are talking directly to them, while in reality they are addressing the whole group. It may also be hard for training analysts to talk to their patients in a seminar.

"Sibling" rivalry is often constellated in candidates who "share" their analysts with other students in a seminar. In the analytic hour, the trainees have their analysts all to themselves. They may have the fantasy of being the analyst's only patient, or at least the most special one. In the seminar situation, on the contrary, trainees see others who are in analysis with their analyst, and fantasies of rejection or of being less preferred than others may surface under these conditions. Furthermore, how others in the seminar react to their analyst becomes an issue. The candidates want their analyst to look good in the eyes of their peers. Thus, transference issues are carried out of the consulting room into other areas.

These transference factors, inherent in training situations, allow more contact between analyst and analysand than in the therapeutic analysis. As a result, the candidates tend to have more real knowledge about their analysts than ordinary analysands, and consequently there are more "hooks" on which to hang projections. Now there occurs a temptation for the training analysts to be more self-disclosing in an effort to validate their patients' perceptions and to welcome them prematurely as colleagues. A certain collegial attitude can enter into the analysis, which affects the transference-countertransference relationship. Perhaps this temptation also reflects the isolation and loneliness of being an analyst and the desire to share one's experiences. Casualness may mask deep unresolved problems.

Such emphasis on the transference and countertransference causes the analysis to last longer, as more of the unconscious material is interpreted in the light of the transference. In London, where one group of Jungians practice analysis using the couch, a regressive transference is fostered, and hence more infantile psychopathology is evoked. This can be extremely helpful to trainees, for they can experience certain psychopathological states in themselves within the transference relationship rather than merely learning about them from textbooks and clinical exposure. Fordham specifically encourages providing conditions wherein psychopathological states can be experienced in the training analysis (1971). His thesis depends upon the concept that psychopathology is the result of quantitative, not qualitative, variations in the experience of unconscious conflicts. The hope is that the candidates can experience and transform their own areas of psychopathology so that they can help patients who have similar problems. Equally, the trainees can learn what parts of themselves are healthy and therefore do not require analytic work.

In line with the view that the training analysis should involve the maximum exposure of a candidate's complexes, it has been suggested that training should include more than one analyst/analysis, as they would most likely emphasize different aspects of the analysand's psyche according to the dialectic that is established. On the other side, it has been argued that this dilutes the intensity of analysis. Proponents of both points of view expressed themselves in a symposium on training published in the *Journal of Analytical Psychology* (Fordham 1962, 26; Plant 1961, 98; Hillman 1962b, 20). A review of the debate was published by this author (Kirsch, 1976).

Multiple analyses – that is, the practice of seeing more than one analyst during training – has long been an accepted pattern among analytical psychologists. It dates back to Jung, who would often refer his analysands to a female analyst at the same time that he was seeing them himself (Wheelwright, 1975). Multiple analysis has two main advantages. First, if carried out with a male and a female, it may activate the inner polarity between male and female components of the psyche. A man's anima will be experienced differently with a woman analyst than through the anima of a male analyst. Obviously, sexual fantasies will also be experienced differently depending upon the sex of the analyst.

In addition, seeing a second analyst gives the analysand an opportunity to experience a therapist of a different psychological type. As mentioned earlier, an analysand often starts analysis with someone who is of a similar psychological type. Later in the analysis it may be important to have the experience of someone of an opposite type and function. Theoretically, therefore, a wider consciousness of anima and animus and of one's psychological type will be experienced through multiple analyses.

Against the practice of multiple analyses is the justified concern that this practice leads to transference "leakage." An analysand may transfer to another analyst when resistance develops with the first analyst. Analyst and analysand may, with the best of intentions, work out a transfer or an addition of another analyst without consciously realizing that this was all done to avoid a resistance. Therefore, the practice of multiple analyses – extremely common in Jung's day – is no longer recommended; the risk of "acting out" in the transference is too subtle and too great. Of course, most candidates do see more than one analyst during their training, so that multiple analyses in a serial sense occur often and do widen the perspective and consciousness of the trainee.

This leads us into the role of the control analyst and what his or her function is in relationship to the training analysis. The IAAP requires each candidate to have a minimum of 100 hours of individual control supervision by a certified Jungian analyst. Usually the trainee brings three or four analytic hours with the patient for each hour of supervision. Some institutes require more than 100 hours of control, and this can be done with several supervisors. Generally, there is one main control analyst and several others who are seen briefly for a particular perspective. The control analyst is in a peculiar position because he or she represents the values of the institute and at the same time is an advocate of the candidate. Furthermore, control analysts vary in how much they get into personal analytic material of the candidate. How much of the countertransference is dealt with by the control analyst and how much is left to the personal analysis? The boundaries are not clear. Splitting the transference between the personal analyst and the control analyst can and does easily occur. The supervisor needs to be confident in his or her role as supervisor without needing to try and take over the analysis. Also, there needs to be respect between the control analyst and the personal analyst. If not, the candidate ends up buffeted between the two, much like in a conflict between the parents (recent symposium by the International Federation for Psychoanalytic Education, Hillman, 1992). Furthermore, the control analyst is not bound by issues of confidentiality, so that he or she is *expected* to inform the evaluation committees of problems that exist with the candidate. The issue of supervision has received relatively little attention in the literature.

An extremely important issue is how a candidate's analysis ends. The ending of analysis is a difficult and complex subject in its own right. There is the realization that an analyst needs to continue self-analysis forever, and that there will be periods of returning to one's original analyst or going to another one. Fordham has described the termination of a training analysis as depending upon:

> (1) the patient's history, embodying past separations, capacity to feel grief, and gratitude, (2) the overt transference situation, (3) clues obtained from one or a series of dreams, (4) the reality situation of the new Society member, (5) an assessment of the ongoing individuation processes at work in the unconscious, and last but not least, (6) the training analyst's countertransference.
>
> (1971, p. 181)

Fordham emphasizes the idea that an unresolvable pathological nexus exists between any patient and his or her analyst, consisting of the irreducible part of certain complexes in both analyst and patient that cannot be analyzed away. Fordham discusses this idea in terms of the actual traumatic situations that have occurred for both analyst and analysand that can be elucidated but cannot necessarily be changed, and also to the theme of the "wounded healer" referred to by Jung. Fordham maintains that the full elucidation of this pathological nexus is frequently overlooked through insufficient concentration on reconstructing infancy and childhood. I would point out that the elucidation of the pathological nexus is critical in a training analysis, since it may be the only way to help potential analysts recognize the damaged parts of themselves that are likely to come up in their future professional work.

Fordham states that a candidate's pathology is all too often displaced into the local society in which the future analyst will practice. The local professional society carries the projection of family, and members react to it as such. Concurrent with this are all the individual transferences and countertransferences among the individual members that can never be fully resolved. These mutual projections flare up from time to time, and it is hoped that they can be contained within the local society. But, when that unresolved pathological nexus is too large, it becomes a nidus out of which hatch tendencies for one or more members to split off from the larger whole. This situation is what makes the basically rewarding job of being a training analyst disillusioning as well.

This chapter has encompassed a delicate subject. Personal analysis of the candidate is the core experience in the making of a Jungian analyst. It needs to be the most individual and subjective of experiences, and yet, at the same time, candidates are evaluated by review committees that probe their relationship to their own psyches. How does one protect the individuality and creativity of the analytic process, and yet at the same time produce analysts? The very mention of the word *training* constellates complexes, because analysts all have their own strong ideas of what the analysis of a candidate should be. In this chapter I have tried to describe some of the complexities of the personal training analysis as a candidate goes through the training process. It is not easy for a candidate in training to have a successful analysis, and we may marvel that it works as often as it does. Unfortunately, all of us have been privy to the other side as well. The personal analysis is the groundwork of being an analyst, and one needs to protect it from the institutional demands of training.

Note

1 "Analysis in Training." In Murray Stein (ed.), *Jungian Analysis*. La Salle, IL: Open Court Press, 1995. Reprinted with the permission of the publisher.

References

Edinger, E. (1961) Comment. *Journal of Analytical Psychology* 6(2): 116–17.
Fordham, M. (1962) Reply. *Journal of Analytical Psychology* 7(1): 24–6.
Fordham, M. (1971) Reflections on Training Analysis. In J. B. Wheelwright (ed.), *The Analytic Process*, pp. 172–84. New York: Putnam.
Fordham, M. (1976) Comment. *Contemporary Psychoanalysis* 12: 168–73.
Franz, M.-L. von (1979) Beruf und Berufung. In U. Eschenbach (ed.), *Die Behandlung in der Analytischen Psychologie*. Fellbach: Verlag Adolf Bonz, pp. 14–32.
Freud, S. (1912/1958) Recommendations to Physicians on the Psychoanalytic Method of Treatment. In *Standard Edition*, vol. 12. London: Hogarth, pp. 109–20.
Guggenbühl-Craig, A. (1971) *Power in the Helping Professions*. New York: Spring.
Henderson, J. L. (1967) *Thresholds of Initiation*. Middletown, CT: Wesleyan University Press.
Hillman, J. (1962a) Training and the C. G. Jung Institute, Zurich. *Journal of Analytical Psychology* 7(1): 3–18.
Hillman, J. (1962b) A Note on Multiple Analysis and Emotional Climate at Training Institutes. *Journal of Analytical Psychology* 7(1): 20–2.
Jung, C. G. (1913/1961) *The Theory of Psychoanalysis*. Collected Works, vol. 4, pp. 85–226. New York: Pantheon.
Jung, C. G. (1946/1954) *Psychology of the Transference*. Collected Works, vol. 16, pp. 163–321. New York: Pantheon.
Kirsch, T. (1976) The Practice of Multiple Analyses in Analytical Psychology. *Contemporary Psychoanalysis* 12: 159–67.
Kirsch, T. (1982) Analysis in Training. In M. Stein (ed.), *Jungian Analysis*, pp. 386–97. La Salle, IL: Open Court.
Marshak, M. O. (1964) The Significance of the Patient in the Training of Analysts. *Journal of Analytical Psychology* 9(1): 80–3.
Micklem, N. (1980) Paper read at Symposium on Training, Eighth International Congress of Analytical Psychology, September 5, San Francisco, CA.
Newton, K. (1961) Personal Reflections on Training. *Journal of Analytical Psychology* 6(2): 103–6.
Plant, A. (1961) A Dynamic Outline of the Training Situation. *Journal of Analytical Psychology* 6(2): 98–102.
Samuels, A. (1985) *Jung and the Post-Jungians*. Boston, MA: Routledge & Kegan Paul.
Spiegelmann, M. J. (1980) The Image of the Jungian Analyst. *Spring: A Journal of Archetype and Culture* 101–16.
Stone, H. (1964) Reflections of an Ex-Trainee on his Training. *Journal of Analytical Psychology* 9(1): 75–9.
The International Federation for Psychoanalytic Education Conference. (1992). Denver, Colorado
Wheelwright, J. B. (1975) A Personal View of Jung. *Psychological Perspectives* 6: 64–73.

CHAPTER 5

FAMILY MATTERS
The descendants of Jung and Freud

From the *Journal of Analytical Psychology* 43(1), January 1998[1]

It is a great honor to be invited as the keynote speaker for this conference. Our topic, "Family Matters," lies at the heart of the emotionally laden conflicts over theory and practice that have plagued the first one hundred years of depth psychology. Psychoanalysts and analytical psychologists grew from different family trees, although the two trunks touched briefly between 1907 and 1913. The resultant schism has produced much bad blood, which has begun to heal in the last few years. The first JAP conference held here at Sebasco Lodge, Maine, last year (1996) was most helpful in this regard, as both the speakers and the participants were open and respectful. We felt a heightened level of enthusiasm and rapprochement throughout the conference. Clinical issues were presented, and similarities and differences in theory and practice were noted. This year we are examining the history and background behind these differences, and hopefully, by the end we shall have a better understanding of their meanings. We have come a long way from those early days when it was difficult for Jungians and Freudians to be in the same room.

This topic has a living reality for me because my parents were first-generation Jungians who both analyzed with Jung during the 1930s, were Jewish, and were forced like so many others to emigrate from Europe. They settled in Los Angeles in 1940 and remained there until their respective deaths, my mother in 1978 and my father in 1989. They were ardent supporters of Jung and were the founders, along with Max Zeller, of the Los Angeles Jung Institute. The Freud–Jung schism loomed as a large factor in their lives. Just after World War II, when the Nazi atrocities against the Jews and others had just come to light, Jung was being accused of having been a Nazi. The term "racial unconscious" was being attributed to Jung in professional publications, although Jung had always referred to this layer of the psyche as the collective unconscious, never the "racial unconscious." For people like my parents who were both Jewish and strong supporters of Jung, this presented a particular challenge. His alleged anti-Semitism was discussed in several publications, including the *Saturday Review,* a most respected literary and cultural magazine of its time. The Bollingen Foundation, named after Jung's tower in Bollingen and supported by the Mellon family, had awarded their annual poetry prize in 1949 to Ezra Pound, an acknowledged fascist. Jung had nothing to do with the award, as it was awarded by a committee of poets, which included T. S. Eliot among others. Robert Hillyer, a poet who had won the Pulitzer Prize in 1934 and was president of the Poetry Society of America in 1949, wrote two scathing articles on Jung in the *Saturday Review,* which the editors of the magazine supported completely (McGuire, 1982, 213). Many of Jung's followers, analysts and non-analysts, gentile and Jew alike, rallied to his defense. Emotions on both sides ran deeply. Conflict was accentuated

30   *Family matters*

by the fact that many analysts of both persuasions had been in analysis with either Freud or Jung, making it more than a theoretical issue. In Los Angeles Jungians and Freudians rarely met, and when they did, the atmosphere was icy. Though I came to realize later that this was not necessarily the norm, the tension between our two schools has been a leitmotif, both personally and professionally, of my life.

Much has been written about the Freud–Jung relationship, and it is not my intention to rehash it here, but there are a few salient comments that I would like to emphasize. It is absolutely essential to understand the cultural differences between the two men. Freud came from an Eastern European Jewish background, and his family was only a scant two generations removed from the shtetl. Furthermore, in the daily life of Vienna anti-Semitism was endemic, and it was difficult, if not impossible, for him to obtain positions because he was Jewish. Though steeped in nineteenth-century science and materialism, he had little formal training in either philosophy or religion. Jung, on the other hand, was imbedded in the traditions of the Protestant Swiss Reform movement with many ministers in his immediate family. He was educated at the University of Basle, where Nietzsche had recently been a professor, and philosophy had been one of Jung's major interests. He, too, was raised in the climate of anti-Semitism typical of his times, a prejudice that he had to overcome in order to accept Freud. Perhaps Freud's materialistic view of the psyche posed an even greater problem for Jung. They needed one another. Jung was the first non-Jew to become seriously interested in psychoanalysis. His experiments with the word association tests and his research into schizophrenia had already gained him an international reputation by the time that the two met (Kerr, 1993), and Freud was eager to have a gentile with Jung's stature become an adherent to psychoanalysis. On the other hand, Jung, whose own father had deeply disappointed him, was searching for and thought that he had found in Freud a father to respect and understand. Jung developed a powerful erotic father transference, and Freud developed an equally powerful son countertransference. What began as an intense and mutual romance soon began to develop negative overtones, which ultimately dominated, and the break in the relations became inevitable. Transference and countertransference phenomena, although recognized, were poorly understood at the time. I am not sure though that today the outcome would have been any different. One only need think of some of our most difficult cases to realize that, even with our current knowledge, acceptable resolutions may still not be possible in some instances. There has been much sorrow and bitterness expressed over the rupture between Freud and Jung. If only the two had managed to maintain their relationship, would it not have been so much better for depth psychology in general? On the contrary, given the extreme cultural and personality differences, I find it amazing that they could have come together at all. During the six years of their friendship, Jung was an ardent supporter of psychoanalysis, and many of the early pioneers such as Abraham, Jones, Brill, Eitingon, and others began their careers working with Jung at the Burghölzli. Orthodoxy in both camps, while initially effective to consolidate theory and practice, soon evolved at its extremes into a rigid fundamentalism, which has weakened depth psychology on both sides. There is no question that the rupture in the relationship was a life-long wound for Jung, a wound from which he never completely recovered. John Freeman, who interviewed Jung for the BBC in 1958, later stated in the *San Francisco Jung Institute Library Journal* (Boe, 1989) that Jung became restless and agitated when questioned about Freud, and he surmised that Jung, who was 83 at the time, still had not worked out his relationship with Freud.

The Freud–Jung story has been seen as the most dramatic of the many occurring during the early years of psychoanalysis. As Freudian theory and psychoanalysis has dominated the psychotherapeutic scene until recently, analytical psychologists have had to come to terms by necessity with Freud and psychoanalysis. This has been accentuated by the fact that the only person whom Jung writes about at any length in his autobiography is Freud. However, it must be remembered that Jung actually wrote only the first three chapters on his childhood; the rest of the book was written by Aniela Jaffe, who took notes as Jung recounted his life. In the original version there was material on William James, Theodore Flournoy, Pierre Janet, and Toni Wolff, among others, which for reasons that are not clear was withheld from publication by the Jung family and without which Freud's influence on Jung is magnified out of proportion (Shamdasani, 1995). This accentuation of Jung's relationship to Freud is somewhat ironical, as I cannot imagine that this was the intended effect of leaving out the other material. Furthermore, most scholarship on Jung until recently has taken a Freud-centric view of the Jung–Freud relationship. Another of our speakers at this conference, Eugene Taylor, will continue his focus on some of these other influences (Taylor, 1996). A further problem contributes to the complex and confused picture of the Freud–Jung relationship. Psychoanalytic historians often have failed to return to original sources to check the accuracy of their material. For instance, a particular view of the Freud–Jung split prevailed for many years, and every paper repeated the same story. An example of the difficulty in deviating from this orthodoxy can be found in the problems Henri Ellenberger had in getting his work, *The Discovery of the Unconscious,* published because his views did not correspond to the then prevailing attitudes about the Freud–Jung debate (Ellenberger, 1970). Ellenberger had gone back to the original sources and found papers that Jung had written while at university showing a Jung prior to Freud who was consistent with the Jung after Freud. Thus, Jung was not completely different (i.e., psychotic) after the break with Freud. His early student writings, the Zofingia lectures, never meant to be published, showed Jung as a young man to have had a passionate interest in the nature of God, religious experience, psychology, and the limits of exact science. If anything, because of his deep transference to Freud, Jung had put aside his reservations about psychoanalysis; after the break with Freud the thread of his earlier ideas re-emerged. To demonstrate how these errors are perpetuated, I would like to bring up a more recent example. John Kerr states in his book, *A Most Dangerous Method,* that Jung was brought up in the Calvinistic tradition (Kerr, 1993). However, Jung was brought up in the Swiss-Reform tradition of the German part of Switzerland, which derives from Zwingli, not Calvin, who lived in French-speaking Geneva. Subsequently, I have seen Jung the Calvinist erroneously referred to in many recent papers, whose authors have swallowed Kerr's statement without question. Anyone familiar with the Swiss psyche knows the enormous difference between its French and German aspects.

The schism with Freud left Jung alone and isolated. Most Zurich analysts remained with Freud, and Jung went through a profound withdrawal with periods of fear for his sanity (Jung, 1963, 176). An incessant stream of fantasies had been released from within, along with a great deal of emotion, and he had an urgent need to understand their meaning. Intuitively he was drawn back to the symbolic play of age 10 to 11 and returned to his imagination of that time. Jung engaged in an active dialogue with these inner emotions and images, but did not know what to make of them, and so he made the choice to yield to them. Very little in the way of scientific writing occurred during this period. A record of the inner dialogues and paintings was made in his private "Red Book" to express his emotional states. One pivotal document, written in 1916, he called *Seven Sermons to the Dead* (Jung, 1963). Here, in the voice of Basilides of Alexandria, a Gnostic thinker in second-

32 *Family matters*

century AD, Jung expressed his inner experience of what he later called the collective unconscious. This document was privately distributed for almost fifty years and was only published as an addendum to *Memories, Dreams, Reflections* in 1963. A recent paper in the *Journal of Analytical Psychology* (Thibaudier, 1995) directly relates the writing of this manuscript to the loss of the relationship to Freud. Her thesis is that Jung had sought a father in Freud, and when the relationship deteriorated, Jung found in the unconscious a symbolic attitude, personified by a character he called Philemon and expressed through such works as the *Seven Sermons,* which replaced Freud as the father figure. The technique he used to elaborate these images and emotions he called active imagination. In the practice of active imagination, the ego consciously surrenders its energy to the image or symbol so that it can contact the deeper layers of the psyche. Often, the images come from dreams, but the images can come from many sources. However, it is important to state that the ego is not completely obliterated, but rather that it functions at a lower level of awareness. Active imagination is often seen incorrectly as (1) the complete obliteration of the ego, or (2) fixed images being used by the analyst to initiate the process. Out of his own deep subjective experiences, which Jung referred to as "Confrontation with the Unconscious" (Jung, 1963), he slowly began to develop what he would later call analytical psychology to differentiate it from psychoanalysis.

This period lasted from 1913 to 1919, following which Jung emerged from his *nekyia* a changed man. From the end of World War I through the decade of the 1920s, Jung refined his thinking. A clearly defined theory and practice of analytical psychology evolved that lasted relatively unchanged until the early 1970s. The only exception was the London analyst Michael Fordham, a child psychiatrist who was influenced by the Kleinian school and who adopted psychoanalytic methods while espousing Jungian theory. Part of the difficulty in trying to compare theories has been a language confusion with both Freud and Jung using the same terminology, such as unconscious, transference, repression, resistance, ego, self, etc., but with different meanings. This problem still exists today, and it is one of the factors that continues to make dialogue between psychoanalysis and analytical psychology confusing.

Typically, Jungian analysis has consisted of face-to-face sessions of variable frequency from one to five times per week. Jung strongly believed that the reactions of the patient and analyst should be visible to one another, since the analyst and patient were equal participants in the process. An average of one to two sessions per week has been typical. However, those who came to see Jung in Zurich would see him on a daily basis while there. As the analysis of unconscious contents was the primary focus of the analytic work, typed-out dreams were brought to the analyst, and the major focus of the analysis was on the symbolic understanding of the dream. Personal associations and amplifications from mythology, comparative religion, anthropology, and other such sources were crucial in the interpretations. He also actively urged analysands to do active imagination as a way to further understand the nature of their own unconscious processes. He especially encouraged it in the final stages of analysis. The transference-countertransference was considered very important, but its interpretation was not as central as it is today. Jung liked to let the transference do its work and only discussed it when it got in the way, which happened often enough! Jungian analysis emphasized psychological development in the second half of life, the individuation process, and larger existential questions of meaning. Therefore, it was thought to be an especially appropriate process for people over 35 who were suffering a midlife crisis. Although I am attempting to describe the typical way in which Jung and first-generation Jungians worked, it would be difficult to ascertain exactly what a classical analysis consisted of. Jung saw the analytic encounter in individual and fluid terms, and he eschewed the word "technique" because he saw the individual encounter as the single most important factor in analysis.

It becomes immediately apparent that the aims and goals of a classical Jungian analysis were diametrically opposed to the prevailing Freudian model with its emphasis on early childhood development, the Oedipus Complex, and its commonly stated goal of improving the patient's capacity to "love and work." In the United States, Jungians were a small minority, functioning mainly outside the academic and hospital settings, and were professionally small in numbers. One exception was Jo Wheelwright, a psychiatrist known to many of the early American psychoanalysts. Jo was a professor at Langley-Porter, good friends with Erik Erickson and Frieda Fromm-Reichmann, and a prominent member of GAP, Group for the Advancement of Psychiatry, a powerful American psychiatric organization consisting of the most famous psychiatrists and psychoanalysts of the day. Jo's humor and extraversion made him a popular figure among these colleagues. Almost all other Jungians were completely unrecognized by American psychoanalysis, and these were the days when almost all heads of psychiatric departments were psychoanalysts. For example, in 1962 when I told my professors at Stanford that I was going into Jungian analysis, it was made clear to me that any advancement in my career would be difficult.

In England, the early Freudians and Jungians had a much different relationship. The first Jungians were Constance Long, the Eders, Maurice Nicoll, Esther Harding, and other women physicians. Constance Long translated Jung's papers into English in 1916 and wrote her own book in 1920 on phantasy (Long, 1920). She died soon thereafter, and the others all left the Jungian fold or moved to the United States. H. G. Baynes, a physician and psychiatrist who was for a while Jung's assistant in Zurich, became the individual who firmly established the roots of analytical psychology in Britain. He returned to London and began building a Jung group in the 1920s. His most prominent student was Michael Fordham. When Baynes died in 1943 at a relatively young age, Fordham emerged as the leading figure for the next fifty years in analytical psychology. As a child psychiatrist he needed other input than Jung's to aid him in his work of understanding early development on which there was relatively little emphasis in the Jungian literature. Fordham had a good contact with Winnicott, resonated with Melanie Klein's theoretical formulations, and through his psychoanalytic associations was placed on the board of the prestigious *British Journal of Medical Psychology*. He became a founding member of the professional society, the SAP, the founder of the *Journal of Analytical Psychology*, the sponsors of this conference, a prolific writer of many books and articles, editor of the *Collected Works* in English, and an organizer of both an adult and child training program in analytical psychology. Furthermore, Fordham had an extremely complex relationship to Jung. On the one hand he loved Jung deeply and was very committed to furthering his work. However, he had wanted to be a patient of Jung's in the late 1930s and had gone to Zurich with the idea of finding work and having analysis. Upon his arrival in Switzerland, Fordham was not allowed to be gainfully employed, and Jung would not see him as a patient. At the time most of his Jungian colleagues were in analysis with Jung, so he keenly felt the exclusion. My impression is that this left him with a life-long wound so that the transference to Jung was always ambivalent. On the other hand, it kept him from having the kind of idealization that so many of the other first-generation analysts had on Jung, and it freed him to explore the interconnections with psychoanalysis. When Fordham first brought the Kleinian ideas to analytical psychology in the late 1950s, there were strong protestations that he was no longer Jungian. Today Fordham is read by the majority of analytical psychologists and his ideas are widely accepted. Thus, there

34 *Family matters*

have been much closer ties between analytical psychologists and psychoanalysts in England than has generally been the case in the US. Many analytical psychologists in England openly state their clinical and theoretical approach is a combination of Jungian and object-relations models. However, in spite of the unofficial friendly relations between the two, on the official level there still is relatively little contact.

The extensive use by members of the SAP of the couch, frequent sessions, and emphasis on early development and the transference was thought by classically trained Jungians to be heretical; in the early days of the Zurich Institute, returning graduates did not feel comfortable in this setting. Thus, another professional association with a more typical Jungian model was established in London in 1977 to accommodate those returning from Zurich and also to offer candidates who wanted a more classical approach a place to train. For complicated political and personal reasons two more trainings were established in England that sought some balance of the two attitudes towards analysis. As time has passed three of the four London-based trainings have required at least three times a week analysis for their candidates, and so the differences in method have become much less marked.

The development of analytical psychology in the US has followed a different pattern. There never has been a national organization of Jungian analysts in the US. Each geographical region has its own professional society and its own set of standards that must conform to the minimum regulations of the International Association. The individual societies have not been willing to accede their autonomy to a national body. Thus, we have societies that have maintained a fairly classical view of Jungian analysis, and others that have incorporated many of the changes that are going on within psychoanalysis. Many of the American Jungian societies contain a broad outlook, which makes for interesting meetings within their respective societies. There is a much greater use of the couch, increased frequency of analytic sessions, and more emphasis on early development and transference, as the work of Fordham and newer object-relations theorists have been incorporated into our practices. Among the major psychoanalytic influences have been Melanie Klein, D. W. Winnicott, W. Bion, and W. R. D. Fairbairn from England, and Heinz Kohut and Robert Langs in the US. There are many other psychoanalysts who are widely read within the Jungian community, but I would single out these individuals as having the most widespread influence.

There have also been significant changes for those classical analysts who have not incorporated object-relations theory into their practices. Jung's hypothesis of the dialectic nature of the analytic relationship had too often led to an inappropriate use of self-disclosure by the analyst. It had been misused by analysts in a narcissistic manner to tell patients about themselves and others in a manner that was eventually harmful to the analysis. Today, most analytical psychologists are much less self-revealing, and the boundaries of the analytical container are far more secure. The danger of analytic leakage is much better understood.

As I began to think about this paper, I had no idea what would emerge. The Jungian position in both the US and the UK has been a minority one. To be Jungian has been suspect to anyone outside the Jungian community. My own life-long experience as part of the Jungian family has been a deep source of continuity among so many other changes. In my youth it bothered me greatly that Jungians were so easily and absolutely dismissed. Jung was tabooed by Freud and subsequent psychoanalysts in a way that none of the other dissidents were treated (Gallant, 1996). Today the atmosphere has changed or we would not be able to have a conference like this.

What are some of the changes? First of all, Freud and psychoanalytic theory has undergone critical review, and the whole field of psychoanalysis has lost its former hegemony in depth psychology. Second, there is a growing awareness among Jungians that analysis and analytic training is not enough; one must be grounded in basic psychotherapeutic principles as well. Third, subjects like spirituality, soul, and meaning, are now legitimate concerns of analytic inquiry, subjects that had concerned Jung from the very outset of his studies of the psyche. Fourth, it is more generally acknowledged that all analytic therapy is a profound meeting of two souls that cannot be reduced to technique alone. Fifth, on a practical level, all analytic treatment is under severe scrutiny and criticism. The newer biological treatments have often been in direct conflict with analytic principles, and present-day culture is against long-term solutions. If we continue to tear each other down, we shall only be hastening the eclipse of each of our professions. The era where psychoanalysis acts as a dominant cultural force is rapidly changing, and it is important that the factionalization of psychoanalysis lessen. As we have moved away from the actual Freud–Jung controversy, a more objective view based upon the changes both within psychoanalysis and analytical psychology have shown that there is a much larger area of common interest than was formerly thought to be the case. There is an openness to the other's point of view, which has allowed a conference such as this to happen.

Note

1 Reprinted with the permission of The Society of Analytical Psychology. "Family Matters: The Descendants of Jung and Freud." *Journal of Analytical Psychology* 43 (1998): 77–85, 0021–8774/98/4301/77 © 1998, The Society of Analytical Psychology. Published by Blackwell Publishers Ltd, 108 Cowley Road, Oxford OX4 1JF, UK and 350 Main Street, Malden, MA 02148, USA.

References

Boe, J. (1989) Pleasing and Agreeable. *San Francisco Library Journal* 8(4): 75–83.
Ellenberger, H. (1970) *The Discovery of the Unconscious.* New York: Basic Books.
Gallant, C. (1996) *Tabooed Jung.* New York: New York University Press.
Jung, C. G. (1916) *Collected Papers in Analytical Psychology,* trans. Constance Long. London: Bailliere, Tindall & Cox.
Jung, C. G. (1963) *Memories, Dreams, Reflections,* ed. Aniela Jaffe. New York: Vintage.
Kerr, J. (1993) *A Most Dangerous Method.* New York: A. Knopf Publishing Co.
Long, C. (1920) *Collected Papers on the Psychology of Phantasy.* London: Bailliere, Tindall & Cox.
McGuire, W. (1982) *Bollingen: An Adventure in Collecting the Past.* Princeton, NJ: Princeton University Press.
Shamdasani, S. (1995) Memories, Dreams, Omissions in Archetypal Sex. *Spring,* 57: 115–37.
Taylor, E. (1996) The New Jung Scholarship. *Psychoanalytic Review* 83(4): 547–68.
Thibaudier, V. (1995) Seven Sermons for Bringing the Dead Father Back to Life. *Journal of Analytical Psychology* 40(3): 365–81.

CHAPTER 6

JUNGIAN DIASPORA

From *The Psychoanalytic Review* 89(5), October 2002[1]

The diaspora had a profound impact on the spread of psychoanalysis to the far corners of the globe. What is not so well known is that the rise of Nazism also had a profound effect on the spread of Jung's psychology. Before we take on that subject, I would like to make a disclaimer on what will not be covered. This paper will discuss neither Jung's relationship to the Nazis nor his attitude toward Jews in general, although this issue will come up with all the individuals discussed herein. Anti-Semitism comes up whenever Jung's name is mentioned in psychoanalytical circles. When the Nazis came to power, there were no official Jungian institutions outside of a lay organization for analysands – no professional societies, no institutes, no training programs. There were only individuals who had sought out Jung for analysis. At that time, if Jung thought the individual was qualified to practice his methods, he would write a letter of recommendation to that effect. Another caveat, I am going to limit my discussion to those Jewish people who sought out Jung before World War II. There are Jews who became Jungian analysts after World War II who, as children, either immigrated from continental Europe to other countries or survived the concentration camps. They are not the subjects of this paper.

Sabina Spielrein qualifies as Jung's first Jewish analysand but after that there is no definite record. In any case, my father, James Kirsch, began his analysis with Jung in 1928. At the time he was a young psychiatrist in private practice in Berlin. He had had two years of Freudian analysis previously. From 1929 until 1933 he made periodic visits to Zurich where he saw both Jung and Toni Wolff for analysis. One of my father's patients at that time was Gerhard Adler, whom he encouraged to go to Zurich for analysis with Jung and Toni Wolff. Adler's best friend was Erich Neumann, who went to Zurich in 1933 and spent a year in analysis with Jung at that time. Another person in this circle was Ernst Bernhard, a psychiatrist who had been in analysis with Otto Fenichel, but who, in the midst of a spiritual crisis, sought out Jung. There were several others in this small circle of Berlin Jewish men who sought out Jung, but I shall concentrate on these four because they were all instrumental in the formation of new Jungian professional groups.

The least well known among the four, Ernst Bernhard, studied to be a pediatrician, but after a spiritual crisis began an analysis with Jung in Zurich. He went back and forth between Berlin and Zurich, but in 1935 he left Berlin permanently. He was refused entry into England and decided to settle in Rome. He began his practice as a Jungian and became friends with Eduardo Weiss, an early follower of Freud and founder of the Italian Psychoanalytic Association. Weiss became despondent and sought the aid of Bernhard. Weiss did not have a formal analysis with Bernhard, but his wife did. When they immigrated to the United States, Mrs. Weiss, on the basis of her analysis with Bernhard, became a Jungian analyst in Berkeley, California, while Eduardo lived and practiced in Chicago. Bernhard gave a series of lectures on dream interpretation to the Italian psychoanalytic association in 1937. When the Italian racial laws came into effect, Bernhard was forced into hiding for the duration of the war. Through friendship with Giuseppe Tucci, then president of the Italian Institute for Middle and Far Eastern Studies, he was able to remain at his residence under house arrest during the war. Tucci was a member of the fascist party and was thus able to protect him. Immediately after Rome was liberated in 1944, Bernhard resumed his practice as a Jungian analyst and became the founder of the Italian Jungians, which over time has developed into two large institutes with slightly different orientations. The founders of both institutes had their analyses with Bernhard.

Gerhard Adler immigrated to London in 1935. He had received a PhD in psychology in Berlin and had already published papers on Jungian psychology while still in Germany. When he arrived in London, there was already a medical section of Jungian analysts, and he became the leader of the non-medical Jungian section. His book *Studies in Analytical Psychology,* written in 1948, is still used as a basic text in analytical psychology. Theoretical and personal differences developed between Adler and Michael Fordham, child psychiatrist and leader of the medical section of Jungian analysts. Klein and Winnicott heavily influenced Fordham, whereas Adler maintained a position theoretically and clinically close to classical Jung. Eventually a split occurred, and two professional societies ensued. There are many ways in which one could describe this schism, but that goes beyond the scope of this short paper. Adler, as well as Fordham, served on the editorial board for the English translations of Jung's *Collected Works.* Later he served as president of the International Association for Analytical Psychology (IAAP) for two terms. Along with Aniela Jaffe he coedited the collected letters of Jung. He was often asked to present the views of C. G. Jung before the English public, both on radio and television. He died in 1988.

Erich Neumann has been considered by many to be Jung's most creative student. Born in Berlin in 1905 his early studies were in philosophy, psychology, Jewish identity, and poetry. He was most drawn to the mystical side of Judaism without being in any way orthodox. He finished his medical training in 1933 in Germany, and then he and his wife, Julie, spent one year in analysis with Jung. As ardent Zionists, they moved to Tel Aviv, where they lived until his death in 1960 and hers in 1985. At first, they set up an informal study group in Jung's psychology, and by 1958 they were the leaders of a professional group of Jungian analysts from Israel, which became a charter group member of the IAAP. Neumann's son, Micha Neumann, a Freudian psychoanalyst in Israel, has published a paper on Jung's alleged anti-Semitism based on the correspondence between Jung and his father. Space does not permit me to review this entire article.

However, in reading over the excerpts of the letters between Jung and Neumann, one finds that Neumann consistently implored Jung, with little success, to become more involved in the study of Judaism to match his study of Taoism and Buddhism. Also, he wanted Jung to become more aware of the politics in Europe, which Jung refused to do. Instead, Jung discussed his research into the spiritual practices of St Ignatius of Loyola. Even after Kristallnacht, Neumann implored Jung to become involved in the political situation in Europe, but Jung did not.

Micha Neumann concluded that on a personal level Jung and his father had an uncomplicated, warm, and collegial relationship. The fact that Neumann was a Jew and Jung a Christian did not seem to influence the relationship in any way. Jung was interested in what Neumann had to say about life in Palestine, and believed

38 Jungian diaspora

that it was good for the Jews to return to their native soil and roots. In spite of all this, Micha Neumann cannot forgive Jung's public statements in 1934 about the differences between Jewish psychology and Aryan psychology, and concluded that Jung was anti-Semitic at that time, a sentiment that he feels changed only after World War II.

The journey of my father, James Kirsch, is the one best known to me, and therefore I will spend the most time on it. As already indicated, my father began his analysis with Jung and with Toni Wolff in 1928. On October 4, 1930, he gave a lecture to the Analytical Psychology Club in Zurich, titled "A Contribution to the Problem of the Present-Day Jew in the Light of Modern Psychology." It was well received, and in fact it was repeated a second time on that occasion in order to accommodate the great interest. Jung and those close to him were in attendance. The main topic covered in the lecture was the problem of the modern Jew recently liberated from the ghetto and exposed to Western European culture. He discussed dreams in which he deciphered the tensions between the ghetto life and the modern assimilated Jew in Germany. Beyond the substance of the lecture itself, it is of interest to note that this young Jewish psychiatrist was invited to speak before Jung and his students at this particular moment in history. Given what happens soon after this, it takes on even greater significance

When Hitler came into power in 1933, my father applied for emigration to Palestine the very next day. He also advised all those around him to leave as quickly as possible. He settled in Tel Aviv and began a practice of Jungian analysis there. Jung was critical of my father for leaving Berlin and did not think that the situation warranted such dramatic action. A letter from Jung to a German colleague, Wolfgang Kranefeld, written in 1934, states that Jung thought my father was an "ass" to leave Germany at that time. One of those who followed him to Tel Aviv was Hilde Silber, at the time a widow with two small children. She was a patient of his with a strong erotic transference. We all know that sexual liaisons between patients and their analysts happen too often, especially in the early days, and it was the case here. Life in Palestine in the 1930s did not appeal to my father and mother, and so they applied to the Home Office in England to emigrate there. Jung had just given a series of lectures at the Tavistock Clinic, and the man in the Home Office had heard about the lectures. As a result, my father and mother were allowed entry into England. He practiced there until 1940, when it looked as if England, too, was going to be overrun by the Nazis. He had relatives in San Francisco and therefore applied for immigration to the United States. In the meantime, my mother had begun her practice as an analyst. Jung had sent her a patient, and that was how her career as an analyst was launched.

The trip across the North Atlantic in October of 1940 was extremely dangerous. Our boat was attacked several times by German U-boats, and, in retrospect, we were lucky to survive the trip. My parents had plans to practice in New York, but the Jungians there did not welcome them. Instead, they visited relatives in San Francisco and on the way stopped in Los Angeles. Los Angeles appealed to my father, and so he brought the family there. He and my mother became the founders of the Los Angeles Jung group and remained prominent personalities within the Jungian community until their respective deaths in 1989 and 1978.

An added complication to this story is similar to that of many other émigrés from Europe. My father had his medical education at Heidelberg University in Germany and was not licensed as a physician in the United States. In 1944 he spent seven months in New York and passed the medical license there. However, he needed an American internship in order to practice in California. The year before Otto Fenichel had died of a heart attack while doing his California internship. My father had fears that the same thing might happen to him and so did not do an American internship. Therefore, he never was able to use his medical license in California. Eventually an angry patient claimed that he was practicing without a license and sued him. After that he never used his medical degree. The lack of a proper license hampered him for the rest of his career, as he never became part of the larger psychological and psychoanalytic community in Los Angeles. The animosity between Freudians and Jungians during that period and my father's lack of proper California credentials left him and his students marginalized.

I have focused on these four Jewish men, because they were all the founders of new Jungian professional groups in foreign countries. They sought out Jung when they were in the midst of spiritual crises and discovered through him a way to deal with their spiritual quests. They were all forced to leave Germany because of the rise of Nazism, and they were all from Berlin. In many ways their stories were not too dissimilar from what happened to many psychoanalysts. There were no Jungian organizations at that time, and the Jewish influence in analytical psychology was much less than in psychoanalysis. Moreover, all four of these men had the unenviable position of being Jungian, Jewish, and at the same time having to defend Jung against the attacks of being a Nazi and anti-Semite, which began after World War II. Many other Jewish people, such as Aniela Jaffe, Jung's personal secretary late in his life, Rivkah Schaerf-Kluger, Sigi Hurwitz, and others, were in analysis with Jung during the 1930s, but they did not have the same organizational impact on the spread of analytical psychology in the world and so have not been discussed in this paper. The diaspora had a profound effect on the spread of analytical psychology, and it is a bit of the history that is not well known either by analytical psychologists or psychoanalysts.

Note

1 "Jungian Diaspora." *The Psychoanalytic Review* 89(5) (October 2002): 715–20. DOI: 10.1521/prev.89.5.715.22104. Republished with permission of Guildford Publications, from "Jungian Diaspora," *Psychoanalytic Review*, Thomas B. Kirsch, 89, 5 2002; permission conveyed through Copyright Clearance Center, Inc.

CHAPTER 7

TONI WOLFF–JAMES KIRSCH CORRESPONDENCE

From the *Journal of Analytical Psychology* 48(4), September 2003[1]

This correspondence is between two significant figures in the early history of analytical psychology. There are twenty-nine letters from Toni Wolff to my father, spanning a period of twenty-four years, from 1929 to the last one dated February 7, 1953. Half the letters are written between 1929 and 1933, and the other half between 1949 and 1953. I assume that there was correspondence between 1933 and 1949 because I came across a letter from Toni Wolff to my mother written in 1937. I am focusing on the letters from Toni Wolff to my father because, for most of us, myself included, she is relatively unknown, except that she was intimately related to Jung for over forty years and she was his assistant for many of those years. The Analytical Psychology Club of San Francisco has put together reminiscences of Toni Wolff into a small pamphlet edited by Fern Jensen, and Bob Hinshaw and Clarissa Pinkola Estes are putting together a collection of her unpublished papers. There are three letters from my father to Toni Wolff in answer to some of her interpretations of my father's behaviour in particular circumstances. The other letters must have been lost with the many moves that my parents made. The letters are all written in German, except for the last one, which is written in English, and I wish to thank Ursula Egli for the translations.

Let me begin by presenting a short biographical sketch of each. Toni Wolff, the oldest of three daughters, was the favorite of her father, a Swiss businessman. When he died in 1910, she was 22; she fell into a depression, and her mother sent her to Jung for treatment. Jung must have immediately sensed Toni's intelligence and aptitude for analysis, for in 1911 he invited her along with his wife and Miss Moltzer to the Weimar Psychoanalytic Congress (McLynn, 1996, 178). Some months after the end of treatment in 1912, the two began a sexual relationship, which soon became known to Emma Jung. Somehow they worked out their respective relationships and sustained this compromise for the remainder of their lives. Toni came regularly to the home for the Sunday lunch, and the three of them were seen together at meetings of the Club and Jung's seminars. She also travelled with Jung as his companion, as will be seen in these letters. Toni became a founding member of the Analytical Psychology Club in 1916, serving as its president from 1928 until 1945. From the early 1920s she worked as Jung's professional assistant, and many people who saw Jung in analysis also saw Toni Wolff. She was considered more practical and worked more personally with the analysand than Jung, and many found therapy with her to be more helpful. My father was one of those who saw both Jung and Toni Wolff in analysis. It is my impression that he saw Toni Wolff more often than he saw Jung, but I am not sure of this. The number of hours of analysis with both Jung and Toni Wolff was less than 100 each. My father documented the number when he was applying for licensure in California. During her presidency in 1944 the 10 percent quota on Jewish membership in the Analytical Psychology Club was passed. The Jewish issue had a great deal of significance in the relationship between Toni and my father, for it comes up early in the correspondence. Toni never married, and as a matter of fact, she never moved from the house in which she was born. When she became an analyst, she turned one of the rooms in her house into a consultation office. She died on March 21, 1953.

My father was born in Guatemala in 1901 into a Jewish merchant family. In 1906 his mother returned with all the children to Berlin where my father began his schooling. His father remained with the business in Guatemala and only came home every two years, but because of World War I he did not return between 1912 and 1921. My father received his medical degree from the University of Heidelberg in 1922 and joined the Zionist organization. He returned to Berlin to begin a practice of psychiatry. He began Freudian analysis and then, in 1922, switched to a Jungian analysis with Toni Sussman, with whom he had 300 hours of analysis. In 1928 he met Jung and Toni Wolff for the first time in Zurich, and between that time and 1933 he made periodic visits from his home in Berlin to Zurich to continue his analysis with both Jung and Toni. In applying for state licensure in California in the 1950s, he stated that he had about 60 hours with Jung and 50 with Toni Wolf. The first half of the correspondence deals with issues between my father and Toni Wolff while he still lived in Berlin. My parents did not like the atmosphere in Tel Aviv, and so in 1935 they immigrated to London. In October 1940 when it looked as if Hitler might invade Britain, my family made a hazardous trip across the North Atlantic and we eventually ended up in Los Angeles. My mother and father started the Jung group there, and they both taught and practiced in Los Angeles until their respective deaths in 1978 and 1989.

The correspondence begins around a scheduled visit of Jung to Berlin in January 1930. Toni asks my father for recommendations for a hotel near the scheduled meeting place and expresses some concern that she might not be admitted because the lecture was sold out. She writes to my father on January 4, 1930: 'We will arrive on the evening of January 12th and are happy to follow your suggestion and stay at the Bristol hotel. Preferably we would like two quiet, single rooms with a bathroom to share between these rooms.'

Two things stand out for me in this letter. First, a relatively new analysand, and a very young one at that, is brought into the familiar circle around Jung. Jung travels openly with Toni, and my father would have known something about the relationship between them. Second, the tone of Toni's letter demonstrates her well-known formality.

The next subject is a most fascinating one. It involves negotiations around a lecture that my father made to the Analytical Psychology Club in Zurich in the fall of 1930. At that time the Analytical Psychology Club was the only structure where people interested in Jung's psychology met, and it was very difficult to join this élite group. Membership required sponsorship by two members as well as a recommendation from one's personal analyst, and then there was a long wait for an opening. In addition, the activities of the Club were all in German so most Americans and British did not even try to join. On September 12, 1930, Toni Wolff, president of the Analytical Psychology Club, wrote to my father that the Club would indeed be interested in his lecture entitled 'The Problem of the Modern Jew in Germany'. No financial remuneration was offered, but she did hold out the possibility that he might be given membership in the Club after his lecture:

I am pleased to note that under the circumstances you will not expect any financial remuneration. On the other hand, I hope that your possible application for membership would be accepted after your lecture, even though you do not live in Switzerland. Of course, I am just mentioning this as a personal remark between us and it should not be referred to publicly. There will be plenty of time for you to send in the application from Berlin after your return (in the usual manner, with two sponsors, and most importantly with a description of the reasons for wanting to join) since there will be no Executive Committee meeting before then.

Emma and Carl Jung, as well as Toni Wolff, attended the lecture. It has been translated into English, and in fact it was read at the IAAP Congress in Zurich in 1995. In it, my father describes dreams of many Jewish analysands living in Berlin. The image of the Nazi brown shirt had already entered into individuals' dreams. Given what happened in Germany shortly thereafter, and the questions raised about Jung's relationship to Jews, the timing of this lecture is important. There was so much interest in the lecture that it was given twice. In the end the executive committee of the Analytical Psychology Club offered him some compensation for his double efforts. Shortly thereafter he was made a 'guest' member of the Club, with the prospect of eventually becoming a regular member. I do not believe that he ever gained the status of a regular member because of the interruption of World War II and his subsequent emigration.

Another very interesting issue came up around the same time. There was a young German artist who lacked funds for analysis, which the Club decided to subsidize with my father in Berlin. She attempted suicide while in analysis with my father, and this brought the analysis to an end. The attempted suicide outraged Toni Wolff, who wrote to my father 'if she continues with such disgusting behaviour, the Club will no longer support her'. Later she stated:

> If I were in your place I would not receive Miss M. anymore if she wants to commit suicide. In that case analytical discussions have no purpose. She only wants your sanction of her suicide, and that is what you can refuse to give her.

This ended the analysis with Miss M., and there ensued a discussion about payment and how much compensation my father should have and how much should be returned to the Club. Toni Wolff was exacting about the money in a most Swiss manner. I find it interesting that the Club had funds to subsidize someone's analysis. I have never heard of this before, and I do not believe this happened frequently.

Following the success of this lecture, my father wished the next year (1931) to give a lecture on Goethe's *Faust,* especially in relationship to the anima. Toni Wolff did not want my father to give this lecture to the Club. She stated that there had been a lecture on Goethe's anima recently, and the Club did not need a further lecture on the subject:

> I do not think that the lecture would be suitable for the Club. We had a Goethe evening about a year ago, and Dr. Medtner spoke about Goethe's anima problem with reference to the figure of Mignon who is Goethe's outstanding anima figure. In October I repeated my lecture, and now I would like to let Goethe rest for a while.

The subject of the anima came up frequently in these letters because my father had difficulties in this area. Women patients developed strong transferences to him, and he likewise had strong countertransference reactions. Toni Wolff was direct and forthright in addressing this issue. It is a leitmotif throughout the letters.

We now move to February 1949 when the correspondence resumes. My parents, along with Max Zeller, had established a growing Jungian community in Los Angeles. As reported earlier, the letters from the intervening years have been lost. My father had given a lecture in Los Angeles titled 'From Hollywood to the Shores of the Spirit' in which he analysed the dreams of a Jewish screenwriter. He was going to use the same material for a seminar in Zurich, and he wanted Toni's reactions. Her reaction was critical of the way my father worked. One of the symbols in the dream was a uniform, and Toni Wolff had some general remarks to make about the symbol of the uniform, which she felt my father had not expressed in his interpretation of the dream:

> You interpret the uniform as the collective persona which he should lay off. However, in the dream the main concern is for him to find a place where he can put on the uniform, because now it is no longer a joke but it is serious. Do you know what a uniform is in reality? It is duty, discipline, and putting aside everything personal and individualistic. It would seem more likely to me that it signifies the acceptance of the human being, as he really is, without personal and arbitrary delusions, wishes, and ambitions ... I wanted to mention these things to you so that you will be more exact in the interpretation of dreams in your seminar here. We are accustomed to something else, and also our students. We cannot offer them interpretations which are only intuitive and optimistic ... It seems to me that you were seduced to many interpretations because you overestimated the creative forces and consequently under estimated human nature, and thus reality ... this is dangerous.

In the same letter she chided my father for having spoken about her relationship to Prof. Jung at a social gathering.

> Why you know about such things, I cannot surmise; in any case it is nobody's concern and is certainly not a topic of conversation at a party. Such things are unbelievably tactless and tasteless and besides terribly misleading. Do you take your licence to your 'feeling cult' from such things? Do you see so little awareness of reality?

My father responded to Toni Wolff in a letter dated February 27, 1949, in which he stated that many things had gotten mixed up in gossip by the time they reached her. He says that he has been extremely discreet about her relationship to Jung, and that the conversation mentioned had probably taken place many years ago, and he could not remember it exactly. He also explained why he did not go into more detailed amplifications in the lecture, which was because he did not have the time. My father had wished to speak with Jung about these private and personal matters two years before, but he had been told that he should not speak about these touchy matters at that time because of Jung's precarious health.

She replied on March 10, 1949, in a much more conciliatory tone. She stated that she was not judging him, but she wanted him to know that the students at the Institute were expected to learn what careful dream analysis was:

Many thanks for your letter of February 27. It appears that you misunderstood several things I wrote, and I would like to clarify them. As far as your lecture is concerned, I certainly never thought of criticizing your analysis with the person in question. My objections only referred to the interpretation of the cited dreams which I found to be overly intuitive and optimistic. The explanations in your letter just seem to confirm my impression, especially as far as the pathological elements in the first and last dreams are concerned and which you do not touch upon at all in this interpretation. For our students, however, it is particularly important to learn what a careful dream analysis is.

And about the discussion of her relationship to Jung she stated the following: 'It is absolutely unnecessary to give any explanation to people who are curious. Such things are very delicate and easily misunderstood, especially by young people'.

The next letter from Toni Wolff is dated December 31, 1949. In addition to some general gossip and news, Toni Wolff brings up an interesting issue. My father had sent her a redwood plant for Christmas by airmail. Toni Wolff neither knew what it was nor how to take care of it, so she asked my father for advice on its care. I find this quite touching because the redwood tree is so much a part of California, and I interpret this as an effort on my father's part to bring a part of California to her. I do not know what happened to the redwood plant, but my guess is that it did not survive.

The next letter, January 19, 1950, has many subjects of interest. The first item discussed is that of the death of her brother-in-law, Hans Trüb. Hans Trüb was a psychiatrist who was married to Toni Wolff's sister. He had become a student of Martin Buber. Trüb had been an early member of the Club, but then he and Jung had a falling out. He had published a book titled *From the Self to the World* (*Von Selbst zur Welt*) in which he had attempted to connect Jung's work with that of Martin Buber. In this letter Toni Wolff states:

> The alliance of Buber with modern analytical psychology seems somewhat open to question, as far as I am concerned, especially in view of the fact that Dr. Trüb did not quite understand the Jungian ideas, of course, because he thought in Buber's concepts and terms.

The relationship of Hans Trüb to C. G. Jung is a long and complicated business and it is beyond the scope of this paper to present.

Another subject of that letter is one in which my father became extremely involved. Prof. Bruno Klopfer, a leading expert in the field of Rorschach psychology at the time, desired to become a Jungian analyst in Los Angeles. He presented his credentials, and my father questioned his number of hours of Jungian analysis. My father then wrote to other leading Jungian analysts, including Jung and Toni Wolff, asking advice about this situation, which generated many bad feelings before Klopfer eventually was made a Jungian analyst in Los Angeles. In 1959 he started a biennial two-week-long workshop in Asilomar, California. At the time it was the only such intensive study group in the United States, and many future Jungian analysts were introduced to Jung's psychology through this workshop.

Lecturers from Zurich also began travelling to the United States. Frau Ostrowski, a Zurich Club member, brought back some impressions of the Los Angeles Jungians to Toni Wolff. Miss Wolff relayed these impressions to my father:

> She (Frau Ostrowski) believed that in Los Angeles the members of the audience were visibly relieved when she told them that symbols do not have a definite

meaning, but instead – according to circumstances – have different meanings. From this she concluded that you had evidently taught that certain symbols are defined precisely and unequivocally.

Her second impression was that also in other situations you may appear too much as an authority figure ... I have heard the view expressed before that you like to play the role of the pope who decrees infallible dogmas.

She ends the letter by stating: 'I hope that these observations will be of some use'. My father answers her in a surprisingly nondefensive manner, given the strength of her criticisms. He relates several dreams, which relate to the issues she mentioned. It is refreshing for me to see that my father took her comments seriously, but at the same time he defended his point of view. Toni Wolff certainly was not easy on him.

There is one final letter written on February 7, 1953, just six weeks prior to her death. Toni Wolff had had severe arthritis for many years and was always going to spas for treatment, and my father earlier had offered to send her cortisone, which had just come on the market. Her response is so typical of her:

I am sure that I would have declined cortisone, that was not even necessary because, luckily, the physicians here are very sceptical of such wonder drugs and first test them carefully and thoroughly, and if possible only clinically. I have heard about very injurious and dangerous consequences of cortisone from several sources.

This concludes the correspondence in my possession. In going over these letters I have gathered many new insights about my father, and they have acquainted me with Toni Wolff's personality. I never had a chance to meet her, as she died a few months before my first visit to Zurich. In these letters, she appears as a formidable person, forthright–direct, and no-nonsense. She could say things to my father that no one else who I know could, and he seemed to be able to take it. In the correspondence, she is extremely formal, and in all the letters refers to my father as 'Dr. Kirsch', and never refers to him by his first name. In return my father always refers to her as 'Miss Wolff', and never refers to her as 'Toni'.

From early on in the relationship Toni Wolff is at least challenging if not antagonistic towards my father. She challenges him about being a member of a 'feeling cult', making imprecise and sloppy interpretations, being indiscreet regarding her relationship to Jung, and then later as being inflexibly authoritarian and rigid regarding symbolism. My father did feel that she was not very accepting of Jews and he has told me that she was not anti-Semitic, but he thought she had more antagonism towards Jews than Jung did, although her feeling towards Jews was never a subject that he dwelt upon at any great length.

My father had contact with her during a period in which not only he but also much of the world was in turmoil and transition. She, on the other hand, never left the house in which she was born. What a contrast! From the correspondence I can see that my father really listened to her and respected her deeply. In light of his circumstances and the world situation, he was never able to see her on a regular basis. In reading over the correspondence it made me wonder how his life and consequently my life might have been different had my father been able to be in a long-term analysis with her.

Note

1 Reprinted by permission of the Society of Analytical Psychology, "Toni Wolff–James Kirsch Correspondence." *Journal of Analytical Psychology,* 48 (2003): 499–506, 0021–8774/2003/4804/499, © 2003, The Society of Analytical Psychology. Published by Blackwell Publishing Ltd, 9600 Garsington Road, Oxford OX4 2DQ, UK and 350 Main Street, Malden, MA 02148, USA.

Reference

McLynn, F. (1996) *Jung.* London: Bantam Press.

CHAPTER 8

HISTORY OF ANALYTICAL PSYCHOLOGY

From *Analytical Psychology: Contemporary Perspectives in Jungian Analysis*, edited by Joseph Cambray and Linda Carter, Routledge, 2004[1]

The history of analytical psychology is part of the larger history of depth psychology and psychoanalysis, with which it is intertwined and yet separate. Due to the painful and bitter parting between the founders of psychoanalysis and analytical psychology, Sigmund Freud and Carl Gustav Jung, a reliable early history has been difficult to ascertain. In a profound way the cleavage between the two founders has both promoted and at the same time inhibited the growth of the two fields. It is not my intention to rehash the Freud/Jung controversy because it is so fraught with factional disputes that any objective view is hard to establish. However, it is necessary that it be mentioned as a baseline problem that has had a long-term and defining imprint on both schools.

Through study of the history of these two movements, one can develop a deeper understanding of why the founders had to separate and travel their own pathways. Beyond the personal clash between the two men, there was a wide cultural divergence. Simply put, Freud's training was in biology, and his theories of the unconscious developed out of a neurophysiological background. Jung, on the other hand, was deeply influenced by continental philosophy, especially Leibniz's "unconscious perceptions," Kant's "dark representations" and *ding-an-sich*, Schopenhauer's "tendency of the unconscious material to flow into quite definite molds," and finally Nietzsche's ideas from *Thus Spake Zarathustra*.

Any history of analytical psychology must begin with its founder, C. G. Jung. It is not the intent to give extensive biographical material on Jung, but there are salient facts about his life that have influenced the development of analytical psychology.

Jung was born on July 26, 1875, in a small Swiss village, Kesswil, along the Rhine River. He came from a long line of Protestant ministers, including his father. His mother's ancestors had mediumistic experiences, as did she. Jung had powerful dreams at a very young age, which he describes in his autobiography, *Memories, Dreams, Reflections*. As mentioned above, he had a strong interest in philosophy, but he went to medical school in Basel, Switzerland, graduating in 1900.

He then moved to Zurich, where he worked at the Burghölzli clinic under Professor Eugen Bleuler. Jung became Bleuler's first assistant and remained at the Burghölzli until 1909 when he left to enter private practice, which he continued with some interruptions until his death in 1961.

In 1903 he married Emma Rauschenbach, the daughter of a wealthy industrialist from Schaffhausen, and they had five children, four girls and one boy. In 1909 they built a house on Lake Zurich in Kusnacht where they lived the rest of their lives. Jung also developed a very important relationship in 1912 with a former patient

48 *History of analytical psychology*

of his, Toni Wolff. She was the other woman in Jung's life, and she became his assistant. These circumstances were known to Jung's family as well as to his patients and disciples, and the three parties involved appeared to be comfortable with the arrangement. In recent years, this situation has received much attention and has given rise to the belief that Jung was a womanizer.

In 1924 Jung built the tower in Bollingen, mostly with his own hands; he continued working on it for the rest of his life. The tower was also on Lake Zurich, but it was in a very secluded part, and here Jung could live in a simple and introverted way. He spent many weeks at a time in Bollingen.

Jung's work on word association experiments at the Burghölzli led him to contact Freud because he realized that Freud's observations on the unconscious were crucial to an explanation of his own research results. This led to Jung writing to Freud in 1906, and in 1907 the Jungs, along with Ludwig Binswanger, traveled to Vienna, where the first conversation between Jung and Freud lasted for thirteen hours. Freud recognized Jung's talents and later referred to the younger man as his "crown prince." For the next six years, Jung was a leading adherent of Freud's, and he represented psychoanalysis both in Europe and in the United States, becoming the first president of the International Psychoanalytic Association and editor of the major psychoanalytic journal and various books. The bitter breakup of their relationship is dramatically chronicled through the letters they exchanged (see McGuire 1974 on the Freud/Jung Letters).

Sabina Spielrein is mentioned over thirty times in the letters, and I would like to draw attention to her, as a great deal of new material has come out recently. Consulting Freud as supervisor, she was Jung's first patient with whom he used psychoanalytic techniques. Sabina Spielrein was a 19-year-old Russian Jewish woman who was brought in on an emergency basis on the evening of 17 August 1904 with a diagnosis of hysteria. Jung became her doctor and psychotherapist, and an extremely strong transference-countertransference situation developed. By the following spring she was well enough to attend medical school in Zurich and was able to leave the hospital. She continued to see Jung as a patient over the next few years, and a strong love relationship developed between the two of them. The exact nature of what happened in their interaction is unknown, but some, including Bruno Bettelheim, are convinced that they had a complete sexual relationship. After graduating from medical school in Zurich she moved to Vienna, where she became a part of the Viennese psychoanalytic circle and became a psychoanalyst. She married and had a daughter, and after moving around for several years, she returned to Russia where she became a leader in psychoanalysis. She opened a psychoanalytic kindergarten in Moscow in 1925, but as Stalin gained control of the country, psychoanalysis was outlawed and she returned to Rostov; little is known of what she did there. She was killed by the Nazis in 1942 along with other Jews of the city. Much of this material has become available only in the past fourteen years with the breakdown of the Soviet empire. Also, her hospital records at the Burghölzli have been released by surviving family members, so we have a much better idea of her state of being in the hospital. Her story is very dramatic, and recently she has become the object of many new books, movies, and theatrical plays. She is no longer just a footnote in psychoanalytic history, and her papers linking sexuality, destruction, and creativity have become better known. Freud included a footnote on her when he first wrote about the "death instinct" in *Beyond the Pleasure Principle* in 1922.

Let us return to what happened to Jung after the breakup of his relationship with Freud. Jung underwent a profound introversion where images from the unconscious flooded him. He spent much time alone and went through periods of disorientation. At the conclusion of World War I and this period of what he called "confrontation with the unconscious," he felt much more secure and had developed the basic elements of what he was to call his new psychology – analytical psychology. The first use of this term is in his *Psychology of the Unconscious*, written in 1912–13. Although Jung coined the term "analytical psychology," it has often been used interchangeably with the term "Jungian." Many modern-day analysts refer to themselves as Jungian analysts, others as analytical psychologists, and still others as Jungian psychoanalysts. These different identities refer to various levels of commitment, allegiance, and identification with both Jung and analytical psychology. It seems that as we move further away from the life and work of Jung, terms other than "Jungian analyst" are coming more into common usage.

In 1921 Jung published a major work, *Psychological Types*, where he described the now well-known typology introversion/extraversion, along with the feeling/thinking and intuitive/sensation functions. These terms have come into common usage in many languages, and the psychological type theory is used extensively in business applications.

By the 1920s, Jung's reputation and psychology had become well established and his interest in the creative process led him to attract many writers and artists. His psychology particularly attracted students from England and the United States along with others from around the world. He gave seminars during the academic year to his English-speaking students in Zurich, and he lectured and traveled widely throughout Europe and United States, along with trips to Africa and India. In 1934 he became president of the International General Medical Society of Psychotherapy and in that capacity he worked closely with colleagues strongly identified with the political leadership of Nazi Germany. His reputation has been marred by that association, which I will discuss in more detail with the history of analytical psychology in Germany.

In 1928 he received a manuscript from Richard Wilhelm, a renowned sinologist, who had translated an ancient Chinese alchemical text, *The Secret of the Golden Flower* (1929). Through this book Jung became interested in the subject of alchemy, and for the remainder of his life he studied and wrote about alchemy texts (mainly European). Through the language of alchemy, he saw the expression of the unconscious in its symbolic form and could then draw parallels between the dreams of twentieth-century individuals and the imaginings of medieval alchemists.

In the wake of a broken leg, he suffered a heart attack in 1944 and was in semi-retirement until his death in 1961. In 1948 he inaugurated the founding of the C. G. Jung Institute in Zurich with a lecture there, and each year until his death he met with the students from the Institute. Jung was not interested in promoting organizations, because he was concerned that they tended to stifle the creativity of the individual. This impression seemed to result from his leadership experience in the International Psychoanalytic Association and the International General Medical Society of Psychotherapy, which had not gone well.

By the time of Jung's 80th birthday he had sufficiently overcome his aversion to organizations, and the International Association for Analytical Psychology was founded. The IAAP has become the accrediting body for all Jungian analysts in the world and has put on an international congress every three years where new research in the field can be presented. In the same year (1955) the *Journal of Analytical Psychology* was founded in London, and it has become the leading Jungian journal in the English language – more about both outgrowths later.

Jung received many honors during his lifetime, including honorary degrees from Harvard, Yale, Oxford, Calcutta, Clark University, and many others. His books

50   *History of analytical psychology*

have been translated into many languages, and his ideas on the nature of the psyche, including the theory of archetypes, the collective unconscious, extraversion/introversion, complex, Self, individuation, and synchronicity, have coined terms that have come into common usage.

Analytical psychology has had different patterns of development from country to country. It has had a continual presence since the early 1920s in Switzerland, the United States, the United Kingdom, and Germany. There has been a long-standing interest in analytical psychology in other places such as France, Italy, and Israel. The last quarter of the twentieth century saw a rapid expansion of interest in Jung's psychology, including Australia, New Zealand, Brazil, South Korea, Japan, South Africa, Austria, Scandinavia, and more recently the Baltic countries, the Czech Republic, Hungary, Bulgaria, Russia, Poland, China, Mexico, and Venezuela. At this point in time, analytical psychology has become a truly worldwide phenomenon.

Switzerland

The history of analytical psychology begins in Switzerland, where Jung lived and worked. Zurich naturally provided fertile soil for psychoanalysis and by 1912 a well-functioning psychoanalytical association connected to the Burghölzli and the University of Zurich was in place. However, in 1912 the Zurich Psychoanalytical Association separated from the Burghölzli and became an independent organization with no academic affiliation, which contributed to psychoanalysis and analytical psychology developing their own independent institutions.

A further separation took place on July 10, 1914 when Alphonse Maeder led the Zurich psychoanalytic group to an almost unanimous decision to resign *en masse* from the International Psychoanalytic Association and the Zurich Psychoanalytic Association. This happened after Freud's denunciation of Jung and the Zurich school in his *On the History of the Psychoanalytic Movement* (1914: 70), where Freud had established an orthodoxy that did not allow for free and unimpeded research.

On 30 October of the same year it was decided to rename the society the Association for Analytical Psychology on the suggestion of Professor Messmer (Muser, 1984). This group, consisting mainly of medical doctors, met on a regular basis every other week until 1918, when it became absorbed into the newly formed Analytical Psychology Club. During the period between 1912 and 1918 Jung reformulated his major theories of the psyche, the collective unconscious, archetypes, individuation, and psychological types, and the meetings at the club must have been significant.

Shamdasani's recent research (1998) has shown that between 1916 and 1918 there were two separate Jungian groups: a professional one, the *Verein*, and a lay group, the Analytical Psychology Club, which became a model for similar clubs in other cities and countries. The two groups merged in 1918 under the name of the Analytical Psychology Club, and this was the meeting place for both analysts and analysands.

Following the First World War, Jung emerged from his "confrontation with the unconscious" (Jung, 1963) and his fame spread, especially in the English-speaking countries and Europe. Individuals would write to Jung asking to see him in analysis and, if accepted, they would come to Zurich for varying lengths of time. In those days, analyses were usually much shorter for many reasons, not least financial considerations, which prevented protracted stays. Most foreigners' analyses were less than a year, and many lasted only weeks or a few months.

History of analytical psychology   51

In 1925 Jung began to give seminars in English in Zurich (McGuire, 1989), and from 1928 to 1939 he gave a seminar in English each academic semester. Originally the transcripts of these seminars were distributed only selectively, but in recent years many of them have been edited and published. Individuals who were in analysis with Jung were invited to attend seminars, as well as Zurich analysts. In his role as professor at the Eidgenossische Technische Hochschule, Jung gave a weekly lecture on basic aspects of analytical psychology to the general student body, and analysands who could understand German were invited to attend. These lectures were quickly translated into English by these analysands.

The combination of analysis and seminars provided the training for the first generation of Jungian analysts. The analysis was usually done with Jung and Toni Wolff. The analysand would see Jung one day and Toni Wolff either later the same day or the following day. This type of analysis, of seeing more than one analyst at a time, has been called "multiple analyses" (Kirsch, 1976) and became an accepted and usual pattern in Zurich and in other countries following the Zurich model. It was sharply criticized by Michael Fordham (1976) in London because he claimed that the transference-countertransference implications were not being analyzed and interpreted. Fordham and his followers believed that the "multiple analyses" model allowed for too much acting out by both the patient and the analyst, fostering avoidance and splitting. On the other hand, the input of two analysts of different psychological types and genders could be helpful, at times, to the patient. Jo Wheelwright, one of those who experienced multiple analyses in Zurich, stated that Jung was excellent for archetypal interpretations while Toni Wolff was more experienced at working on personal issues and overall he found her to be a better practical analyst than Jung (Wheelwright, 1974). This pattern of multiple analyses has continued into subsequent generations of analysts in Zurich and other places. The increasing importance of analyzing the transference has lessened its practice considerably.

In the early days the path to becoming a Jungian analyst was fluid. Jung would write a letter stating that the person had studied his methods and was ready to practice as an analyst. However, seeing Jung was no guarantee that an individual would receive a letter of accreditation. Many people who expected such a letter never received one, whereas others who did not plan to become analysts received Jung's blessing. In some instances Jung recommended further academic training to an analysand, e.g., Jo Wheelwright, while others were accepted with very little academic training, for instance, Hilde Kirsch.

During the 1930s, Jung did not seem very interested in forming his own school of psychology and psychotherapy. As president of the International General Medical Society for Psychotherapy, he was more interested in finding points of commonality among the different schools of psychotherapy. In 1938, he signed a statement produced by the International General Medical Society for Psychotherapy, which outlined points of agreement among the various psychotherapeutic schools. In Switzerland, he became president of the Swiss Society for Practical Psychology where he was again attempting to form a common, non-sectarian basis for psychotherapy. However, some of his closest associates during that period recognized the need to form an institute in Zurich where Jung's psychology could be studied. Due to World War II, the plan had to be put on hold until 1948.

After the war, a small institute for the study of Jung's psychology was founded at Gemeindestrasse 27 in Zurich, the same building where the Analytical Psychology Club was housed. There was much discussion about the choice of its name. Toni Wolff favored "Institute for Complex Psychology," whereas Jung's chief concern

52 *History of analytical psychology*

was the omission of his name in the title. Jung's followers won out, and it became the C. G. Jung Institute. Jung gave the inaugural speech on 24 April 1948 on the subject of the history of "Complex Psychology," and he suggested areas for research, such as: further experiments with the word-association test and family structure; more fully elaborated clinical case histories; research on dreams in relationship to physical illness, death, catastrophes; research on the normal family in terms of psychic structure; the compensatory nature of marriage; and finally, much more work on symbolism – triadic and tetradic forms and their historical development in relationship to philosophy, religion, and the new field of microphysics. At the end of the speech he recognized that much of the list was "mere desideratum" and "not all of it will be fulfilled" (Jung, 1948, paras 475–6).

The establishment of the Jung Institute changed the way one became a Jungian analyst. It was no longer strictly a personal matter between the individual and Jung. At the Institute, training became part of a larger educational experience where the individual's analysis was still paramount, but where academic criteria had to be fulfilled and formal structures began to play a significant role. However, the Jung Institute was not an international accrediting body, so that individuals still could become analysts by having personal analysis with Jung and receiving a letter of recommendation from him. It was only with the founding of the International Association for Analytical Psychology (IAAP) in 1955 that the authority for accreditation was definitively transferred from Jung personally to a professional association.

The Institute was set up along the lines of a European university with many classes, non-compulsory attendance, and the only requirement being that students pass a test in a given subject at the end of the year. Admissions requirements included the minimum of a master's degree in any field, along with a personal biography and interviews. The lack of specificity in a clinical discipline went along with Jung's idea that a non-clinical background could be an appropriate foundation for becoming an analyst. The profession of Jungian analyst was seen as a separate discipline and one could become an analyst via theology, economics, or philosophy, just as readily as through the traditional disciplines of medicine, psychology, and social work. Such liberal admission requirements have allowed individuals, for instance, to make a midlife change and become analysts by studying in Zurich. In the meantime, clinical requirements to practice any kind of therapy have tightened worldwide, but the Zurich Institute remained, until recently, a training center where non-clinically trained people could become analysts. However, the tightening of requirements clinically has affected the Zurich Institute. The basic tracks include the following subjects: Fundamentals of Analytical Psychology; Psychology of Dreams; Association Experiments; General History of Religion; Fairy Tales; Mythology; and General Psychopathology. After taking the required courses, students have to pass a test, the *propaedeuticum*, in each of the given subjects. After passing the test they attend case colloquia, where patient material is discussed, and further courses to deepen their knowledge of analytical psychology.

In the early years, symbolic understanding was emphasized over clinical training. In order to graduate from the Institute, students then had to pass another set of examinations, write and defend a thesis, and write up analytic cases demonstrating Jungian methods. The Institute offered tracks in German, English, French, and Italian. The vast majority of the early students were American, British, or Swiss. For many years the number of students hovered around thirty at any given time; the atmosphere was lively and intimate and the discussions intense. Jung would visit the Institute from time to time to meet with the students and he often attended the

History of analytical psychology   53

yearly students' party. Although the Institute in Zurich was not the first Jungian training center in the world (London and San Francisco having started in 1946), it was by far the most organized and the largest. With the presence of Jung in the background and many of the first generation of analysts providing the bulk of the teaching and analysis, Zurich was the center for analytical psychology.

During the first twenty years of its operation, the Institute was a very creative place to be; there was an intimacy and an intensity that the students attending there really enjoyed. Jung and the first generation of analysts around him were the primary teachers and there was an atmosphere of congeniality. Then there was an episode of a sexual transgression by the director of studies at the time, which involved the entire Institute as well as governmental structures in both the United States and Switzerland. The affair produced a heated division within the Institute community and, as a consequence, the director of studies was forced out. This event was a harbinger of change in the Jungian world as the question of boundary violations was at issue in many other Jungian training programs at the time. Clinical boundaries were to assume greater importance in the future of all training programs, including Zurich. Perhaps change happened more slowly in Zurich because the influence of Jung's own interest in archetypal symbolism and mythological amplification of dreams held sway over clinical traditions more dominant in other training centers, as well as Jung's relationship to Toni Wolff.

The Jung Institute was the central cohesive structure for analytical psychology in Zurich as it provided the training and the exchange of intellectual ideas. However, there was a need for a professional organization in Switzerland that could deal with the political, administrative, and professional issues that faced the growing number of graduates working there. Another important development was the establishment of the Klinik am Zurichberg, an inpatient facility utilizing Jungian theory and practice. Many students from the Jung Institute did part of their clinical training at this facility and, at the time, it was the only Jungian-oriented hospital in the world. When the founders of the Klinik retired, the divisions within the remaining staff resulted in the hospital philosophy reverting to a more traditional one.

As Jung's ideas became more popular, the Jung Institute in Zurich could no longer accommodate all the students. In 1973 an old mansion, which was owned by the community in Kusnacht on the Lake of Zurich, became available, and Adolf Guggenbühl-Craig, as the president of the Institute, was able to arrange a favorable lease agreement. Located close to Jung's home, the building seemed ideal to house the growing Institute. Student enrollment increased steadily and by the end of the 1980s, out of a total of 400 students, over 100 were American. At the same time, the Institute had widened its international character with the addition of students from Asia, Africa, and the smaller European countries. As geographical boundaries expanded, so did the curriculum. Clinical issues had greater emphasis and the number of required clinical colloquia, as well as individual supervisory hours for students, increased. This broadening of analytic theory was anathema to some of the first-generation analysts, especially Marie-Louise von Franz, who felt that Jung's contributions were being diluted by the addition of psychoanalytic theory and practice. These changes within the Institute curriculum demonstrated to von Franz that not enough attention was being paid to the individuation process going on in the unconscious. Honoring her strong beliefs about the nature of Jung's work, she withdrew from teaching at the Institute in the early 1980s. Other analysts and candidates joined her, and they began to meet informally on a regular basis.

This resulted in the "von Franz group" eventually forming their own institute, the Research and Training Centre in Depth Psychology, which came into being on

54 *History of analytical psychology*

8 May 1994 and was incorporated as a foundation the following day. On the surface, the programs of the Jung Institute and the Centre seem very similar. However, as one probes more deeply into the heart and soul of this new program, meaningful differences emerge. In the Centre, the collective unconscious, or objective psyche, becomes the most central guide for each individual and the value of the outer collective is minimized. Students at the original Jung Institute have more concern for the collective values and the persona than do their Centre counterparts. Former members of the Jung Institute whose allegiance moved to the new Centre gave up their membership in both the IAAP and the SGfAP (the Swiss Society for Analytical Psychology). Candidates graduating from the Centre will not be eligible to become members in the IAAP as their training will not be with IAAP members. The Centre has much the feeling of the old Institute during the 1950s and 1960s, when the number of students was small and the courses were similar in nature to the curriculum at the Centre.

At this time we have two trainings going on in Zurich. Those who want to study mainly von Franz and Jung go to the Research Centre, whereas those wishing a more traditional Jungian training attend the Jung Institute in Kusnacht.

I have gone into much greater detail with Switzerland than I will with the other training institutes because of its long history and the centrality of its position. It is also the only Institute that is run on a university model; all the other Institutes are part-time and additional to other professional activities such as private practice, hospital practice, or working in a clinic.

The United States

The next country where analytical psychology developed was the United States. Jung made his first visit there in 1909 when he, along with Freud, gave lectures at Clark University in Worcester, Massachusetts, where they received honorary doctorates. This was the first of many visits for Jung, but it was Freud's only trip to America.

Analytical psychology first took root in New York, and two decades later it was established in San Francisco and Los Angeles. These three centers developed relatively independently of one another and have unique histories. They developed during Jung's lifetime, and he had contact with individuals at each center. Other Jungian groups did not develop in the United States until the early 1970s.

Jung made three trips to the United States between 1909 and 1912 as an adherent of psychoanalysis and a colleague of Freud. These visits were mainly to the eastern seaboard, centered on Boston and New York. Both Freud and Jung were widely acclaimed on their first visit and were enthusiastically greeted by the medical elite and the intellectual establishment. When Jung returned for the third time in 1912 to deliver a series of lectures on psychoanalysis at the medical school of Fordham University in New York, he publicly expressed his differences with Freud for the first time. Although we know from the Freud–Jung correspondence and Jung's publication of the *Wandlungen und Symbole der Libido* in the *Jahrbuch* (English translation: *Psychology of the Unconscious,* 1916/1991) that differences in viewpoints were emerging, it was only in the Fordham lectures that Jung made these differences explicit and public. While accepting Freud's view of infantile sexuality, he relativized its importance and began to state that a neurosis develops out of a conflict in the present and that one must analyze the here and now to rid the person of suffering. Furthermore, Jung expanded the concept of libido beyond Freud's conception, which primarily focused on sexual and aggressive drives. Jung defined libido as psychic energy in general, including sex and aggression but also consisting of other primary drives such as the nutritive or the spiritual.

The first Jungian in the United States was Beatrice Hinkle, a physician who made the first English translation of *Wandlungen und Symbole der Libido* as *Psychology of the Unconscious* in 1916. Beatrice Hinkle has the further distinction of having set up the first psychotherapy clinic of any kind in the United States at the Cornell Medical College in New York in 1908. She studied and analyzed with Jung in 1911 and then returned to New York, where she joined Constance Long, a British physician who had also analyzed with Jung, and two American physicians, Eleanor Bertine and Kristine Mann. The four physicians formed a small study group. The two younger women, Bertine and Mann, had met as medical students at Cornell Medical College where Hinkle held a position in the Neurology Department. In 1919 Bertine arranged for Drs. Hinkle and Long, established analysts, to speak before an International Conference of Medical Women. Dr. Mann was also a participant at that conference. Following the conference Mann and Bertine went to Zurich for analysis with Jung. While there, they met Esther Harding, an English physician, who was also in analysis with Jung. Harding and Bertine developed a close relationship that was to continue for the next forty years. In 1924 they decided to relocate to New York. They returned to Zurich for analysis two months each year and spent summers at their residence on Bailey Island, Maine, where they also saw analysands. In 1936, after Jung received an honorary degree from Harvard University, he gave a seminar on Bailey Island where many of his students at the time came to hear him.

Beginning in the 1920s, other Jungian analysts began to practice in New York who were not so closely aligned with Drs. Mann, Bertine, and Harding. The most influential individual was Frances Wickes, a lay analyst, whose book *The Inner World of Childhood* (1927) became a best seller, followed by *The Inner World of Man* (1938) and *The Inner World of Choice* (1963). Henderson (1982) describes her work as being inspirational rather than analytical. There was a tension between Frances Wickes and the three women doctors. Wickes, as a lay person, had a different perspective from the three single professional women, and there was a distant but respectful relationship between them.

Following the model of Zurich and London, New York started its own Analytical Psychology Club in 1936. The format was similar to that of other clubs with monthly meetings and papers presented by analysts, lay members of the club, and guest speakers. An enduring achievement of the Analytical Psychological Club was the establishment of the Kristine Mann Library. When Mann died of cancer in 1945, the club library was named in her honor. The library has assembled a press archive of Jung and his work starting in the early 1900s and has amassed a large collection of related material on mythology, comparative anthropology, psychology, and religion. Many unpublished manuscripts can be found there.

During Jung's 1937 visit to New York, Paul and Mary Mellon consulted him, and the following year, they attended the Eranos conference in Ascona, Switzerland. They remained in Zurich until the fall of 1939 in analysis with Jung. Prior to leaving Zurich, Mary Mellon discussed her idea of having Jung's *Collected Works* translated and published in English. Before the Mellons were able to return to Zurich and finalize the negotiations, Mary Mellon died tragically in *status asthmaticus* in the spring of 1946. In her memory, Paul Mellon created the Bollingen Foundation, named after Jung's tower. The first volume of the *Collected Works* to be published in English was *Psychology and Alchemy* in 1953. The Bollingen Foundation subsidized the publication of Jung's writings in order to make them available to the general reader. The Foundation dissolved in the early 1980s, and at that time Princeton University Press took over the publication of the *Collected Works*.

At the conclusion of the Second World War, the Medical Society for Analytical Psychology was formed, and in 1954, a division of psychologists was formed. Realizing that they had more in common than divided them, they combined to form the New York Association for Analytical Psychology in 1957, which became one of the founding members of the IAAP at its inaugural meeting in Zurich in 1958.

C. G. Jung Foundation

Interest in Jung's psychology continued to grow, and the Analytical Psychology Club had neither the financial resources nor the personnel to meet the growing need. The analysts in New York, spearheaded by Esther Harding, decided to form a foundation that would serve as a central point for all activities concerning Jung's analytical psychology. Initially the scope of the foundation was national, and it included analytical training, a clinic, book publishing, a library, and an information center. It became operational in 1963. The New York Foundation is basically a lay organization with membership open to any individual regardless of prior experience, either academic or analytic. For financial reasons, it has ceased publishing books, and it no longer has a clinic. It has lost its national character, but it remains a valuable resource for those living in the Greater New York area.

A significant event was the establishment of the Archive for Research in Archetypal Symbolism (ARAS), a large collection of pictures and commentary on their archetypal significance from numerous cultures and ages. The collection was begun by Olga Froebe-Kapteyn in Ascona at the behest of Jung in the 1930s and had been supported by the Bollingen Foundation. When the Bollingen Foundation was phasing out its operations, the New York Jung Foundation was offered the ARAS collection if it would provide housing and continued care for its development. Mrs. Jane Pratt agreed to underwrite and guarantee the costs for the first ten years of its existence so that ARAS became an integral part of the Foundation in the late 1960s. Paul Mellon also lent support to ARAS with a generous grant that has helped to put ARAS on firm financial ground. Eventually, ARAS separated from the Foundation and formed its own national board and administration. It continues to thrive today with an ever-growing collection and wider distribution.

Although a New York professional association was formed in 1946, the training program was informal until the establishment of the Foundation. When the Foundation was formed, the New York Institute became a part of it. The training center developed its own board, which has governed policies with regard to training and which has been separate from the Foundation board.

The first candidates graduated in 1963. Before the Foundation existed, training consisted of a long period of personal analysis and supervision of cases with another analyst, after which the prospective analyst would be invited to join the professional group. There was no special requirement for admission beyond a degree in psychology or medicine. One of the unique features of training in New York has been the requirement that all candidates attend a two-year, once-a-week group therapy. This developed out of a two-year, leaderless group therapy experience of six senior analysts from 1960 to 1962 who found it so useful personally that they made it a requirement of the training program. Christopher Whitmont, one of those six original senior analyst members, recognized how much conflict there was among members and how individual analysis did not prepare one for dealing with professional conflict. Personal analysis helped with the intrapsychic and some interpersonal issues but it did not necessarily help the individual to relate within a group.

Theoretically, analytical psychology in New York has stayed close to its roots in Jung's theory. The founders, Esther Harding, Eleanor Bertine, Kristine Mann, and Frances Wickes, all had close ties to Jung, and this connection has continued. The professional group numbers over 100 members. Over the years there have been numerous personal tensions within the membership, with some members changing their voting membership to other professional societies. At present, approximately fifteen members of the New York society have applied to form their own new society with their own view of training. This has produced a great deal of tension, and, at the time of writing, the situation has not yet been resolved.

San Francisco

The second region in the United States to develop an interest in Jung's psychology was the San Francisco Bay Area. Elizabeth and James Whitney Sr spent time in Zurich in the early 1920s and returned to Berkeley to become the first psychoanalysts of any persuasion west of the Mississippi River. James Sr died shortly after returning, but Elizabeth had a long and illustrious career as a Jungian analyst. By 1940 Joseph and Jane Wheelwright had returned from Zurich and Joseph Henderson had returned as well with an intermediate stop in New York. An Analytical Psychology Club was formed, and several doctors and psychologists wished to begin training. During World War II, Drs. Henderson and Wheelwright worked at a rehabilitation clinic examining returning military personnel from the South Pacific. Here they worked alongside their Freudian counterparts and a collegiality developed that was highly unusual at that time.

In 1943, the Medical Society for Analytical Psychology (MSAP) (same name but separate from New York) was formed and the professional group differentiated from the Analytical Psychology Club. Joseph Wheelwright became a founding member of the Langley Porter Neuropsychiatric Institute in 1941 and was a professor there for the next thirty years. Joseph Henderson began teaching at the Stanford University Medical Center in San Francisco and remained there until 1959 when the complex moved to Palo Alto. Through these positions, many young doctors were attracted to Jungian training and the early composition of the San Francisco Jung Society had a predominance of medically trained analysts. This was different from New York, where there was little contact with the medical and psychotherapeutic communities. Also, there was relatively little contact between the New York group and the San Francisco one.

In 1948, four psychologists, who had their analyses with the medical analysts, were accepted as trainees within the professional group. These four immediately formed the Association of Analytical Clinical Psychologists as a counterpart to the medical group. In those days, the rivalry in the United States between medicine and psychology was acute and each discipline felt the need to have its own organization. However, both groups quickly realized that analysis should not be restricted to a single discipline and they formed the Northern California Society of Jungian Analysts.

Two psychologists, Elizabeth Howes and Sheila Moon, had analysis with Elizabeth Whitney and also had seen Dr. and Mrs. Jung in Zurich. Drs. Howes and Moon and their professional work were strongly influenced by a Christian viewpoint. In 1944 a decision had to be made as to whether they should be a part of the newly forming professional group. The two women elected to go their own way and in

58 *History of analytical psychology*

1955 formed the Guild for Psychological Studies, of which Mrs. Emma Jung was a founding sponsor. To this day, the Guild has functioned as a separate organization, presenting lectures and workshops to interested participants. This early cleavage was significant because it established analytical psychology in Northern California as a clinical discipline, and individuals with a predominantly Christian orientation found a niche in the Guild. The separation of the Guild from the MSAP, as well as the fact that most of the professional members were physicians, led to criticism that the San Francisco Jungians were more interested in their medical persona than in the deeper values of analytical psychology.

On July 13, 1964, the C. G. Jung Institute was created as a nonprofit organization; subsequently the training was restructured, a low-fee outpatient clinic was formed, and a building to house these activities was purchased. In 1972 a most significant event occurred for the San Francisco Institute. On her 80th birthday, friends and former analysands established a foundation in Frances Wickes' name. Over the years, the foundation distributed small grants, but in 1972 the board decided to dissolve the foundation and to make a terminal grant of $1,500,000 to the C. G. Jung Institute of San Francisco. With the grant, the San Francisco group bought its present residence for $150,000 and with the remainder established an endowment. For the following several years the financial stability of the Institute was assured by the earnings from the endowment as well as by contributions from interested lay public. The existing programs of the Institute grew rapidly and new ones were developed. New staff members were employed to manage the library, public programs, the clinic, and overall administration.

The training of analysts has been the core activity of the Institute. The evaluation of candidates, for many years, was conducted by an equal number of San Francisco and Los Angeles analysts. When the joint evaluating committees were instituted, it was unique in the Jungian world. No other Jungian group included outside evaluators passing judgment on its candidates. The initial reason was the small size of both societies, but over time it was recognized that sharing was beneficial for both the candidates and the analysts doing the evaluations. In spite of major differences in outlook, the joint board worked well until recently. The joint board and the yearly California North–South Jungian Conference also promoted a general working relationship between the two societies.

Because of its large size and endowment, the San Francisco Institute has numerous programs; a large library; an active ARAS collection; its own journal, the *San Francisco Jung Institute Library Journal* [since 2007 published as *Jung Journal: Culture & Psyche*]; and an active clinic.

Changes have occurred in the make-up of the San Francisco Jung Institute as fewer medical doctors have applied for training with the general movement in psychiatry away from psychotherapy to a biological-pharmacological approach. Currently applicants come from the fields of psychology or social work, with the occasional psychiatric nurse practitioner or marriage and family counselor. Women predominate among the present applicants and candidates, representing a shift away from the early days when applicants were mainly male medical doctors. The San Francisco Jung Institute has approximately 125 active members and 50 candidates in various stages of training.

The San Francisco Jung Institute has long been considered one of the most well-established and respected Jungian institutes in the world. From the very beginning it established good relations with psychoanalysis. The Wheelwrights, Joseph Henderson, and Elizabeth Whitney worked well together to found the early professional group. At the time of writing there have been no serious splits within the professional group, and an air of respect generally prevails among the membership. From the outset there have been monthly dinner meetings of the membership so that there is ample opportunity for members to get to know each other in a less structured setting.

Los Angeles

The third area where analytical psychology developed was Los Angeles. German Jewish refugees, James and Hilde Kirsch, and Max and Lore Zeller, arrived in 1940 and 1941, respectively. None of them had the proper credentials to practice as psychotherapists or analysts, so the development of analytical psychology occurred outside the mainstream of psychotherapeutic and analytic training. Nevertheless, many people were attracted to analytical psychology and an Analytical Psychology Club was formed. There was a strong connection between Zurich and Los Angeles, and in 1950, twenty individuals from Los Angeles were in analysis in Zurich. A fund was developed to bring Zurich lecturers to Los Angeles, and there has continued to be a connection between the two Jungian centers.

In 1952 the San Francisco and Los Angeles groups cautiously planned a joint meeting in Santa Barbara, California, to explore areas of mutual interest. They hoped that a meeting between the two societies could lessen mutual projections. The initial meeting proved to be fruitful, and the two societies decided to get together on a yearly basis from then on. The annual event became known as the North–South Conference, and it was the first-ever meeting between two Jungian societies.

In the mid-1970s, Edward Edinger arrived in Los Angeles from New York. Although Edinger brought with him the knowledge and experience of a classical Jungian, he did not have a personal analysis with Jung. Edinger's intellectual focus was on the works of C. G. Jung and Marie-Louise von Franz, and his published books reworked Jung's ideas into a language that seemed easier to grasp than Jung's. For over twenty years, Edinger influenced many Los Angeles analysts who have shared this point of view. On the other hand, many candidates were interested in the new developments in psychoanalysis that had relevance for analytical psychology and this led to an enormous tension within the Los Angeles Jungian community. In the 1990s, the division between those who adhered closely to the words of Jung and von Franz and those who wished to incorporate psychoanalytic concepts into Jungian practice widened. Finally, after the death of Edinger in 1998, a second professional society was formed that has been closely aligned to Edinger's point of view.

Analytical psychology has developed in Los Angeles from a small German Jewish émigré enclave to a substantial professional Jungian community. Currently the Society of Jungian Analysts of Southern California includes approximately seventy members (the majority having been certified within the past six years) and fifty candidates. The Institute, founded in 1967 without an endowment, has managed to survive and grow throughout this period. The Institute components include its own ARAS collection, the Hilde Kirsch Children's Center, the Max and Lore Zeller Book Store, the James Kirsch Lecture Room, the Kieffer Frantz Clinic, the journal *Psychological Perspectives*, and numerous ongoing projects. There is an active training program with many candidates. A second professional society has recently formed in which classical works of Jung and Marie Louise von Franz are emphasized.

Later developments of analytical psychology in the United States

I have presented the development of New York and the two California societies in some detail, first because they all were formed while Jung was still alive, and there was communication with him about their formation. Second, there were no new Jungian groups for another thirty years, until the early 1970s, in the United States. Third, the United States has been the only country within which independent Jungian societies have developed. In all other countries, the development of groups has been on a national level.

By the early 1970s, there were Americans who had trained in Zurich and returned to different areas in the United States. In order to lessen the isolation of these individuals and to promote a broader training program, these individuals came together to form the Inter-Regional Society of Jungian Analysts (IRSJA). The analysts and their respective candidates have continued to meet twice a year for seminars and examinations, and when enough analysts from a particular area have been certified, the group has separated and become an autonomous society. This has been partially successful, but often a large enough group has not wished to disaffiliate. As the Inter-Regional group has become larger, it has accepted candidates from areas where there is an existing society. This has caused some tension within the different American groups, as this was not part of the original intent of the IRSJA.

At the time of writing there are groups in most parts of the country, including Chicago, Texas, New England, and the Pacific Northwest, as well as parts of Canada. Space does not permit me to follow the development of these various groups, but they all have evolved out of a combination of the Inter-Regional training and graduates from the Zurich Institute returning to the United States or Canada. In New England, all the founders were Zurich graduates, and there were no IRSJA members for a long time.

As the Inter-Regional Society grew, there was concern from the existing societies about territorial issues. As there was no national American group, the existing societies at that time – Boston, New York, San Francisco, and Los Angeles – met with representatives from Inter-Regional and formed the Council of American Societies of Jungian Analysts (CASJA). As new societies have formed, they have all become members of CASJA, now broadened to North America and called CNASJA. CNASJA has no official position or authority, but it does host a regular meeting and provide a forum for issues that emerge among the societies. It has proved to be effective for airing disputes.

The newer societies have a range of attitudes with respect to analytical psychology, from largely developmental to highly symbolic. How long the societies can remain separate and not form a national organization remains to be seen. If one adds up the membership of all the American societies, it presents close to one quarter of the total membership of the IAAP. Analytical psychology in the United States is vibrant, and it takes on many shapes and forms.

United Kingdom

The United Kingdom provided fertile soil for the development of psychoanalysis and analytical psychology. The early followers of Jung did not conform to an intellectual orthodoxy; it was only when H. G. Baynes, an extraverted English physician, went for analysis to Jung after World War I that a firm foundation for Jung's psychology was established (Jansen, 2003). Jung gave his first professional talk in England in

History of analytical psychology   61

1914, and his last visit was in 1938 when he received an honorary doctorate from Oxford. In between, he made numerous professional trips, held seminars for his students, and gave a series of five lectures at the Tavistock Clinic in 1935, which were attended by many prominent British physicians and psychotherapists.

An Analytical Psychology Club, modeled on the club in Zurich, was formed and held its first meeting on September 15, 1922, at the home of Esther Harding, then living in London before she moved to the United States in 1924. The Analytical Psychology Club quickly grew from the initial five in 1922 to approximately twenty-five members. In the beginning, in order to qualify for membership, all the members had to be analyzed by either Jung or Toni Wolff, but this requirement was quickly changed, and analysis and recommendation by any qualified Jungian analyst became acceptable. Regular lectures, discussion groups on a variety of subjects, and a large library became the main aspects of the club. As with the Zurich Club, important and ongoing issues were: how to relate as a group; the relationship of the individuation process to group process; and the purpose of the group – whether to focus on inner archetypal issues or on social and political questions. H. G. Baynes, later known as Peter, was the leader of the Jungians in England until his untimely death in 1943. He became Jung's assistant in Zurich in the early 1920s, and in 1925 he arranged a safari to Africa for himself and Jung. He returned to England in 1929 and practiced there until his death. By the late 1930s there was both a medical and a lay group of analysts.

One of Baynes' leading students was Michael Fordham, who, at that time, was still beginning as a child psychiatrist. Fordham was not able to have analysis with Jung and instead saw a neophyte Jungian in London. Fordham became the leader of the Jungians after Baynes' death, and he initiated the founding of a professional society, the Society of Analytical Psychology (SAP), as well as inaugurating a clinical Jungian publication, the *Journal of Analytical Psychology*. Fordham's interest in child analysis led him to have both professional and personal contact with Melanie Klein and Donald Winnicott. He was strongly influenced by both of them, and he incorporated many of their theories into the classical Jungian model. This led in the 1960s to the evolution of what became known as the "London developmental school" versus the "Zurich classical school." The London school emphasized infancy and early child development, whereas the Zurich school focused primarily on archetypal imagery and amplification of those images.

As the developmental approach within the SAP became more firmly established, the analysts and candidates who adhered to a more classical Jungian approach became uncomfortable. The tension between the two perspectives has often been described as a personal conflict between Michael Fordham and Gerhard Adler, which Fordham denied, claiming that the differences were theoretical. Adler complained that his trainees were not acceptable at the SAP, and that his seminars were badly attended. By 1975 Adler and his colleagues were ready to form their own group, where the more traditional Jungian positions could be expressed; this resulted in the formation of the Association of Jungian Analysts (AJA). However, AJA began to have its own internal conflicts when analysts arrived from Zurich and were asked to do further training in London. This split the group once again into those analysts who trained in Zurich and the ones who trained in the UK. Consequently, more Zurich-oriented analysts founded the Independent Group of Analytical Psychologists (IGAP). To have two more classically oriented Jungian societies was politically untenable for the SAP, which was the original group and the one with the longest history. The SAP members had long been active in the British Association for Psychotherapy (BAP), which had a Jungian section. A compromise was worked out so that the Jungian section of BAP would become another UK-based group, with the result that there would be two "developmentally oriented societies" and two "classically oriented societies." That decision was reached in 1986, and in the following years each of the four societies evolved on its own path.

Two much larger umbrella organizations have been founded in Great Britain, the United Kingdom Council for Psychotherapy (UKCP) and the British Confederation of Psychotherapists (BCP). The UKCP is the true umbrella organization for all psychotherapists in the UK, and numbers over 3,000 psychotherapists of all persuasions. All the Jungian organizations were members of this umbrella organization. In 1992 the BCP was formed to be an umbrella organization for all psychoanalytic organizations. The members of the BCP were not comfortable having the broad spectrum of psychotherapists representing psychoanalytic issues. Both SAP and BAP and, more recently, AJA have become members of the BCP, but IGAP has not been invited to join the BCP. Standards are the issue, and this is expressed in terms of the frequency of sessions per week for analytic candidates and the frequency with which clinic patients are seen by the candidates.

It was in this atmosphere of *Sturm und Drang* (storm and stress) in London that Andrew Samuels published his classic book, *Jung and the Post-Jungians* (1985), wherein he developed a classification of analytical psychologists that included a classical, a developmental, and an archetypal school. Briefly summarized, the classical school, consciously working in Jung's tradition, focuses on self and individuation. The developmental school has a specific focus on the importance of infancy in the evolution of the adult personality, and an equally important emphasis on the analysis of the transference and countertransference. The developmental school has a close relationship to psychoanalysis, although influence in the opposite direction is not as significant. The archetypal school focuses on imagery in therapy with little emphasis on overt transference and countertransference. When Samuels' book came out in 1985, most analysts did not like being labeled in this way, as it went against the grain of individuality and authenticity.

Since the book's publication, there has been a continual evolution of the tripartite division. The classical and developmental schools still exist, but the archetypal school as a clinical discipline never gained acceptance as a separate entity in the UK. The archetypal school has either been integrated or eliminated, probably a bit of both. Further evolutions in the classical and developmental schools, respectively, have led to additional philosophical and theoretical divisions that stretch the limits on both ends. On the classical side, a new (ultra-classical) group has emerged that emphasizes the original works of Jung and Marie-Louise von Franz. This view is championed by the Research Centre in Zurich and the second society in Los Angeles. At the other end of the spectrum are those analysts who have become primarily psychoanalytic but originally trained at Jungian Institutes. These analysts have adopted the rules of abstinence and neutrality in a psychoanalytic way, valuing the psychoanalytic frame over the working alliance and valuing transference-countertransference exploration over explicit fantasy and dream images. The enthusiasm for psychoanalysis has come about through Jungian analysts who were not satisfied with either their classical or developmental Jungian analyses. They have not coalesced to form any definite professional societies.

Analytical psychology in the UK has been heavily influenced by psychoanalytic thinking, but formal contacts between the two have been minimal. Michael Fordham was an exception since in 1945, through his friendship with the psychoanalyst John Rickman, he began a forum between psychoanalysts and analytical psychologists in the Medical Section of the British Psychological Society (Astor, 1995). In 1962, Fordham was elected chairman of the Royal-Medico Psychological Association, which later became the Royal College of Psychiatrists. However, in spite of these important positions, analytical psychologists have not been able to obtain formal recognition from the British psychoanalytic community, which is something they have very much wanted.

In 1993, a Centre for Psychoanalytic Studies at the University of Essex was founded. It offers a range of postgraduate degree courses, public lectures, short specialist courses, and opportunities for research (Papadopoulos, 1996). Subsequently, the Society of Analytical Psychology established a Chair in Analytical Psychology for that Center. Since the fall of 1995 Renos Papadopoulos and Andrew Samuels have been sharing the half-time position equally. The placement of the Center structurally in the midst of a university has been a positive opening for analytical psychology. There is contact with other departments within the university, and the students participate in a rich and varied psychoanalytic curriculum.

Currently, most analytical psychologists in England practice some hybrid of analytical psychology and object-relations psychoanalysis, with those of a more classical Jungian persuasion in the minority. The political issue of an umbrella organization of all analytical psychologists in England has not been settled. It is important to emphasize that the historical developments in the UK have foreshadowed similar events in other countries. As a result of Fordham's individual relationship to psychoanalysts and his particular relationship to Jung, these events occurred in the UK decades earlier than in other countries.

Germany

The story of Jung and analytical psychology in Germany is intimately connected with the general history of Germany in the twentieth century, and the spectres of Nazism and Hitler are a persistent presence. Jung personally, and analytical psychology in general, were closely connected to the Nationalist Socialist regime; much has been written about this period in Jung's life. Both Jung's detractors and his apologists have argued for over half a century as to whether Jung was a Nazi and/or anti-Semitic. (A brief discussion of this important issue will follow; for a more detailed elucidation the reader is referred to Samuels, 1993; Kirsch, 2000; Maidenbaum and Martin, 2002; Bair, 2003.)

There has been a Jungian presence in Germany since the early 1920s when Richard Gustav Heyer and Kathe Bugler returned from Zurich to Munich having had analysis with Jung. Several individuals from Berlin also had analysis with Jung, and in 1931 they formed the C. G. Jung Society of Berlin. What was called a "Society" in Berlin was equivalent to an Analytical Psychology Club elsewhere; it included both analysands and analysts. When the Nazis came to power in 1933, those of Jewish descent were removed from the official membership. Jung gave several workshops to the Berlin Jungian Society during the 1930s.

The story becomes more complicated after the Nazis come into power. There are two overlapping structures with which both Jung and Jungians became involved. The first is the General Medical Society for Psychotherapy, which had been founded in 1926 for psychotherapeutically oriented physicians. It had yearly meetings with participants from all of Europe and the United States. Jung was made honorary vice president of this organization in 1931. When Ernst Kretschmer, the president, resigned in 1933 for political reasons, Jung was asked to take over the organization. He insisted that the name be changed to the International General Medical Society for Psychotherapy and that Jewish members from Germany be allowed to be individual members. Jews had been banned from the Nazified German section, and he wanted them to remain as individual members of the International Society. He also made a statement comparing Aryan psychology and Jewish psychology, which was quite unfortunate and which has been the basis for attacking Jung as an anti-Semite as well as a Nazi. Jung remained president of this organization until 1940, when he finally resigned and gave up trying to keep the organization out of the political fire.

The man who headed up the Nazified German section was named Matthias Goering, a self-styled Adlerian psychiatry professor who was also a distant cousin of Hermann Goering. Professor Goering, through his cousin, had close connections with the Nazi hierarchy and in 1936 became head of a psychotherapy institute called the Goering Institute. This became the main training center for psychotherapists until the end of the Nazi regime. Analytical psychology was one of the subjects taught at the Goering Institute by Jungians who were members of the Nazi party (Cocks, 1997). Although Jung himself had nothing to do with this, his psychology was perpetuated by Dr. Heyer and others in this system throughout the war. Heyer protected Bugler, who was half Jewish. Bugler, although not a physician, had been the first German to be analyzed by Jung in the early 1920s.

After World War II, all the different schools of psychotherapy and analysis had to rise from the ashes. As a consequence of his Nazi affiliation, Jung discredited Heyer, who then returned to Munich. Kathe Bugler did not like the direction that Jungian psychology was taking in Berlin; she disaffiliated herself from the analytic organizations that were forming but continued to practice as a Jungian analyst. Many of the early Jungians after the war went to her for analysis. Harald Schultz-Henke, a neo-Freudian who attempted to bring together all the psychoanalytic theoretical perspectives, founded a neo-Freudian institute that those interested in Jungian psychology also attended. By graduating from this program, the Jungians gradually formed their own section from within. Candidates from the two schools took the same seminars but then branched out to study and analyze with their own respective teachers and analysts. These conditions continue to the present day. The Berlin Jungians have one of the largest groups in the world.

During this same period after the war, Wilhelm Bitter in Stuttgart founded a Jung Institute much more closely aligned to Zurich. Professor Bitter had been in Switzerland during the war, and he was not politically associated with the Nazis. In 1958 these two groups combined to form the German Association of Jungian Analysts. Over time, satellite institutes have developed in other cities in Germany such as Munich, Cologne, and Bremen. The Stuttgart group has remained more closely aligned to Zurich, whereas the Berlin group has been much influenced by psychoanalysis.

Germany was also one of the first countries where government health insurance paid for psychoanalytic treatment, so that a large number of psychoanalytically oriented therapists have had economic support. Since East and West Germany combined, the economic support for psychoanalysis has had to be modified. Germany and other European countries are struggling with the issue of financial reimbursement by the government, which requires that psychoanalysts be accredited in some standard way. Thus, who is and who is not a Jungian analyst according to governmental policy has profound economic ramifications.

IAAP

Jung had a decidedly ambivalent relationship with organizations. The only Jungian organizations that existed prior to the formation of the Institute in Zurich were the Analytical Psychology Clubs in some of the major cities of Europe and the United States. Even there, Jung kept his distance and was never closely involved with the administration of any of the clubs (including the one in Zurich); however, he did lend support by giving lectures and seminars.

In 1955, Jung celebrated his 80th birthday and some of his Zurich followers urged him to consider the formation of an international professional organization (Meier, 1992, personal communication). Thus, the IAAP was founded in Switzerland in 1955 and was structured according to Swiss law.

At its inception, the aims of the IAAP were (1) to promote analytical psychology, (2) to accredit professional groups and individual members where no group existed, and (3) to hold congresses on a regular basis. In order to accredit analysts, minimum standards of training were stipulated in the Constitution.

The work of the IAAP has increased markedly since its founding and the leaders have many duties, including: resolving conflict between groups and individuals; evaluating new groups and individuals; reaching out to new areas of the world seeking development, such as Russia and Asia; organizing congresses; and publishing congress proceedings, an annual newsletter, and a membership list. Politically, the association has broadened from its Northern European roots to encompass the rest of Europe, the Americas, and parts of Asia and Africa. The IAAP, with its many functions, has played an increasingly prominent role in the growth of analytical psychology with a primary mandate to accredit analysts and offering an organizational identification.

Analytical psychology in the rest of the world

In this chapter I have focused on Switzerland, the United States, the United Kingdom, and Germany because they have all had a continuing Jungian presence from the time that Jung first established his independent psychology in the early 1920s. Furthermore, these Jungian professional groups were established during Jung's lifetime, which meant that he knew and influenced them to some degree. However, there are other countries where analytical psychology developed and that were within Jung's purview.

One example is Israel. Erich and Julie Neumann originally established residence in Palestine in 1934. They began a small group in Tel Aviv, and it has grown slowly over the years. Erich Neumann was arguably Jung's most creative student and the themes of his books follow Jung's line of archetypal theory. The Neumanns taught both child and adult analysis, and Israel was a charter member of the IAAP. In recent years there have been many personality conflicts within the Israeli professional society, and now it has divided into three separate groups based on these personal alignments.

Italy is another country where there has been a Jungian presence since the mid-1930s. Ernst Bernhard, a German Jewish Jungian who saw Jung in 1933 for a spiritual crisis, settled in Rome in 1935. He was protected during World War II and began to practice again in 1944. At the present time there are two major Jungian associations in Italy, and the founders of both had their analyses with Bernhard. The conflict between the two groups began as a personality conflict, but the two now work together on many projects of mutual interest.

66 *History of analytical psychology*

France is another country with an early Jungian presence, which began in 1929. Before World War II, there was an active Analytical Psychology Club in Paris, which the Jungs visited and where both lectured, Jung in 1932 and Emma in the late 1930s. During World War II there was a cessation of Jungian activity, which did not begin again until well after its end. Elie Humbert, a Catholic priest, saw Jung in analysis during the late 1950s. He was probably one of Jung's last patients. Humbert returned to Paris, and through the force of his intellect and his personal dynamism, a group of individuals began to train to become Jungian analysts. This group has grown rapidly and is one of the largest and most active in the world today.

During the past thirty years there has been a tremendous increase in analytical psychology. Many countries in Europe have developed Jungian societies, including Belgium, Denmark, Sweden, Spain, and Austria, with individuals in the other European countries. Mexico, Venezuela, and Brazil have developed strong Jungian groups, and other countries in Latin America have an emerging interest. Australia and New Zealand have formed a combined group that requires a lot of travel for its members. South Africa has its own Jungian society, as does Japan.

Since the fall of communism and the Soviet state, the countries of Eastern Europe and Russia have shown a strong interest in analytical psychology. It has been difficult for people from these areas to afford personal analysis, which is, of course, fundamental to becoming an analyst. Various scholarships and foundations have helped to support analytic training for a few individuals, and analysts from the West have committed themselves to teaching in these countries. The most prominent example of this is the work of Jan Wiener and Catherine Crowther who have gone on a regular basis to St Petersburg, where many of the students have graduated from a two-year course.

The end result is that analytical psychology has become a worldwide phenomenon. What began as Jung's psychology has truly developed into analytical psychology, with Jung as its founder but many others contributing to its body of literature and knowledge. As with any discipline that has such an inherent subjective factor, the theory and practice have undergone many revisions. Each individual analyst is somewhere on a continuum and is influenced by his/her analytic training and own individual nature.

Analytical psychology, along with other forms of depth psychology, has been under attack in recent years. New antidepressants have changed the way many depressions are treated, and psychotherapy is no longer the first treatment of choice. Health insurance, private and governmental, no longer reimburses long-term psychotherapy, threatening the economic viability of many psychotherapists, who continue to increase in number. Conditions vary from country to country, but the trend is the same the world over. Fewer people enter psychoanalysis of any sort, including Jungian analysis.

Psychoanalysis is over 100 years old, and it is no longer the young and exciting discipline that it once was. It has failed to live up to its promises of healing the individual and of transforming society; in the 1950s it was seen by many as a panacea for the ills of the world. Although Freudian psychoanalysis bears the brunt of disillusionment, Jung and analytical psychology come in for their share of criticism. Yet many of Jung's ideas are now part of mainstream Western culture, and much of his specialized terminology is incorporated into everyday language.

One might ask: what is it that makes one Jungian? That is not an easy question to answer. For some, Jung may be like some distant relative in the past with whom they have some tenuous connection. For others, the connection may be more immediate and personal. Whether it was his broad view of the unconscious, his thoughts on

History of analytical psychology   67

individuation, or his interest in the more esoteric aspects of the psyche, Jung spoke to us in some immediate and personal way. Maybe we have moved away from that initial experience, but we still hold on to it at some deep level. Jung emphasized the reality of the unconscious, especially as seen through one's dreams, and it seems that most Jungians take this seriously. The reality of the dream, its potential for opening ever wider aspects of one's psyche, is something Jungians value above all.

Clearly, there is room for a clinical discipline of Jungian analysis. Jung, among others, has shown us that openness to forms of experience beyond everyday reality is essential to our humanness. Whether we call the level of the psyche that is in touch with that other reality the collective unconscious, the Self, the God-image, the objective psyche, or something else, it has always been, and will always be, part of us.

Note

1   "History of Analytical Psychology." In Joseph Cambray and Linda Carter (eds), *Analytical Psychology: Contemporary Perspectives in Jungian Analysis*, pp. 5–31. Hove, UK: Brunner-Routledge, 2004. Reprinted by the permission of the publisher.

References

Astor, J. (1995) *Michael Fordham: Innovations in Analytical Psychology*. London: Routledge.
Bair, D. (2003) *Jung: A Biography*. Boston, MA: Little Brown & Co.
Cocks, G. (1997) *Psychotherapy in the Third Reich: The Goering Institute*, 2nd edition. New Brunswick, NJ: Transaction Publishers.
Fordham, M. (1976) Discussion of T. Kirsch's Article "The Practice of Multiple Analyses." *Contemporary Psychoanalysis* 12(2): 159–67.
Freud, S. (1914) *On the History of the Psychoanalytic Movement*. Standard Edition, vol. 14. London: Hogarth Press.
Freud, S. (1961) *Beyond the Pleasure Principle*. New York: W. W. Norton & Co.
Henderson, J. (1982) Reflections on the History and Practice of Jungian Analysis. In M. Stein (ed.), *Jungian Analysis*. La Salle, IL: Open Court Publishing, pp. 3–26.
Jansen, D. B. (2003) *Jung's Apprentice*. Einsiedeln, Switzerland: Daimon Verlag.
Jung, C. G. (1916/1991) *Psychology of the Unconscious*. Princeton, NJ: Princeton University Press.
Jung, C. G. (1921/1923/1964) *Psychological Types*. Collected Works, vol. 6. Princeton, NJ: Princeton University Press.
Jung, C. G. (1948) *Symbolic Life*. Collected Works, vol. 18. Princeton, NJ: Princeton University Press.
Jung, C. G. (1953/1980) *Psychology and Alchemy*. Collected Works, vol. 12. Princeton, NJ: Princeton University Press.
Jung, C. G. (1963) *Memories, Dreams, Reflections*. New York: Pantheon Books.
Kirsch, T. (1976) The Practice of Multiple Analyses in Analytical Psychology. *Contemporary Psychoanalysis* 12(2): 159–67.
Kirsch, T. (2000) *The Jungians*. London: Routledge.
McGuire, W. (1974) *Freud/Jung Letters*. Princeton, NJ: Princeton University Press.
McGuire, W. (ed.) (1989) *Analytical Psychology: Notes of the Seminar Given in 1925 by C. G. Jung*. Bollingen Series 99. Princeton, NJ: Princeton University Press.
Maidenbaum, A., and Martin, S. (eds) (2002) *Jung and the Shadow of Anti-Semitism*. Berwick, ME: Nicolas-Hays Publishing.
Meier, C. A. (1992) Personal communication.
Muser, F. E. (1984) *Zur Geschichte des Psychologischen Clubs Zurich von den Anfangen bis 1928*. Zurich: Analytical Psychology Club.
Papadopoulos, R. (ed.) (1996) Report on New Center. *IAAP Newsletter* 16: 94–97.

68 *History of analytical psychology*

Samuels, A. (1985) *Jung and the Post-Jungians.* London: Routledge.
Samuels, A. (1993) *The Political Psyche.* London: Routledge.
Shamdasani, S. (1998) *Cult Fictions.* London: Routledge.
Wheelwright, J. (1974) Jung and Freud Speak to Each Other. *Psychological Perspectives* 5(2): 171–6.

CHAPTER 9

THOMAS B. KIRSCH INTERVIEWS EDWARD EDINGER, DECEMBER 4, 1996

From *The San Francisco Jung Institute Library Journal*, 23(2), 2004[1]

Figure 9.1 Edward Edinger in the 1980s (photograph: Lore Zeller, used with permission)

70 *Thomas B. Kirsch interviews Edward Edinger*

Editor's Note: Edward F. Edinger (1922–98) is well known for his many lectures and writings on the application of Jungian psychology. He was an influential teacher and analyst, first in New York and later in Los Angeles. His books, *Ego and Archetype* (1972) and *Anatomy of the Psyche* (1985) have become classics, while his published lectures on Jung's work, such as *The Mysterium Lectures* and *The Aion Lectures* (1996), are uniquely valuable companions to reading Jung's more difficult works. His most recent book, published since his death, is *The Sacred Psyche: A Psychological Approach to the Psalms*. Tom Kirsch interviewed Dr. Edinger while preparing his book on the history of analytical psychology, published as *The Jungians* (2000).

Thomas Kirsch (TK): I am really curious about the history of analytical psychology, which is developing beyond Jung. Jung is by far the most important person, but there is actually a field developing at this point, and you have been a central part of that in New York, and I think in Los Angeles, too. So, I just wanted to get a little bit of history about you, is that alright?

Edward Edinger (EE): That's fine. I'll try to answer whatever questions you can come up with, and the more specific the question, the more specific the response.

TK: The first question I have been asking people is how they first heard about Jung, in what context, what was happening, or who introduced them and what happened.

EE: I encountered Jung through reading, through his books, and I also encountered fairly early Esther Harding's book, *Psychic Energy*. That was in 1949. I was through medical school and my Army service, and I was doing post-graduate work in internal medicine, but I was not satisfied, I was quite dissatisfied, as a matter of fact, and had not really found my bearings. I knew that physical medicine was not it for me: it did not carry [the] meaning dimension.

TK: Were you a resident in medicine at that time?

EE: At that particular time, in 1949, I was a research fellow at Barnes Hospital in St. Louis, and then I did go back to New Haven and had a residency in medicine there. It was in the midst of that that I woke up one morning with the realization that I had to become a Jungian analyst.

TK: Really! What was the first book of Jung that you read?

EE: I think it was *Modern Man in Search of a Soul*.

TK: That was the first thing I read, too. And then you did a psychiatry residency, didn't you?

EE: That's right. I got in touch with Esther Harding in New York and started a psychiatry residency at Rocklin State Hospital in Orangeberg, New York, and personal analysis in New York. That all started in 1950–1.

TK: That's interesting to me. I had not realized, when you talk about Barnes, then Yale, you were on a kind of achievement, academically oriented [trajectory]. I went to Yale Medical School, too. Then going to Rocklin State Hospital and the Jungian thing was really a switch for you.

EE: It was a switch out of the academic locale, but I wanted a place close to New York, and I made inquiries as to where there might be people who had some interest in Jung, and there was a chap at Rocklin State, and that contributed to it, too.

TK: Is that somebody I might even know?

EE: No, he never got into general visibility.

TK: Then you started your analysis, and would you say that was a positive experience for you?

EE: Are you kidding?

TK: I have to ask you that because there are so many people who talk about their analysis where it was not a positive experience.

EE: Is that so?

TK: Absolutely! That's why I put it that way to you, and I did not want to just assume it.

EE: Isn't that interesting?

TK: Without mentioning names, there are a lot of people who are/were very disillusioned by their analyses.

EE: I am sorry to hear that.

TK: Well, it has been very disturbing to me to hear it, too.

EE: I am afraid it is a symptom of the times, too, because things have changed from my days.

TK: Right. For you it was an absolutely transforming experience, I knew that intuitively, even though I have never talked to you about it, but I just sensed that. Can I ask how long you were in analysis?

EE: It trailed off gradually; it was about six or seven years.

TK: Did you have any supervisory work at that time, too?

EE: Yes, but at that time there was no organized training program in New York, and training was done on an *ad hoc* basis. There were occasional lectures and seminars that would be put on by the Professional Society.

TK: I thought there was just the Club at that time.

EE: There was a Professional Society ever since about the mid-forties, I'd say. It was called the New York Association of Analytical Psychology, but there was no Institute, no Foundation. The Club and the Professional Society would do things jointly, and the Club would bring over people from Zurich so that there would be seminars. The main training was done on an *ad hoc* basis and emphasis was on the individual analysis and supervised analysis.

TK: Who was your supervisor?

EE: I did that with Eleanor Bertine. Are you familiar with her?

TK: I saw her once as a possible analyst, but then she became ill, and I could not see her. I was at Yale in 1958. As a matter of fact, I saw Esther Harding once, too. I don't know what would have happened if I had done that. I saw you once, too.

EE: Yes, I remember that. You finally worked with Eugene Henley, didn't you?

TK: I did, and that was very wonderful for me.

EE: I would think so; he was a pretty sound fellow.

TK: I liked him a lot. ... Later I came to San Francisco, and I have been seeing Joe Henderson on and off ever since. I have the same feeling about my analysis as you do about your experience with Esther Harding.

EE: That's what happens when you get hooked up with quality.

TK: I really feel very fortunate. When or how was it decided that you became a Jungian analyst?

EE: Well, that was my intention right from the beginning, and I was told to get started and to see how far I could go. Get into some analysis, get psychiatric training, and see what unfolds. It unfolded, and I was accepted.

TK: This is what I am trying to get clear on, the New York Association for Analytical Psychology then accepted you as a member.

EE: That's right, I'd say the decision really was up to my analyst and my supervisor. That's how it worked in those days.

TK: In other words, Esther Harding and Eleanor Bertine said, "You are ready."

EE: They presented my name to the Professional Association, and I was accepted.

72   *Thomas B. Kirsch interviews Edward Edinger*

TK: You did not have to do anything special, like write a paper or present a case?

EE: No, I did not.

TK: What year was that?

EE: Probably 1957. Maybe it was 1956. I remember giving my maiden paper to the Analytical Psychology Club in 1956.

TK: What was that on?

EE: Let me see if I can find it in the files: "Reflections Concerning the Transference Phenomenon."

TK: Very interesting.

EE: It is a perfectly acceptable paper, and I am not ashamed of it.

TK: There is nothing that you have written which is not, as you say, absolutely quality. I am sure that one would be, too; I have not seen it. Now you are an analyst, and there is the professional group, and what happened for you then? Did you become active in the teaching? When did teaching start there? [Was it the] kind of the seminar format that we know today?

EE: As I said, there were occasional seminars given by different people, but the formal program did not start up until the early sixties, the same time that the Foundation was formed. What is currently called the Institute ... was originally called the Training Center [and] ... thought of as really an arm or a portion of the Jung Foundation. Since then they have become more separated, but originally they were quite closely connected.

TK: That is also very interesting to me because that meant that the Foundation was to be the major organization.

EE: That was the original idea, that it would have different arms; it would promote public programs in one aspect, but that it would also have a professional training arm.

TK: Were you actively involved in the founding of that professional arm of the Foundation?

EE: Yes. I was very active in that whole thing, and I was one of the original members who got the original incorporation for the Foundation. Originally, the Institute did not have a separate incorporation, and now it does. Originally, the incorporation was just the Foundation. I am one of the original three or four individuals who set up that corporation.

TK: Who were the other three or four?

EE: You can check it out for sure by inquiring, but I remember Anneliese Aumüller was one; I am sure Esther Harding was one; Christopher Whitmont might have been one; and myself – these are the only ones I remember.

TK: So that is in the early 1960s. Then were you also active in the Foundation, in the public part of it, too?

EE: Yes, very much so. I gave public seminars quite frequently.

TK: What subjects were you speaking on then?

EE: In the early 1960s I gave a seminar, or a series of lectures and discussions over a period of four to six weeks, on "The Relation Between the Ego and the Self," which later became the first part of *Ego and Archetype*. I gave a long seminar on "Alchemy," and it was the first phase of what became *Anatomy of the Psyche*. I gave a long seminar on "Greek Mythology"; due to the efforts of Deborah Wesley, it is now edited in the book, *The Eternal Drama*. I gave a seminar on "Gnosticism."

TK: Really! I would say, Ed, that you have been the strongest student of Jung in the sense that you do not have the ambivalence toward the religious aspect that, I think, somewhere Jung was always struggling with.

EE: Well, Jung was not ambivalent.

TK: No, he was not ambivalent, but he would not take the religious step, he always wanted to be … (maybe this is getting off the track), but there was a kind of scientific attitude that he always held to. I am sure you do, too.

EE: I don't think you are adequately understanding him. I don't think there was any ambivalence, and I don't think there was any ambiguity. The ambiguity is only apparent to people who cannot fully understand Jung's empirical position. We have lots of so-called Jungians who are indeed ambivalent about the religious dimension of the psyche, no doubt about that, but I do not believe that is true of Jung. What you are referring to, what seems like the two strands, the scientific strand and the religious strand, are not antithetical or problematical once one has reached the depth of understanding of the psyche that Jung is working from.

TK: I guess there is a way – I don't know how to put it – when I read you it comes out clearer than it does in Jung.

EE: Do you know why, I think, that is? I have been told that a number of times, and I know what you are referring to. I think there are several reasons for that. One reason is a typological difference. My good perceptive function is sensation, and Jung's was intuition. That temperamental difference leads me to be more concrete and clearer and more specific. But that is also because with my lesser intuition I am not as keenly aware of all the secondary and tertiary interconnections that the images and ideas refer to, and that means although I am clearer, I do not have Jung's depth.

TK: Yes, but it is experientially very different to read you. It is somewhat easier: there is a clarity that I can grasp.

EE: On the one hand, that is an advantage, but it is also a disadvantage in that some of the resonating depths are left out of the account.

TK: I want to correct myself. I did not mean to say that Jung was ambivalent about religion, but there is a way in which the fluidity, the intuitive fluidity, of his writing is very different from reading you. I feel a directness, and maybe I need to go back and read Jung again.

EE: Jung is dealing with more data, more psychological data, than I am. He plumbs depths that I have not reached and that nobody else has reached, either. In trying to be true to his full experience, he necessarily then cannot be more clear than all his data warrant.

TK: I appreciate your putting it out so clearly for me because that helps me to formulate it. You see, one of the questions that I am asking myself here is that today there are so many Jungians who are related to psychoanalysis, and it's always very questionable what is going on when they pair up that way, and I am curious what it was like for you in New York with this strong introverted bias and your experience of the unconscious, what your relationship to psychoanalysis was, if there was one, or to other non-Jungian psychotherapies.

EE: I thought I had an understanding of what Freudian psychoanalysis was, what Adlerian analysis was, and in my days Sullivan was also pretty well known, and I was familiar with all those approaches. They all have their elements of truth and validity. They are not erroneous really: it's just when a partial truth is assumed to be and is used in practical application as though it is the whole, then it becomes erroneous in my understanding. But as far as what we euphemistically call the Jungian community, it was a much more agreeable place to me in those days than it is now.

TK: I can imagine.

EE: The people I associated with, I had personal respect for all of them; they had a good level of analysis, and they had a reasonably good understanding of Jung, and they were devoted to the Jungian view, and that state of affairs has progressively diluted as the so-called community has enlarged.

TK: Do you have a sense that the Jungian point of view is just going to become so diluted that it will become part of a larger depth psychology?

EE: Yes, I think that has already happened, but I am not too unhappy about that phenomenon. I have given a lot of thought to the question of "Why there are so many different schools of psychotherapy?"

TK: I would love to hear what you have to say about that.

EE: We have got several schools of psychotherapy within our so-called Jungian organization even. I am sure you are well aware of that.

TK: I am acutely aware of that.

EE: More aware of it than I am given the political responsibilities you have carried.

TK: Which I am very glad to be out of now!

EE: Anyway, it is a fact that there are a number of different schools of psychotherapy, and it is a fact that expresses something about the nature and variety of the psyche. That tells me that different people, for different reasons, find certain formulations as to the nature of the psyche more compatible and comfortable and more serviceable to their own development than others. I think there are probably different reasons for that. The first one, of course, that springs to mind, and that Jung has already pointed out in the difference between Freud and Adler, is the difference in the attitude types, and function types too most likely, or in part … I really do see the mass of humanity as psychologically spread out along the course of history. What I mean by that is that there are now not a few cave dwellers still amongst us.

TK: You think there are?

EE: A few. That psychological level. There are now not a few ancient Greeks: I am thinking about the ones we hear about in the *Iliad*, for instance. As I have alluded to in various places, I see the psychology of inner city gangs as very similar to the psychology of the Greeks and Trojans during their war, the way it is described in the *Iliad*. And so on through history. We certainly have a lot of people from the Middle Ages, and a great number of people in eighteenth-century Enlightenment. In fact, not very many people passed that level. To get up into the twentieth century to what Jung talks about in his work as the really modern man, that person is quite rare. Those will be the only ones, I think, that really have the capacity to grasp what Jung is talking about. So, we have these different schools of psychotherapy, and everybody has to find what fits for himself, and it's futile to have argumentation between the different ones because they are experiencing different realities.

TK: I wonder when you were in New York – I am assuming in Los Angeles you have been much more introverted, seeing patients, writing, and you have not been involved in the training per se …

EE: That's right, I give some courses, but I don't participate in the organizational functioning.

TK: And in New York you were central …

EE: I paid my dues then, and I feel entitled now not to do that anymore, and it does not fit my current reality at all. I am not on any committees, and I don't want to attend meetings and things like that at all.

TK: I am very sympathetic to that point of view. Did you get into discussions or did you have this formulated about the different schools of psychology when you were in New York, or would you get involved in discussions among different psychotherapy schools in New York?

EE: Very early on, when I was quite young, I attended a few panels put on, not by our organization, but [by] some of the other organizations in New York, where representatives of different schools came together and would have panel discussions before an audience. I did that a few times. It was a very unsatisfactory experience, and I learned very quickly that this was not a profitable way to spend my time.

TK: Were you active in the New York professional organization until you left, which was in 1976 or 1977?

EE: I left in 1979, and I was the Chairman of the Institute for ten years up till I left.

TK: So they had to replace you. I know that whenever I go back to New York and see people like Beverley Zabriskie, or others, you are still very much thought of there.

EE: I have been back a few times and have given talks. I went back last year, for instance, and also in 1984, to give them a chance to be reminded of me.

TK: That's good. When you there, were you Chairman of the Training Board when the professional group separated from the Foundation?

EE: I was, but I don't have a clear memory of exactly when that was.

TK: Was that a friendly separation, or a difficult separation?

EE: As far as my experience of it, it was friendly, but I cannot speak for everybody because people have different reactions to those things.

TK: But from your point of view it was ...

EE: The separation amounted to the training center getting a separate incorporation, and I don't recall in detail all the surrounding dealings about it, but the general sense was that I think we were a little concerned about how well the Foundation was going to be maintained, and that we [had] better look after ourselves, and during the mid-1970s the Foundation was spending more than it was taking in, and I was quite dissatisfied with the direction it was taking. I was serving on the Foundation Board at one time, I remember, that was the time when Skip Wyles – I do not know whether you remember him – was the Foundation Director, but I was so dissatisfied with the way the majority was taking the Foundation, I resigned from that Board.

TK: I came on the Board in about 1979, and you were already gone at that time. Philip Zabriskie was the head of it and Charlie Taylor – they were the two, and Joshua Sherman was the Executive Director. I was on the Board for a long time and then pulled away, too. What was the relationship of the Analytical Psychology Club to all this? The New York Analytical Psychology Club was an important organ.

EE: That's very true. It was the original organ, and it is the repository of the Kristine Mann Library, which is probably their finest asset. It was a separate entity (it shared the building as soon as we got the building) and it has maintained its separateness, and – to tell you the truth – along the way I have had more faith in the continuity of the Analytical Psychology Club than I have had in the Foundation.

TK: I can understand that, too. There is a soul in these clubs. They are outdated in some external way but internally they have a life of their own.

EE: Exactly, it has got some soul. They are founded on and rooted in authentic experiences of the psyche that people come together to share.

TK: As I have gone into this, I am so much more aware of how important the clubs were, and I am really going to emphasize this. I talked to C. A. Meier before he died, and he said, in the 1930s and 1940s it was in the club where all the intellectuals congregated, where the life of the psyche and of Jung's psychology were.

EE: On this subject, you might be interested to pick up a tape of a lecture I gave in New York last year, in 1995, entitled "The Question of a Jungian Community," in which I elaborate some of my thoughts about these different entities we have, and what their significance is ... I gave two talks in September 1995 and the other one was on "The Vocation of Depth Psychotherapy." ... I gave that talk down here, and it's going to be published in *Psychological Perspectives*. The other one was a little more informal and is available on tape.

TK: We have candidates who have never heard of the Analytical Psychology Clubs.

EE: I know, because for some reason the young analysts did not connect with the clubs, and I think the young people also are afraid of mixing the professional and the social. They are trying to be very rationally separate, and the result has been a kind of disconnection.

TK: I'll try to talk about some of the positive aspects of what those experiences were like for people, and what went on in the clubs because they were the meeting points. How would you compare your experience practicing in Los Angeles and what it was like for you in New York? Or are they such different phases in your life that you cannot make any kind of comparison?

EE: What aspects do you want me to compare?

TK: What is it like having a practice, what is your life style as a Jungian in Los Angeles? It seems to me so different from New York. You say you paid your dues in New York. You were much more involved in the outer world there ...

EE: There are all sorts of differences. To start with, I lived in Rocklin County and commuted to Manhattan, and here I do not have to commute anymore. That's a big difference to start with.

TK: It gave you at least two hours a day.

EE: About an hour each way. I guess the clientele is subtly or not so subtly different, and my mode of function has relaxed more and more, which is partly due to age and partly due to location and cultural atmosphere, but the big change, of course, was that – although for a few years I served occasionally on an Admissions Committee or something like that – I did very little of that sort of thing and soon bowed out of that completely. That's the big change.

TK: I noticed that you are not a member of the IAAP.

EE: Yes, I am.

TK: You are? Good.

EE: What made you think that?

TK: I could not find you in the book.

EE: Sure, I am. I am a member of both the New York and Southern California Associations, and my voting membership is in Southern California.

TK: Here it is. Good.

EE: It probably has a symbolic significance.

TK: I am interested in that.

EE: To tell you the truth, I am not particularly proud of being a member right now.

TK: I don't know whether that was my intuition about it.

EE: I attended the first three international congresses: in 1958 in Zurich ...

TK: Did you meet Jung?

EE: Oh, yes, a couple of times. The second one was in 1962, again in Zurich, and the third one in 1965, in Montreux, and that was my last one. By that time it had gotten so collective and unwieldy that it made me a little sick, and I have never attended a congress since then. It has gotten bigger and bigger, and less and less to my taste ever since.

TK: It may seem strange, but I have a certain sympathy with that. Although I have made a certain niche for myself with certain friends, the last congress was very difficult for me. I am very happy to be out of the organizational structure. I have also paid my dues! But has there also been something that happened, what the IAAP represents today compared to five or ten years ago, which upsets you or is there something that you are strongly against?

EE: No, it's the total drift of things. It is very disappointing to me to see what Jung fundamentally represents getting lost even while his name is still functioning. It is quite remarkable to me that there are really quite widespread undercurrents of hostility to Jung in the organization. Some of it is right on the surface, and there is a lot of it just below the surface. I have reflected a lot on what that can mean, and I'd be interested to hear what you think it means. What I think it means is that what Jung has achieved requires more of people than they have to give to it, and it generates a sense of inferiority and inadequacy, which then has to be defended against.

TK: That's very interesting. I am a feeling type, and I put it on another thing – that there was a kind of over-idealization of Jung among certain people in the first generation, that Jung could do no wrong or had no shadow or anything like that. And in a sort of compensatory way people are going through a period of Jung-bashing at this point, to kind of compensate.

EE: You are offering a collective explanation while I am offering an individual explanation.

TK: You are right.

EE: I would like to carry this issue a little further with you because, as you are well aware, people consider that I am one of the prime over-idealizers of Jung.

TK: I have heard that said.

EE: I am sure you have.

TK: I grew up with two parents who were very strongly identified with Jung.

EE: That may make it a little difficult for you to be objective. I appreciate that thought very much.

TK: I don't say that I am objective about this, believe me. Jung has always been part of my life.

EE: What separates me from practically all the other so-called Jungians is that I have a perception of Jung's magnitude that other people do not share. That's not something one can argue about or prove. It's just an individual perception, and either it is way off base or it is approximately correct, and only history will determine that. But I do have it; it is my deepest conviction, and so I must live out of it, and I judge people on the basis of whether they have it or not too.

TK: It is so hard, Jung was a great, great thinker, and he is central in my life, too, and I don't know how to answer that.

EE: There is nothing to answer, and I just wanted to take the opportunity to spell it out because ordinarily these things go on behind one's back, and you don't usually have a chance to have a direct interchange on these matters.

TK: I am very touched by that because in some way, in my own limited way, I feel the same way about Jung, and what Jungian psychology has done in my life is so central. I get identified with that, too, and I hear this said about me too, maybe in a family way or ...

EE: Cheap analytic remarks!

TK: We live our lives. I really respect that you are living out your conviction, your deepest inner position.

EE: It is a continual surprise to me that people who are confronted with everything that Jung has left us – his works, his letters, his seminars – and if one had made a serious study of those things, it is obvious that this man has plumbed depths that nobody has ever touched before, and it amazes me that this is not generally recognized. I continue to be amazed that it is not recognized.

TK: My sense was that people like Esther Harding, Joe Henderson, my parents, that generation felt something very deeply about Jung and recognized it.

EE: Well, they had had the experience to some extent. They had the depth experience, and the depth experience is now very rare.

TK: It is. You look at the candidates we have now ...

EE: And the requirements for graduation are now so watered down, the psychological requirements, and that has been progressing for twenty or thirty years now, getting worse and worse, and lower and lower requirements.

TK: And people have to read less and less of Jung, and they read instead other authors. The London group, for instance, SAP: Jung probably is not even the major author they have to read; it might be Winnicott or Fordham. It's very different.

EE: It's a very different school of psychotherapy.

TK: This may be a good point to stop. I have been very touched, especially the last few minutes, and I appreciate talking with you.

EE: I have enjoyed it, Tom.

TK: Would you like to see this?

EE: If you are going to work up a transcription of it, I would like to see it.

TK: I'll send it on to you. Thank you.

Note

1 Thomas B. Kirsch Interviews Edward Edinger, December 4, 1996, *San Francisco Jung Institute Library Journal,* 23(2) (2004): 48–66: http://dx.doi.org/10.1525/jung.1.2004.23.2.48. Reprinted with the permission of the C. G. Jung Institute of San Francisco.

CHAPTER 10

CULTURAL COMPLEXES IN THE HISTORY OF JUNG, FREUD, AND THEIR FOLLOWERS

From *The Cultural Complex: Contemporary Jungian Perspectives on Psyche and Society*, edited by Thomas Singer and Samuel L. Kimbles, Routledge 2004[1]

The term "cultural complex" arises from two different aspects of Jung's psychology. Let us start with the term "complex," because this was the first area of research for Jung. Through the word association test Jung noted that there occurred a delayed reaction time to certain words which was experimentally repeatable. Jung observed that the delay was caused by the arousal of particularly strong emotions in connection with specific trigger words. He coined the term "complex" to account for this phenomenon. Indeed, it was Jung's pioneering work on the word association test and the development of the complex theory that led Jung to first make contact with Freud. Now the term "complex" is used in ordinary language to define an individual's particular sensitivity to a place, person, or thing. It is part of his or her personal psychology. When we speak about a cultural complex, we are moving away from an individual psychology to the psychology of the group – which can dwell both within the "collective" psyche of the group and the group level of the psyche embedded within the individual.

Let us now try to locate the term "cultural" in the context of Jung's psychology. We begin with Jung's notion of the archetype. Briefly, archetypes are the inborn, innate predispositions of the psyche. Jung describes them as the "self-portrait of an instinct," and they are the factors that an individual brings to any given situation, internal or external. It is rare that one sees an archetypal experience without it being embedded in historical or cultural patterns. Although the historical and cultural context has always been assumed in analytical psychology, the delineation of this level of experience has not been emphasized. In general terms, Jungians have spoken either of the personal psychology or the archetypal psychology of the individual, but have not emphasized the cultural context. In 1962 Joseph Henderson presented a paper at the Second International Congress for Analytical Psychology titled "The Archetype of Culture" where he defined this layer of the psyche, which he postulated as existing between the personal and the archetypal (Henderson, 1964). Dr. Henderson's paper was received with great enthusiasm, but the cultural level of the psyche is still not frequently referred to. In the last few years Tom Singer (2002) and Sam Kimbles (2000) have coined the term "cultural complexes" to elaborate on this level of psychological experience.

With the goal of further elaborating the concept of cultural complexes by applying it to the specific "case history" of Jung and Freud and their followers,

80 *Cultural complexes*

I am going to focus on the relationship between these psychological pioneers and the groups that developed around them as seen from the perspective of cultural complexes. First, there are the underlying "cultural complexes" that Jung and Freud each separately brought to their intensely creative and destructive relationship. Second, there are the "cultural complexes" among the Freudian and Jungian groups that were actually generated by Freud and Jung's coming together and falling out. In this chapter, I will address both of these separate but interrelated categories of cultural complexes.

The central thesis of this chapter can be stated as follows: how we carry the relationship between Freud and Jung inside our individual and group psyches – their collaboration, their fight, the subsequent history of the groups that formed around each of them, and the theory and practice that grew out of their work and their "schools" – constitutes and has contributed to the creation of "cultural complexes" that dwell inside each of us and the groups we identify with and/or see as our rivals. These "cultural complexes" of the Jung–Freud traditions that we carry within ourselves and our groups help define our professional identities and how we interact with our professional world – for better or worse. The "cultural complexes" brought to and born of the Jung–Freud relationship have been a most heated subject for almost one hundred years and have touched the deepest levels of emotion in those who practice psychoanalysis and analytical psychology. We can be certain that we are in the realm of complexes because of the intense reactivity that any mention of the topic usually provokes. A contemporary word association test administered to psychoanalysts and analytical psychologists that included the names of Jung and Freud would quickly demonstrate this fact. Although the backdrop for the tension between Jungians and Freudians goes back to the very beginnings of a Christianity born out of Judaism, my own attention in this chapter will focus on the different cultural backgrounds of Freud and Jung, and then on my own experience as a Jew and Jungian in a predominantly Freudian psychoanalytic culture since the early 1960s.

Freud was born in Bohemia in 1856, and his family moved to Vienna when he was a still a very young boy. During the time of his growing up, Vienna was strongly anti-Semitic, and there were few professions that a Jew could enter. Freud studied medicine, became a neurologist, and did some of the pioneering research in discovering the anesthetic properties of cocaine and related substances. He was a docent at the University of Vienna medical school, which meant that he was at the lowest level of the academic hierarchy, and he knew that as a Jew his chances for promotion were slim. In 1895 Freud and Breuer published their pioneering studies titled *Studies in Hysteria* and the field of psychoanalysis was born. A small group of individuals, all of whom were Jewish, formed around Freud, and they began to meet on a weekly basis. Freud's theories on the nature of infantile sexuality were being roundly criticized in both the medical and lay press. Both the nature of his ideas and his being Jewish led him to feel ostracized and an outsider.

Jung's background was entirely different from that of Freud's. In Jung's family there had been many generations of Protestant ministers. Only in the preceding two generations had his father's family moved from Germany to Switzerland where Jung was born in 1875. On his mother's side the family had lived many generations in Switzerland, and several members had written about their psychic paranormal abilities. When Jung was growing up in the rural countryside surrounding Basel, there were just a few Jews in the entire canton of Basel. It was only in the late 1800s that Jews were allowed to live within the city walls of the Swiss cities. Prior to that they had to live outside the cities, and they were allowed to come into the cities to do their business only during the day. One does not know when Jung met a Jew for the first time, but it most likely would have been at the university in Basel during his studies between 1895 and 1900 (Gossman, 2000).

Through Jung's work on the word association test and complex theory, he became acquainted with Freud's theories of the unconscious. Jung utilized Freud's theories to explain the results of his own research. In 1906 Jung sent his papers on the word association test and complex theory to Freud, and in March of 1907, Jung, his wife, and Ludwig Binswanger, a colleague at the Burghölzli and later founder of Existential Psychoanalysis, visited Freud in Vienna. There was an immediate fascination between the two men, and very quickly Jung was anointed as the "crown prince" of the psychoanalytic movement, much to the chagrin of Freud's Viennese colleagues. Freud saw in Jung an established psychiatrist from a famous institution, the Burghölzli, who was not Jewish and who came from a central part of Europe, who would make an excellent representative for psychoanalysis to the world. Meanwhile, Jung saw in Freud the father that he had been looking for since the disillusionment with his own father, and so the relationship blossomed quickly.

The Freud–Jung correspondence documents the tremendous hopes and expectations that the two had of each other. It also demonstrates the eventual demise of their relationship, which is a sad chapter in the history of psychoanalysis and analytical psychology. By the end of their relationship in 1914, mutual accusations were made of the other, including Freud asserting that Jung was anti-Semitic, and Jung accusing Freud of being materialistic and stereotypically Jewish. Freud wrote in *On the History of the Psychoanalytic Movement* that "he [Jung] seemed ready to enter into a friendly relationship with me and for my sake to give up certain racial prejudices which he had previously permitted himself" (Freud, 1914/1957). There is no question as one reads the letters that both men suffered deeply from the loss of the relationship. Jung withdrew from many of his psychiatric activities and went through a period of profound introversion and disequilibrium, and one sees in Freud's writings and correspondence a bitterness that one seldom sees elsewhere in his work. Ernest Jones, Freud's biographer, remarked that "his [Freud's] daughter tells me that it [the break with Jung] was the only time she remembers her father being depressed" (Jones, 1953–7: 99). The two men were never to meet again.

Ever since that time, many professionals have mourned the fact that the two men had to split. The consensus is that, if the two men had been able to continue their work together, many of the issues that split psychoanalysis and analytical psychology would not have happened. Although we can fantasize what might have happened had the two been able to continue their collaboration, it is noteworthy that they were able to come together in the first place. Given their differences in cultural backgrounds and upbringing, the fact that they worked together for the time that they did is remarkable. Freud continued to be active in developing a strong psychoanalytic organization in many European countries and in the United States. Most of those attracted to Freud's work were Jewish, and the early psychoanalytic association was more than 90 percent Jewish. On the other hand, Jung withdrew from organizations, but he did slowly develop a group of students around him. No formal international Jungian professional association was organized until 1955, when Jung was 80 years old.

Between 1914 and 1955 Jung did become involved in one other professional organization, and the nature of his participation in that organization has negatively influenced his reputation up to the present. Jung was made honorary vice-president of the German Medical Society for Psychotherapy in 1931. This society was formed in 1926 in order to provide a forum for medically trained psychotherapists who

82 Cultural complexes

were interested in psychoanalysis but who did not wish to become members of the Berlin Psychoanalytic Institute. The German Medical Society for Psychotherapy put on yearly conferences that attracted participants from the rest of Europe and the United States. In 1933 the president of this group was Ernst Kretschmer, a professor of psychiatry at Tübingen, who resigned because he did not agree with the Nazi philosophy. The group was in a predicament about who the new president should be, and as Jung was the honorary vice-president, he was urgently asked to take over as president. He eventually agreed to become president with the stipulation that the organization change its name to the International General Medical Society for Psychotherapy, and that Jewish members in Germany could retain their membership as individual members. All Jewish members in Germany had been excluded from the national German group as part of the then new Nazi ideology. In 1933 in his introductory remarks to the newly resuscitated *Zentralblatt* (the official organ of the German Medical Society for Psychotherapy), Jung made the following statement:

> The differences which actually do exist between Germanic and Jewish psychology and which have been known to every intelligent person are no longer to be glossed over, and this can only be beneficial to science. At the same time, I should like to state expressly that this implies no depreciation of Semitic psychology, any more than it is a depreciation of the Chinese to speak of the peculiar psychology of the Oriental.
>
> (Jung, 1964, pp. 533–4)

This statement of Jung's has been picked up by psychoanalysis and scholars of other disciplines interested in this period to demonstrate that Jung was both anti-Semitic and a Nazi sympathizer. There is no question that the tone of Jung's comments and the timing of them could not have been worse. One can see how Jung's statement could be melded into Nazi propaganda, although those familiar with Jung at the time knew of his interest in national character and differences in cultural heritage.

A second problem associated with this organization is that the German president was Matthias Goering, a distant cousin of the future close associate of Hitler, Hermann Goering. Matthias Goering was a professor of psychiatry as well as a Nazi, and from 1936 until 1945 he was the head of the major psychotherapy training institute in Nazi Germany. Jung and Matthias Goering had an extensive correspondence connected with the International General Medical Society for Psychotherapy, which still has not been released by the Jung family. Jung's association with Matthias Goering has often been confused and thought to have been with Hermann Goering, with whom Jung had no contact (Cocks, 1997). In 1934 Matthias Goering published an issue of the journal for German members only, which was completely Nazified, but by mistake it went out internationally, and it also included an article by Jung, which was meant for the international edition. Jung protested this mistake by Goering, but the damage was done. Jung's association with the International General Medical Society for Psychotherapy throughout the 1930s gave credence to the assertions of Jung's anti-Semitism made by Freud in 1914 (Freud, 1914/1957: 7).

What has been most remarkable is that from that time until the present Jung has been labeled as an anti-Semite. Although it is known that many of Jung's most important students were Jewish, and there has been much evidence to show that Jung aided the Allies during World War II, the linkage between Jung, Nazism, and anti-Semitism continues until this day. This will be described later in more detail. Is it possible that a cultural complex is at work in the persistence of the notion among Freudians that Jung was a Nazi? Certainly it could be part of a cultural complex that any criticism of Freud's work by a non-Jew is evidence of anti-Semitism. From the point of view of Freud as a Jew, his "cultural complex" would lead him to conclude that any criticism of him by a non-Jew is *prima facie* evidence of anti-Semitism. It would certainly be natural to view Jung, as a part Christian/part Swiss-German, associating with any Goering in the 1930s as evidence of Jung's being both a Nazi and an anti-Semite. Cultural complexes contaminate people and their thinking. What if both Freud and Jung had cultural complexes – Jung about Jews, Freud about non-Jews. By the way, it is important to note that we do not see Jung's interest in and early ideas about "national character" to be the same as the notion of "cultural complexes." They may intersect, but they are not the same. There can be a "national character" or identity without it being a "cultural complex."

It is at this point that my own personal history comes into play. Both my father and mother, who were Jewish, were in analysis with Jung during all of the 1930s. They did not live in Zurich but traveled there first from Berlin, later from Tel Aviv, and finally from London. Jung had several other Jewish analysands during this period, including Erich Neumann, Gerhard Adler, Rivkah Schaerf, Aniela Jaffé, and others. Specifically, Neumann, Adler, and my father warned Jung not to make the statement about national character that he did in 1934. Jung refused to listen to their counsel, but after World War II acknowledged that he had made a mistake in not listening to them. Jung never made a public apology. What is of further interest is that my father gave a lecture twice at the Analytical Psychology Club in Zurich in October 1930 on the subject of "A Modern Jew in Germany," which Jung attended and enthusiastically endorsed. Patients' dreams already had the images of Nazis showing up frequently. At the time my father was only 29 years of age and was a relatively new analysand of Jung's. My father, along with Jung's other Jewish analysands, all questioned him about his alleged anti-Semitism and none of those in analysis found him to be anti-Semitic.

When the extent of the Nazi destructiveness became apparent at the conclusion of World War II, this provided fuel for those who believed that Jung was a rabid anti-Semite and Nazi. The hostility between Freudians and Jungians in most parts of the world except London and San Francisco was tremendous. The period immediately following World War II was the pinnacle of influence for psychoanalysis, and prominent psychoanalysts wrote about Jung as a Nazi sympathizer and anti-Semitic, noting his association with Matthias Goering, the International General Medical Society for Psychotherapy, and the Nazis during the 1930s. For example, in the *History of Psychiatry* by Alexander and Selesnick there was a special appendix on the subject of Jung and his affiliation with the Nazis (Alexander and Selesnick, 1966: 407–9). Freudians had their rationalizations for dismissing Jung, and when I first entered psychiatric training in 1962, I encountered these "reasons" as potent manifestations of what I now recognize to be the symptoms of a cultural complex. I have come to think that at least one of the underlying, perhaps not totally conscious, purposes of the Freudian cultural complex about Jung and his followers was to annihilate the heretical Christian Jungian sect of psychology.

If one thinks that at least some cultural complexes originate in the fear and/or real experience of a group of people being extinguished, it makes sense that the group fearing such a threat may in turn seek to deny the right to exist of other similar, rival groups. For whatever reasons, the Freudians were almost successful in annihilating the rather small Jungian group in the United States. I discovered that one of the most successful ways of achieving this goal was for Freudians to

84 *Cultural complexes*

plead ignorance about Jung. Feigning or indeed truly not knowing anything about Jung was an effective way of denying his existence. In my case, I was told on many occasions during my psychiatric training that my Jungian analysis would hurt my psychiatric career. If my professors had succeeded in dissuading me from entering Jungian training, they would have effectively denied my existence as a Jungian. In addition to simply denying Jung's existence, the Freudian complex about Jungians expressed itself to me as skepticism about Jung's supposed mysticism and hostility to his alleged political views, especially as they related to World War II. In spite of these dire warnings, I obtained Jungian training and became a Jungian analyst. This meant that I had to overcome the intensely negative emotional reactivity of Freudians toward Jung. Such emotional reactivity is characteristic of cultural complexes. Proceeding with my Jungian training was a very difficult thing to do as a young person. My livelihood was at stake, and I feared that I would not get patients or be taken seriously as a psychiatrist and an analyst. Whenever Jung's name was brought up during that period, his association to the Nazis was inevitably mentioned. As I had heard a great deal about Jung from my parents and their Jewish colleagues, I knew that the charges against him could not be entirely valid. I had conversations with many Jewish analysts who had been in analysis with Jung during this period.

From the other side of this cultural complex, most early Jungians had a completely negative opinion of Freud and psychoanalysis. As psychoanalysis was the dominant psychology of the time, almost all early Jungians had begun with some form of psychoanalysis, and it had not answered their need. In the process of looking at other alternatives, they had come upon Jung and Jungian analysis, and it had been more compatible and rewarding. As Jung was so marginalized, the early Jungians developed a defensive superiority which denigrated anything to do with early developmental issues, personal unconscious conflicts, and defense structures. Meanwhile they tended to emphasize the spiritual, the archetypal, and the transcendent. Anything to do with personal unconscious material was seen as less important and less relevant than the larger "archetypal issues." Freud was seen as reductive, materialistic, anti-spiritual, and neurotic. There were obvious exceptions to these gross generalizations, i.e., the stereotyping is pathognomonic of a complex, but the attitudes expressed here were generally shared and can now be considered part of the Jungian cultural complex about Freud and Freudians. The conditions have now changed markedly. Individuals often begin with Jungian analysis, and it is no longer marginalized. Also, there no longer is the same stigma if one crosses the party line and sees an analyst from the other camp. For instance, people who identify themselves as Jungian can openly speak of a positive experience with Freudian analysis. But that is just beginning to happen now.

Many years ago, when I began to become more comfortable with an identity as a Jungian analyst, I started to give talks and write about Jungian themes. Because of my background and experience, my lectures often included personal anecdotes about Jung and early Jungians. Therefore, questions often came up about Jung and his relationship to the Nazis and to the Jews. My answer would always include the fact that my parents were Jewish, and that they had been in analysis with him during the period when he was supposed to be anti-Semitic, and they had not found him to be so. This at least quieted most people. I do not think that it necessarily changed anyone's mind. However, even when my lectures have had nothing to do with Jung the man, often I was questioned about Jung's complicity with the Nazis, etc. I continued to give talks and lectures about Jungian subjects, and my interest in the history of Jung and analytical psychology grew. I was elected as vice-president and then president of the International Association for Analytical Psychology. In that capacity, I continued to give lectures on Jung in various parts of the world, including Europe, Korea, South Africa, and Australia. No matter where I went the questions about Jung and his relationship to the Nazis and to anti-Semitism arose, and the exact subject matter of the lecture was not relevant.

Since the early 1980s there have been many changes in psychoanalytic theory and practice with the result that there are now many kinds of psychoanalyses in the world. Furthermore, pharmacological agents have become much more prevalent in the treatment of psychological disorders, and the esteem with which psychoanalysis has been held has decreased considerably. Freud himself has become the subject of much criticism, and the number of people entering psychoanalysis has decreased markedly. At the same time the work of some dissidents, such as Sandor Ferenczi and others rejected by Freud, has become increasingly accepted. The cultures of both psychoanalysis and analytical psychology have begun to shift dramatically – both as separate movements and in relation to one another. An opportunity arose for me to speak about Jung to a primarily psychoanalytic audience. In the year 2000 the International Association for Analytical Psychology became one of the co-sponsors of the International Association for the History of Psychoanalysis conference in Versailles, France (Kirsch, 2001). This meant that the Jungians could have one speaker in each of the English, French, and German sessions. I presented a short paper on the topic of Jung as Freud's first critic. The areas of Jung's criticism of Freud that I spoke about were:

- Jung's criticism of libido theory.
- Jung's criticism of Freud's undervaluing the importance of the manifest content in dreams.
- Jung's criticism of Freud's idea that culture was fundamentally "derivative".
- Jung's inability to accept the concept of analytic neutrality; Jung believed in the dialectical process in analysis, i.e., that the analytic relationship is a two-person psychology.

I presented these criticisms with the idea that there would now be a much greater receptivity to Jung's ideas and even his criticisms of Freud than in 1913 and in the subsequent early years of psychoanalysis.

There were two or three questions about the content of my lecture. Then an American woman psychotherapist from New York stood up and made a statement that there was "an elephant in the room." She stated that Jung was an anti-Semitic Nazi and that he was connected to the Holocaust. She went on to say that there were relatives of people in the room who had died indirectly because of Jung. Her emotional outburst brought a moment of silence and an end to rational discussion. It also brought an emotional reaction from me. I mentioned my family history and told her and the rest of the audience that it was not possible that Jung could have been as she described him. I made these statements with a great deal of feeling, and I felt very emotionally shaken by the experience. Later, I wondered what it would have been like if I had been able to react calmly to her exaggerated statement against Jung. But, in the moment, we were plunged into the emotional reactivity characteristic of both personal and cultural complexes. During the remainder of the conference several people came up to me and were either critical of my outburst, supportive of my response to the old, familiar accusations, or had other questions about Jung. For instance, some asked if Jung had in fact been Jewish and later converted to Christianity. Most of the questions about Jung revealed such a level

86 *Cultural complexes*

of naivety about the man and his work that I realized it was still too early to bring Jung into the mainstream of psychoanalytic thought. Once again, I discovered that when I tried to present a rational discussion on the differences between Freud and Jung, Jung's alleged anti-Semitism took over the center stage and inhibited any meaningful discussion. I have asked myself many times what if Jung had been anti-Semitic; does that mean that one cannot discuss his theories objectively? Does that discount them automatically? Given the worst-case scenario, which my personal experience tells me is not true, it is both important and necessary to discuss these ideas in as objective a manner as possible.

Obviously, the subject of the Jung–Freud relationship has deep personal meaning for me and the painful exchange that took place at the Versailles conference can easily be formulated at that level. Subsequently, however, I have also come to think of this disturbing episode in terms of the notion of a "cultural complex" and its power in the unconscious at the level of both the individual and group psyche. The conflict and its emotion can feel intensely personal – as it did to me at Versailles – but in fact much of the affect comes from a cultural or group level of the psyche that is highly charged for both the individual and the group. Reflecting on this experience from the perspective of the concept of "cultural complexes," I see the cultural complex "taking over" the Versailles experience in the following ways:

- The level of affect that it aroused in me and the audience.
- The way in which the "cultural complex" shaped the memory of the participants at the conference in a highly selective way.
- Through its shaping of memory, the "cultural complex" created its own history and perspective.

The Jung–Freud relationship has become a "cultural complex" through the meaning it has taken on in the followers of Jung and Freud, and through their separate tellings of the history of the relationship. Communication of this "history" transmits the "cultural complex" and its tremendous emotional charge to successive generations of Jungian and Freudian analysts. The emotional charge of the cultural complex in the individual and group psyche can easily carry the day when the complex is triggered, altering memory, history, and meaning.

A further complicating level of the problem for me has been that, as a Jew, I have been defending Jung, who was purportedly anti-Semitic. Although not a religiously practicing Jew, I have always strongly identified culturally as a Jew, and this has put me at times in an awkward situation when defending Jung against Freud. The experience in Versailles was certainly one of those times. Another question that has always puzzled me is why Jung has received so much negative criticism about his problematic contact with the Nazis, whereas Heidegger, a known member of the Nazi party throughout the war who sacked his Jewish teacher, Edmund Husserl, does not receive the same level of criticism. It must go back to the original relationship between Freud and Jung, which ended so bitterly and which on both the personal and cultural level still has not been assimilated completely on either side. Of course, Heidegger did not have the followers and students in quite the same way Jung did – and groups have a particularly potent way of transmitting complexes and their tremendous emotion. All of this points to the psychological fact that when speaking about the Freud–Jung relationship, the cultural differences and the unconscious cultural complexes that underlie both their personal relationship and the groups that sprang from their pioneering work must be considered. The readiness with which the unconscious can break through when discussing differences and similarities between Freud and Jung is very much with us. Singer and Kimbles have made us more aware of the profound effect of cultural complexes on our personal lives and our lives as members of groups – be they family, ethnic, professional, regional, or national. As part of our growth process, we need to learn to integrate into consciousness these cultural complexes in the same way that we work towards integrating personal complexes. If we disregard this level of the psyche, we are susceptible to the effects of cultural complexes in unexpected ways. My experience with psychoanalysts in Versailles has confirmed that for me. Even more than that, it has confirmed for me the emotional fact that when individuals and groups get caught in the grips of unconscious cultural complexes, more often than not we are left with very sad stories to tell.

I would like to conclude by reiterating the point that I consider central to this chapter: how we carry the relationship between Freud and Jung inside our individual and group psyches – their collaboration, their fight, the subsequent history of the groups that formed around each of them, and the theory and practice that grew out of their work and their "schools" – constitutes and has contributed to the creation of "cultural complexes" that dwell inside each of us and the groups we identify with and/or see as our rivals. These "cultural complexes" of the Jung–Freud traditions that we carry within ourselves and our groups help define our professional identities and how we interact with our professional world – for better or worse.

Note

1   "Cultural Complexes in the History of Freud, Jung, and their Followers." In Thomas Singer and Samuel L. Kimbles (eds), *The Cultural Complex: Contemporary Jungian Perspectives on Psyche and Society*, pp. 185–95. Hove, UK: Brunner-Routledge, 2004. Reprinted with the permission of the publisher.

References

Alexander, F. G., and Selesnick, S. T. (1966) *The History of Psychiatry*, appendix B. New York: Harper & Row.

Cocks, G. (1997) *Psychotherapy in the Third Reich*. 2nd edn. New Brunswick, NJ: Transaction.

Freud, S. (1914/1957) *On the History of the Psychoanalytic Movement*. Standard Edition, vol. 14. London: Hogarth Press.

Gossman, Lionel (2000) *Basel in the Age of Burkhardt*. Chicago, IL: University of Chicago Press.

Henderson, J. (1964) The Archetype of Culture. In A. Guggenbühl-Craig (ed.), *Der Archetyp: Proceedings of the 2nd International Congress for Analytical Psychology, 1962*. Basel and New York: S. Karger, pp. 3–15.

Homans, P. (1998) We (Not So Happy) Few: Symbolic Loss and Mourning in Freud's Psychoanalytic Movement and the History of Psychoanalysis. *Psychoanalysis and History* 1(1): 69–86.

Jones, E. (1953–7) *The Life and Work of Sigmund Freud*. 3 vols. New York: Basic Books.

Jung, C. G. (1933/1964) Editorial. Collected Works, vol. 10. New York: Pantheon.

Kimbles, S. (2000) The Cultural Complex and the Myth of Invisibility. In T. Singer (ed.) *The Vision Thing: Myth Politics and Psyche in the World*. London: Routledge, pp. 157–169.

Kirsch, T. (2001) Reports on the VIIIth International Meeting of IAHP. *Journal of Analytical Psychology* 46(3): 496–8.

Singer, T. (2002) The Cultural Complex and Archetypal Defenses of the Collective Spirit: Baby Zeus, Elian Gonzales, Constantine's Sword, and Other Holy Wars. *San Francisco Jung Institute Library Journal* 20(4): 4–28.

CHAPTER 11

THE ROLE OF PERSONAL THERAPY IN THE FORMATION OF A JUNGIAN ANALYST

From *The Psychotherapist's Own Psychotherapy: Patient and Clinical Perspectives*, edited by Jesse D. Geller, John C. Norcross, and David E. Orlinsky, Oxford University Press, 2005[1]

A personal analysis is central to becoming a Jungian analyst; it is the aim of this chapter to describe the evolution of training analysis in analytical psychology and to present some issues which pertain to its practice.

Historical introduction

Jung was the first to recognize the necessity of a training analysis and did so in 1912 while still collaborating with Freud, who acknowledged this important contribution when he stated, "I count it one of the valuable services of the Zurich school of analysis that they have emphasized this necessity and laid it down as a requisition that anyone who wishes to practice analysis of others should first submit to be analyzed himself by a competent person" (Freud, 1912).

After the break with Freud, Jung entered a long period of introversion, experiencing many images and fantasies that he could not explain using Freud's theories. At first he referred to them as "primordial images" (Jung, 1913), later as "archetypal images." These events, central to his self-analysis and described in *Memories, Dreams, Reflections* in the chapter "Confrontation with the Unconscious," form the basis of all his subsequent theories (Jung, 1961). Jung then described a collective level to the unconscious, which he believed contained creative potential, extending Freud's picture of the unconscious as the repository of repressed infantile material. Within his own theoretical framework the personal analysis was the core of an analyst's professional training. In 1946 Jung wrote the following about the training analysis: "anybody who intends to practice psychotherapy should first submit to a 'training analysis,' yet even the best preparation will not suffice to teach him everything about the unconscious ... A complete emptying of the unconscious is out of the question if only because its creative powers are continually producing new formations" (1946, 177).

At the conclusion of World War I people from around the world, especially English-speaking individuals, came to Jung for consultation and analysis. As a result of their analyses and their transference to Jung, many wished to become analysts. They had come out of personal need, but they literally were transformed into practitioners of a new profession. In addition to analysis, Jung offered a seminar in English during the academic year, to which he invited many of his analysands. The English seminars continued until 1939 when World War II intervened, and were never resumed because after his first heart attack in 1944 he went into semi-retirement. Most of those who sought out Jung in the 1920s and 1930s also saw a second analyst during their stay in Zurich. Usually this was Toni Wolff, who served as Jung's main assistant. According to Joseph Wheelwright, one brought the "big dreams" to Jung, while Toni Wolff handled more personal material (Wheelwright, 1975). This practice was called "multiple analyses," with the analysand consulting more than one analyst concurrently. Those who spoke German could also attend Jung's weekly lectures at Zurich's Eigenosse Technische Hochschule (ETH, Switzerland's equivalent of MIT, where Jung was professor of psychology).

After an undetermined period of time an individual would receive a letter from Jung affirming that he or she was qualified to practice analysis according to Jung's methods; often the person returned to practice Jungian analysis in the home country. Jung's criteria for eligibility to receive this letter of approval were never made explicit. To some he suggested more education, a medical or psychological degree, while to others he made no such recommendation. As in the early days of Freud, many individuals lacking academic credentials became analysts on the basis of a personal analysis alone.

This was the state of affairs until 1948, when the C. G. Jung Institute in Zurich opened its doors to begin formal training, ending the period when a personal analysis with Jung or one of his immediate associates became the sole criterion to become an analyst. After 1948 an academic curriculum, in addition to the personal analysis, was required for graduation. These requirements became worldwide in 1955 when the International Association for Analytical Psychology was established. Though now part of an institutionalized process, the personal analysis has remained central to training. Before going into greater detail, I would like to present some core concepts of analytical psychology.

Core concepts

Dreams

The importance of working with dreams is paramount, with an emphasis on the manifest content. The dream is seen as an "interior drama," compensatory to the attitude of consciousness. Not only is the retrospective origin, the "where from" of the dream, examined but also its prospective "where to" – that is, the potential development to which the dream points.

Psychological type

Important factors influencing many analyses are Jung's two attitudes of introversion and extraversion, and his four functions: sensation, intuition, thinking, and feeling.

Transference and countertransference

Although borrowed from psychoanalysis, these terms have a different meaning for analytical psychology. The transference includes not only projections from past family figures but also potential for future development, still dormant in the unconscious, which is projected onto the analyst.

Dialectical relationship

The analysand and analyst are equally involved in the analytical relationship. The analyst's subjective reactions are an integral part of the therapy and are not seen only as neurotic countertransference. Neither is the Jungian analyst considered a blank screen.

Symbolic versus developmental

There is a basic divide between those Jungians who utilize a more developmental approach and include post-Freudian psychoanalytic theories in their orientation, and those who adhere closely to Jung's basic writings and his methods of working, as handed down by those who analyzed with him. The majority of Jungians fall somewhere between the two extremes. Depending on the approach, this will affect the frequency of sessions per week, the use of the couch versus chair, the emphasis on transference-countertransference interpretations, the importance of early development, and the nature of dream interpretation.

US and European training guidelines

In addition to the theoretical and technical differences among Jungians, there are also political issues that account for the wide variation in what constitutes the training analysis. For instance, in England the influence of Kleinian and British object-relations theorists is very strong. In the United States, which lacks a national Jungian organization, the training situation is very different from all other countries, where a national organization determines training standards. In the United States, each locally accredited institute within the International Association for Analytical Psychology needs only to adhere to the basic minimal standards of the International Association and is free to set its own standards. There is wide variation among US training institutes in the emphasis on developmental or classical Jungian theories and methods.

Another important issue is the category of "training analyst." Most of the major training institutes have established such a category. The San Francisco Institute, where I trained, makes no such distinction. Its founders believed that the category "training analyst" would create a problematic hierarchy; they also wished to provide the candidate in training a wide choice among personal analysts; however, they stipulated that to supervise control work with a candidate, the analyst must have been a member in good standing for five years. This policy seems to have promoted openness to both developmental and classical Jungian theory, and enabled the inevitable tensions that arise to be contained without divisive splitting.

A further political issue is the role of the personal analyst in evaluating an applicant during the admissions process or the candidate during training. In the early days of the Jung Institute in Zurich, the personal analyst was intimately involved in the evaluation process (Hillman, 1962b, 8). Until recently, many other major institutes followed this example. In the San Francisco Institute, the personal analyst was forbidden to participate in his or her analysand's admission or evaluation processes, so as not to overburden the already difficult work of analysis and to prevent potentially disturbing analytic material from being withheld by the candidate, fearing that this information might prevent passage to the next phase of training.

Current training issues

Now, as we are aware of boundary issues in analysis, and what happens when they are transgressed, this policy has changed in every training institution around the world. The philosophy is to preserve the privacy of every candidate's personal analysis. The task of evaluating candidates has now fallen to reviewing committees that collect information from seminar leaders, supervisors, and control analysts.

In spite of these provisions, the analyst is still likely to regard the candidate in analysis differently from other analysands. First, the person who enters analysis with the idea of becoming an analyst has a definite aim or goal beyond his or her own therapy. This person wishes to have the analysis serve the ego aim of becoming an analyst, which means forming some kind of identity with the analyst, often raising unresolved issues for both the analyst and analysand. Such an aim is clearly different from that of a person who comes for the relief of symptoms. In the nontraining analysis, there is an endpoint at which the analyst and analysand separate, whereas in the training analysis there is a continued connection in their shared professional world. Another way to express this is in terms of the tension between individuality and collective responsibility. The personal training analysis must, on the one hand, honor the individual expression of the analysand; on the other, it has a collective responsibility to the Jungian community to affirm certain basic values. Each analyst has an individual relationship to the professional group, and the candidate must forge his or her independent relationship to this same professional community. Much of this work happens through the personal training analysis, but the question remains whether a truly independent relationship, free of transference residuals, is ever possible.

Academic knowledge helps orient the developing analyst, but personal analysis provides the model for his/her own professional work. With time and experience the new analyst develops a unique style, which continues to evolve over the course of his or her professional career.

The training analysis

In my experience most Jungian analysts acquire a great deal more analysis than is required for graduation or certification. The usual requirement is that the entering candidate have a minimum 100 to 200 hours of personal analysis before beginning training. Most programs require candidates to be in analysis during the training period. Many trained Jungian analysts go back for further analysis as different life circumstances arise. In fact, analysts are encouraged to return for analysis at nodal points. Freud also believed that one should go back every five years for further analysis, although in those days the analyses were much shorter. As the Jungian community is relatively small and members are likely to know each other, many analysts seek further analysis with non-Jungians. Furthermore, today there is much more crossfertilization between analytical psychologists and psychoanalysts than formerly, so that many Jungian analysts want the experience of having their personal material dealt with in the language and philosophy of another school.

Often a candidate in Jungian training is advised to have analysis with both a man and woman, or with an analyst of a particular psychological attitude or type, in the belief that gender and psychological type influence the nature of the dialectic in ways deemed desirable for that candidate's development. The practice of seeing more than one analyst concurrently, referred to as *multiple analyses* and examined in greater depth elsewhere (Kirsch, 1976), has been much debated within Jungian circles. On the one hand, it dilutes and splits the transference; on the other hand, new and valuable material is evoked. Today, with our greater sensitivity to transference issues, this practice of seeing more than one analyst during training has become less common.

92 *The formation of a Jungian analyst*

Fordham (1962) has provided a rationale for the many hours of personal analysis that Jungian analysts have today. He says that it is important for trainees to experience as many psychopathological states in themselves as possible. In fact he encourages candidates to experience these psychopathological states in their training analyses, because then they will be able to cope with them more readily when they face the same issues as analysts. Equally, the trainees can learn to identify the parts of themselves that are healthy, not requiring analytic work, and serving as a source of strength (Fordham, 1962).

Limits of personal analysis

Fordham also says that an unresolvable pathological nexus exists between any patient and his or her analyst, regardless of the length of analysis. This factor will also influence the training analysis. Full elucidation of infancy and childhood will minimize the influence of unresolved complexes upon the analytic relationships that the new analyst will form with subsequent analysands. However, some traumatic experiences can be elucidated but not necessarily changed, hence the concept of the "wounded healer."

All too often a candidate's unresolved complexes are projected onto the local society in which he or she will practice. In this way the professional community, to some extent, is seen through the scrim of one's family of origin, in both its positive and negative lights. Concurrent with this are the many transference-countertransference residuals between individual members that are never fully resolved and exist in every society, regardless of its philosophic school or analytic method; the extent and intensity of these differences, far more than any philosophical disagreement, determines whether a group will remain together or divide (Kirsch, 2000).

A life-long pursuit of inner growth and personal development is the *sine qua non* of the Jungian analyst. Analytical psychology has undergone many changes in its evolution as a profession and a psychoanalytic discipline, yet throughout, a personal analysis remains at the core in shaping the present-day Jungian analyst.

Note

1   Extracts from pp. 27–33 chapter 3, "The Role of Personal Therapy in the Formation of a Jungian Analyst" by Tom Kirsch from Jesse D. Geller, John C. Norcross, and David E. Orlinsky (eds), *Psychotherapist's Own Psychotherapy* (2005). By Permission of Oxford University Press, USA, www.oup.com.

References

Edinger, E. (1961) Comment. *Journal of Analytical Psychology* 6(2): 116–17.
Fordham, M. (1962) Reply. *Journal of Analytical Psychology* 7(1): 24–6.
Fordham, M. (1971) Reflections on Training Analysis. In Joseph B. Wheelwright (ed.), *The Analytic Process,* pp. 172–84. New York: Putnam.
Fordham, M. (1976) Comment. *Contemporary Psychoanalysis* 12: 168–73.
Freud, S. (1912/1958) Recommendations to Physicians on the Psychoanalytic Method of Treatment. In *Standard Edition of the Complete Psychological Works of Sigmund Freud,* ed. and trans. J. Strachey, vol 12, pp. 109–20. London: Hogarth.
Guggenbühl-Craig, A. (1971) *Power in the Helping Professions.* New York: Spring.
Hillman, J. (1962a.) Training and the C. G. Jung Institute, Zurich. *Journal of Analytical Psychology* 7(1): 3–18.

Hillman, J. (1962b) A Note on Multiple Analysis and Emotional Climate at Training Institutes. *Journal of Analytical Psychology* 7(1): 20–2.

Jung, C. G. (1913/1961) *The Theory of Psychoanalysis.* Collected Works, vol. 4, trans. R. F. C. Hull, vol. 4, pp. 85–226. New York: Pantheon.

Jung, C. G. (1946/1954) *Psychology of the Transference.* Collected Works, vol. 16, trans. R. F. C. Hull, vol. 16, pp. 163–321. New York: Pantheon.

Jung, C. G. (1961) *Memories, Dreams, Reflections.* New York: Random House, Vintage Books.

Jung, C. G. (1971) *Psychological Types.* In Collected Works, vol 6, trans. R. F. C. Hull, vol. 6, p. 197. New York: Pantheon.

Kirsch, T. (1976) The Practice of Multiple Analyses in Analytical Psychology. *Contemporary Psychoanalysis* 12: 159–67.

Kirsch, T. (1995) Analysis in Training. In Murray Stein (ed.), *Jungian Analysis,* 2nd edition, pp. 437–50. LaSalle, IL: Open Court.

Kirsch, T. (2000) *The Jungians.* London: Routledge.

Marshak, M. O. (1964) The Significance of the Patient in the Training of Analysts. *Journal of Analytical Psychology* 9(1): 80–3.

Newton, K. (1961) Personal Reflections on Training. *Journal of Analytical* Psychology 6(2): 103–6.

Plaut, A. (1961) A Dynamic Outline of the Training Situation. *Journal of Analytical Psychology* 6(2): 98–102.

Samuels, A. (1985) *Jung and the Post-Jungians.* Boston, MA: Routledge & Kegan Paul.

Spiegelmann, M. J. (1980) The Image of the Jungian Analyst. *Spring: A Journal of Archetype and Culture:* 101–16.

Stone, H. (1964) Reflections of an Ex-Trainee on his Training. *Journal of Analytical Psychology* 9(1): 75–9.

Wheelwright, J. B. (1975) A Personal View of Jung. *Psychological Perspectives* 6: 64–73.

CHAPTER 12

THE LEGACY OF C. G. JUNG

From *Who Owns Jung?* edited by Ann Casemont, Karnac Books, 2007[1]

Who owns Jung is a question that can be answered in two words: No one. One may rightfully ask how someone can own another person's name? I could end my article right now. However, since I was asked to consider this question, I have been mulling over the notion of ownership of Jung as a symbol. Having been in and around Jung's psychology since my childhood, which is coming upon sixty years, I thought this might be a time to write about the issue. The present impetus for discussing this topic came up when psychoanalysts of different persuasions in the UK hotly debated who owns the title "psychoanalyst" and, therefore, who is entitled to be registered as a psychoanalyst. At that time, it was concluded that only members of the British Psycho-Analytical Society could be registered as psychoanalysts, and everyone else had to use some other title such as psychoanalytically oriented psychotherapist for their identity. Ann Casement, at the time the head of the licensing body for psychotherapists in the UK, was then asked to edit a book entitled *Who Owns Psychoanalysis?* to discuss this topic generally. This book was a success, and the editor thought that a companion book on who owns Jung also would prove to be of interest.

I do not believe that a book on who owns Jung has the same meaning as who owns psychoanalysis. Jung was the person who founded a movement which he called analytical psychology, so to own Jung feels different than to own psychoanalysis, which is a generic term for all those who practice that specialty. Granted that Freud stated that he "owned" psychoanalysis (Freud, 1914), but psychoanalysis today has developed in many different directions, some of which would not be recognizable to Freud. The only way that one can make the two books comparable is if you use the word "Jung" symbolically to stand for something which in its own way is equivalent to psychoanalysis. As the personage of Jung has become more distant, it is easier to make "Jung" a symbol for an attitude towards the unconscious and separate it from Jung the person. Perhaps as more time elapses, we will distance ourselves even further from Jung the man and find another name that seems suitable for our field. Even now many analytical psychologists, which is our official title from Jung, call themselves Jungian analysts, or Jungian psychoanalysts, as well as analytical psychologists ... Our identity as "Jungian analysts" is evolving, and we are developing different personas depending upon which part of Jung we wish to be identified with.

Since my experience with Jungian psychology dates to a time when Jung was still alive, I remember a favorite past time among those who knew him was to quote him on various topics. Whether these quotes were actually what Jung said to these particular people or not always left me with some doubt. Now I look back at some of these statements and realize that these quotes from Jung arose out of their respective strong transferences. Because Jung was charismatic, his words took on an authority that was nearly impossible to refute. Each of these people who knew Jung and had been in analysis with him thought that they had the real Jung, unknown to the rest of us. These people were part of the first generation of analysts, scattered around the globe, who had analyzed with Jung from the early 1920s until 1939 and then came back to see him after World War II for an occasional session. This was my first memory in response to the question asked to me by the editor of this book. Every one of these people had a different experience of Jung, and each felt that his or her own experience was the real Jung. The fact that Jung was severely criticized for his activities during the 1930s and during World War II only intensified these disciples of Jung and their sense of loyalty and ownership. Jung was being badly misunderstood and ill regarded by the dominant psychoanalytic culture.

Jung's influence has reached across the globe through his writings and those of his students, lectures given about his work, filmed interviews with him, etc. His books have been translated into many languages, and many of his theories have become part of our everyday language such as complex, archetype, introvert, extravert, synchronicity, and individuation. Jung has been a leading figure in demonstrating the value and importance of paying attention and deepening our inner experience through dreams, active imagination, expressive arts, and the like. In our increasingly technological world, he has showed us a way to rekindle our deepest spiritual yearnings.

Jung's work touches people in different fields. On the one hand, Jung started out as a psychiatrist and moved from studying psychosis, namely schizophrenia, to studying neuroses and then to normal people. His study of psychological types was a study of normal differences in psychological attitudes and functions in the so-called normal person. His seminal work, *Psychological Types,* influenced Myers and Briggs who developed a test to show how these different attitudes and functions – introversion, extraversion, thinking, feeling, intuition, sensation – work in the normal population, and which ones were dominant and which ones were less well developed. This test has become widely used both in academia and business to assess potential strengths and weaknesses of the individual. I mention this part of Jung's work in particular because, although Jung's influence is acknowledged, it is largely practiced by people who have no other connection to Jung's psychology. Here is a part of Jung's psychology that is no longer really "owned" by Jungians; it has become a separate discipline of its own. One remarkable exception is John Beebe who has made an extensive study of Jung's psychological types and who has bridged his work with that of the psychological type discipline.

During most of Jung's professional life he practiced and wrote about his way of doing analysis. He never wrote detailed case histories as he did not want to give the impression that analysis could be done one way only and, secondly, for reasons of confidentiality. However, he gave numerous examples of working with dreams and active imagination among his writings. This meant that the first generation of Jungian analysts used their own personal analytic experience with Jung as their model for both doing analysis and for training others. Given that this first generation of analysts was comprised of people from many different cultures, the practice of Jungian analysis has evolved differently depending upon the founder/founders and their cultural milieu.

In the second half of Jung's life he discovered medieval alchemy, and his interests turned to the study of this discipline in terms of what it could reveal about the nature of the collective unconscious. He also became the dominant figure of a yearly conference titled Eranos, where leading philosophers, theologians, mythologists,

96   *The legacy of C. G. Jung*

and scientists would speak about the nature of the psyche from their respective viewpoints. This chapter will not attempt to discuss what part of Jung they own, as that would take us into a study of cultural ideas and history of consciousness, which is beyond the scope of this chapter. Instead, the focus will be on the development of the Jungian professional analytic community from the time of the Freud/Jung split in 1913 until the present. Also, some discussion of where the state of Jung scholarship is today will be part of this chapter.

Jung's own family descendants comprise another group of people with a claim on Jung to which I will return later in the chapter. This is a complex story. Also, there are archives and libraries with documents from Jung, and accessibility to these institutions influences what we know about Jung. Later in this chapter I will return to a description of them.

Analytical psychology as a term for Jung's psychology begins after the break with Freud. Jung was the leader of the psychoanalytic group in Zurich at the time of the split in 1913. Zurich was the second leading psychoanalytic center at the time of the split. Most of the people in Zurich followed Jung when the split occurred. Jung underwent a period of disorientation which he described in *Memories, Dreams, Reflections,* as "Confrontation with the Unconscious." He was flooded by images from his unconscious that became the prime material for all his future scientific writings. These images and writings are contained in a book titled *The Red Book*.[2]

As an integral part of the analytic process as expressed by Jung, analysands were expected to do a comparative study of the images which appeared in their dreams. This required the reading of books that were often difficult to obtain. In order to facilitate making this material available to analysands, an Analytical Psychology Club was formed in Zurich and had its first meeting on February 26, 1916. The "Club" was to be a meeting place for analysands so that (1) social interaction could take place among the members, (2) reading material could be made available to analysands, (3) lectures by authorities on symbolism and related topics could be given. These meetings took place monthly, and a library of relevant books was accumulated. Analysts and analysands mixed freely, and membership in the Club required hours of personal analysis as well as written approval from the personal analyst. Prior to World War II Analytical Psychology Clubs formed in London, New York, and San Francisco, and the model was always the same. The Analytical Psychology Club in Los Angeles formed in 1944. Other Analytical Psychology Clubs formed in Europe but did not survive World War II. These Analytical Psychology Clubs were the main structures which existed in the Jungian world until the formation of the Society of Analytical Psychology in London in 1946, and the C. G. Jung Institute in Zurich in 1948. Rudimentary professional organizations were formed in New York and San Francisco, but their influence only grew after World War II. Jung himself was extremely ambivalent about organizations, as his only two ventures into organizations, the International Psychoanalytical Association (IPA) and the International General Medical Society for Psychotherapy, had ended disastrously for him. Jung had at times an ambivalent relationship to the Analytical Psychology Club in Zurich. For instance, he withdrew from the Club in the early 1920s when Hans Trüb became the leading figure. Trüb later withdrew to follow Martin Buber and Jung returned and attended meetings. His colleague, Toni Wolff, was the president of the club in Zurich for more than twenty years.

The importance of the Analytical Psychology Clubs cannot be underestimated. To become a member was not easy, and especially in Zurich one needed to have the approval of some of the influential women members (Reid, 2001). Thus, to be a Jungian meant that one was a member of one of these Analytical Psychology Clubs.

The legacy of C. G. Jung   97

They did not lose their influence until the formation of the IAAP in 1955 when the IAAP became the accrediting body of Jungian analysts in the world. This coincided with Jungian analysts beginning to form their own professional organizations and separating from their Analytical Psychology Clubs. The clubs still exist in those original cities, but their importance as forming a part of the Jungian identity has markedly decreased. They still have their monthly lectures, and their libraries contain a large number of volumes on symbolism.

How did one become a Jungian analyst before the formation of the IAAP in 1955? Jung's period of deep introversion ended at approximately the same time that World War I ended. Jung's book *Psychology of the Unconscious* had been well received in the English-speaking world, and his book *Psychological Types* was to be published in 1921. His fame spread and people from all over the world, but especially from the United States and England, clamored to see him for analysis. Analyses in those days were extremely short by present-day standards, often lasting only three to six months. Travel in those days was also much more difficult and time consuming so that it was not easy for people to stay a long time in Zurich unless they were independently wealthy. Furthermore, Jung himself did not practice analysis more than half of each year, as he spent increasing time at his tower in Bollingen as well as making several long journeys, such as the one to Africa in 1925, which lasted for six months. The pattern was for analysands to see both Jung and Toni Wolff concurrently. Also, there were so many English-speaking analysands that Jung instituted a Wednesday morning seminar during the academic year so that his analysands would have something other than their personal analysis.

How one became a Jungian analyst under these circumstances was not completely clear. Some people came expressly for the purpose of becoming Jungian analysts, and others arrived to work on personal problems and then found that they also wanted to become Jungian analysts. Jung signed letters stating that the individual in mind had attended seminars and had had personal analysis and was now authorized to practice his methods. What criteria Jung used to write these letters of recommendation was not clear. His intuition about the person's relationship to his or her own unconscious was the primary factor. His attitude to formal education was contradictory. In some cases he required that the individual get an advanced degree, and in other cases he did not mind that the individual involved did not have much formal education.

Some who came expressly for Jung's recommendation never got it, and others who had no intention of becoming analysts would unexpectedly receive a recommendation from Jung. An example of the latter was my mother, Hilde Kirsch, who was a nursing mother in London in 1937 when she received a call from a medical doctor who had seen Jung. This doctor had met my mother at an Analytical Psychology Club meeting in London and had liked her. When this doctor contacted Jung about her, Jung recommended that he follow through and go into analysis with her. This was how she became a Jungian analyst. Jung continued this pattern of individual recommendation until the time of his death in 1961. In the last ten years of his life he used this method sparingly. By that time, the Jung Institute in Zurich was functioning, and the IAAP had come into existence and one of its main functions was to accredit analysts.

The Jung Institute in Zurich had already been thought about prior to World War II, but the war put all plans on hold. The Institute opened its doors in 1948, and it was organized along the lines of a European University. Courses included the study of dreams, complexes, word-association studies, mythology, comparative religion, fairy tales, Freud, psychiatry, and related subjects. Clinical colloquia were added as the student progressed in his studies. The Jung Institute emphasized academic studies and the individual's personal analysis. A thesis was required to graduate. After that one could practice as a Jungian analyst. There were approximately thirty students a year in attendance and the courses were in German, English, and French. The size of the Institute did not change much until the 1970s when it moved from the English quarter in Zurich to Kusnacht, a suburb of Zurich where Jung had lived. As Jung became more popular, the student population increased up to a maximum of 400. Political struggles have caused two splits from the original Institute. The first split occurred in 1992 when students loyal to M. L. von Franz left to form the Zentrum. They felt that the original Institute had lost the essence of Jung. The students from the Zentrum have not in general been interested in an official accreditation from the IAAP, although some graduates from the Zentrum have desired the accreditation. The second split occurred in 2004 and had to do with the finances of the Institute. The original Institute ran into financial difficulties, with fewer students, etc., and the governing board, the Curatorium, wanted the training analysts and teachers at the Institute to contribute money to help with the Institute's financial shortfall. This produced a massive protest on the part of some analysts, and those analysts decided to form their own Institute. There were not any basic theoretical differences between the two, but the money issues loomed large. Both the original Institute and the one formed in 2004 are member institutes of the IAAP, and their graduates are accredited through the IAAP. As the original Jung Institute in Zurich was in place prior to the formation of the IAAP in 1955, it has had an anomalous position within the IAAP structure. It does not represent a geographical entity, unlike all the other professional societies within the IAAP. The graduates of the Institute in Zurich became and still become members of IAAP by being part of a graduates organization, the Association of Graduate Analytical Psychologists of the C. G. Jung Institute of Zurich (AGAP). AGAP has no geographical boundaries, and those graduates from outside of Switzerland who return to their country of origin often do not belong to the local group in their country. This has produced tensions in many parts of the world (Kirsch, 1995).

I have mentioned the IAAP in passing several times, and as it is the main accrediting body of Jungian analysts, it is important to discuss its influence and authority in deciding "Who Owns Jung?". The IAAP, or International Association for Analytical Psychology, was founded on July 26, 1955. This was given to Jung on his 80th birthday as a gift from his disciples. The IAAP was incorporated in Switzerland with the aim to (1) accredit individual members, (2) accredit new groups, (3) have congresses, (4) adjudicate disputes within professional groups. From an initial membership of around 150 members it has grown to a membership closer to 3,000. The tasks and responsibilities of the IAAP have grown as the membership has spread worldwide.

The first Congress was held in Zurich in 1958. Jung attended the opening session and the banquet. Only analysts could attend, and no outsiders were let in. This meant neither trainees nor spouses. The second Congress was held in Zurich again in 1962, one year after Jung's death. At the second Congress a dispute which had already been brewing in the first Congress came out into the open. A clear differentiation between the classical methods used by Jung and Jungians in Zurich came into conflict with the newly espoused developmental model championed by Michael Fordham and others in the English professional group, the Society for Analytical Psychology (SAP). Esther Harding from New York who championed the classical position on archetypes and amplification sharply criticized a newly trained London analyst, Murray Jackson, who she felt had no understanding of what Jung meant by the term "symbol." She criticized him for reducing the term "symbol" to sign, just as Jung had criticized Freud earlier. She received strong approval for her position from the predominantly Zurich audience, and the British were not pleased with how they were received. For many years after that there was a deep tension between the positions of the SAP and Zurich. Most Jungians in the world sided with the Zurich position. Meanwhile, the *Journal of Analytical Psychology*, published by the SAP, presented the London clinical developmental position strongly and forcefully. Both groups claimed their Jungian identity, and both claimed their positions directly from Jung. They were both correct as Jung did espouse both positions, and he actually strongly urged the Zurich analysts to respect the developmental position (*Time Magazine*, 1958). In terms of "Who Owns Jung?" both had equal claims to representing Jung.

This dispute became a central question for the next several IAAP Congresses. Finally, in the 1983 Congress in Jerusalem this became the actual topic of the Congress. By that time the tension between the two sides had abated considerably. Clinical innovations from psychoanalysis and object-relations theory had begun to creep into many classical Jungian ideas, and the developmental theory of the London Jungians fitted into the overall zeitgeist of Jungian psychology.

In 1985 Andrew Samuels wrote his classic *Jung and the Post-Jungians*, where the differences among Jungians were first described. He based his classification on the emphasis that different analysts placed on the theory of archetypes, the self, transference, and the role of developmental issues in their work. The classical analyst pays greatest attention to the emergence of archetypal themes, especially the self, in his/her analysands. Transference phenomena are not emphasized and developmental issues are minimally acknowledged. The developmental group places greatest emphasis on early childhood issues, relies heavily on transference interpretations, and pays less attention to imagery and the symbolism of archetypes. To developmentalists bodily parts represent the archetypes rather than images, and they also have modified the use of the term "self" to include a primal self in the first half of life. The third group, following Hillman, who chose the term "archetypal psychology" to designate his particular school, emphasizes archetypal images and experiences and pays relatively little attention to the childhood developmental issues as well as to the transference. When Samuels' work was published in 1985, many analysts did not like this categorization, but it did provide a heuristic way of describing the development of analytical psychology, and it continues to be useful in describing the way different Jungian analysts work. All three groups see themselves as being centrally located in the psychology of Jung, and so all claim ownership to Jung.

Analytical psychology and Jung's work have continued to spread throughout the world. There are now analysts on every continent, and the IAAP's function is to help developing analysts in these far-off places where no accredited training is taking place. This has taken up an increasing amount of time for the IAAP. As I have stated earlier, the IAAP was founded in Switzerland, and in the early years the primary influence was Swiss and British. It needs to be mentioned that most of the member groups in the IAAP, except the United States, are national groups. Each country has a national group, and when there are enough members within a certain region of the country, satellite institutes are formed within the national group. This is the case in Germany, France, and Italy. The United States has never formed a national group within the IAAP, but instead there are regional geographical societies such as New York, Northern California, Southern California, and many others. The North Americans do meet on a yearly basis to discuss issues of mutual concern, but they have not formed a national group, although it has been proposed from time to time.

100 *The legacy of C. G. Jung*

In the 1980s there was a shift in influence from Switzerland and England to the United States. Politically the United States Jungians became some of the dominant figures within the IAAP. In 1989 and shortly thereafter the opening of the former Soviet Union brought an interest in analytical psychology from those areas plus Latin America, South Africa, Australia and New Zealand, and Asia. At the present time there has been a great interest in analytical psychology from much of Latin America and China, and the IAAP has truly become a worldwide organization. There are now five official languages of the IAAP, including German, English, French, Italian, and Spanish.

The IAAP holds Congresses every three years in different parts of the world, mainly Europe and the United States, but the next Congress in the year 2007 will take place in Cape Town, South Africa. In between these Congresses regional and topical conferences have been held. These Congresses are an opportunity for analysts to meet their colleagues and to exchange views on analytical psychology. It is also a time when the delegates from all the societies elect new groups and new individual members.

The IAAP has no official connection to either academia or to any government. Therefore, the IAAP has no legal authority to decide who can call himself/herself a Jungian analyst or not. There have been instances where individuals have called themselves Jungian analysts when they are not members of the IAAP. They have been asked to use another name to identify themselves, and in most cases, they have agreed to that. The point is that the IAAP, like the IPA, was formed outside governmental channels and therefore has no legal claim to the name Jungian analyst.

The Jung family and the Eidgenosse Technische Hochschule, (ETH) archive

The Jung family naturally has an interest in how Jung is viewed in the world. At the time of Jung's death in 1961 a trust was formed to handle Jung's personal estate. His English-language intellectual property was handled by his American and British publishers, respectively, the Bollingen Foundation, later transferred to Princeton, and Routledge, while the Jung family made decisions on the German edition. It was and is named the Erbengemeinschaft C. G. Jung, and members of the extended family are part of the trust. At first the spokesman for the trust was Jung's son, Franz, but in 1981, the heirs adopted a legal structure to adapt to the growing size of the Jung family. An executive committee exists which consists of one member from each branch of the family. At present it includes two grandsons and three great grandchildren. The president of the trust is Ulrich Hoerni, an architect by training who has devoted much of his life to the large number of issues around Jung's work. Two other important members are Peter Jung, a psychiatrist, and Andreas Jung, an architect, who has lived in his grandfather's house since 1975 and who is the archivist and librarian. Decisions on the many unpublished works, such as seminar notes, correspondences, lectures, etc., have yet to be made. Earlier I also mentioned the publication of *The Red Book,* by Sonu Shamdasani, of Jung's paintings and writings during his "Confrontation with the Unconscious" between 1912 and 1930. Translations of Jung's works into different languages continue, and the international copyright laws concerning them are complex. The fact of the matter is that staying abreast of all the ways that the name of Jung comes up is a rather time-consuming job.

In 1977 a Jung Archive was founded at the ETH in Zurich. Jung had been a professor there between 1933 and 1941, and Jung had it as a stipulation in his will that his papers should be preserved in an archive there (Ulrich Hoerni, personal communication, 2006). Today it has over 1,000 manuscripts and 35,000 letters from and to Jung. The Archive has grown with the acquisitions of the papers of Professor C. A. Meier, Jung's successor at the ETH; Aniela Jaffe, Jung's secretary; and Jolande Jacobi, a close associate of Jung's; as well as the important correspondence between Sigmund Freud and Jung. Access to the Archive is public, but only the "Press Archives" and "Separata Archives" are available (*Tages Anzeiger*, December 3, 2005). Most of the material in the Archive has already been published, and the original manuscripts exist in the Archive. Unpublished material is open to any scholar, but the documents in question need to be vetted by the Erbengemeinschaft beforehand in order to assess that confidential material is not being released. Confidentiality and "privacy laws" are all important in Switzerland and the rest of Europe. The result of this procedure is that it requires some preplanning to obtain the requested manuscripts. In the words of the curator, Yvonne Voegeli, "We house the Archive, but we do not administer the Archive" (*Tages Anzeiger*, December 3, 2005). A further problem is that the ETH Archive has had budget cuts and there is no longer the personnel available to do the necessary work of administering the documents quickly. Thus, it can sometimes take many months to obtain documents that one would think would be readily available. Both the Erbengemeinschaft and the ETH have come under criticism from Jung scholars, because it has appeared that documents relating to Jung are being withheld, when in fact the process of vetting and administering the documents is the real problem.

Philemon

In the year 2003 a new non-profit foundation called Philemon was created in the United States in order to fund the complete works of Jung in both German and English. Let me quote extensively from their announcement:

> In distinction to the widely known *Collected Works,* the *Complete Works* will comprise manuscripts, seminars, and correspondence hitherto unpublished or formerly believed "lost" that number in tens of thousands of pages. The historical, clinical and cultural importance of this material equals and, in some instances, surpasses the importance of that which has been already published. Given the volume of material yet unpublished extant in various public and private archives, the Philemon Foundation conservatively estimates that it will prepare for publication an additional 30 volumes beyond the 20 volumes of the *Collected Works,* and that the time frame required to complete this task will be at least 30 years. Once this is complete, a new English translation of the existing *Collected Works* is envisaged. Philemon Foundation will make the completed body of C. G. Jung's work available as volumes in The Philemon Series. As such, the Philemon Foundation is the successor to the Bollingen Foundation that originally made possible the publication of Jung's *Collected Works,* cornerstone of their Bollingen Series. Philemon Foundation has the support and collaboration of the Heirs of C. G. Jung. This unique relationship ensures access by the Philemon Foundation to the wealth of unpublished material by C. G. Jung, thus entrusting the Philemon Foundation with the task of bringing that work to the widest reading public. All existing contractual rights and agreements remain unchanged.

102 *The legacy of C. G. Jung*

The president of this new foundation is Stephen Martin, a Jungian analyst in Philadelphia, and the general editor is Sonu Shamdasani, Jungian scholar and historian and author of books on Jung. Recently, he has been appointed to the Philemon Readership in Jung History at the Wellcome Trust Centre for the History of Medicine at University College London, initially for ten years. In progress are the publication of Jung's ETH lectures, the correspondence between Jung and Victor White, and Jung's Children's Dreams seminar.[3] The correspondence project had run out of funds, and the ETH lectures, the correspondence between Jung and Victor White, and the English version of the Children's Dreams seminar, though part of the original prospectus for the Jung seminar series, had been abandoned. All of us in the Jungian world are delighted by the prospect of more of Jung's works being made available. Unpublished manuscripts, seminars, and correspondences will be published as the funds become available. Depending upon how many of these get published, the Philemon Foundation will play an important role in the future of how Jung is seen.

Conclusion

In this chapter I began with Jung the person and those who were in analysis with him. Their extremely strong positive transferences influenced many of us who came in contact with Jungian psychology shortly after World War II. The formation of the IAAP in 1955 established an accreditation procedure for Jungian analysts throughout the world, which has only grown since then. The influence of the IAAP and of Jungian analysts has been described in a major portion of this chapter.

Before concluding this chapter I would like to present my own assessment of "who owns Jung" at this time. As with documents pertaining to the life and work of Freud and psychoanalysis, a similar pattern is emerging with regard to accessing material about the historical Jung. Much of the material is in private hands, and where it is in the public domain, access is not always readily available. The ETH, Jung family, the Library of Congress, the Countway library, and numerous private persons have many documents relating to Jung's life and work which have not yet been published. How available these documents become to the interested scholar has become more problematic over time. Jung scholarship is seemingly getting into many of the same kind of difficulties that happened in Freud scholarship. The interested parties in Jung scholarship have different aims, and the various groups are being protective about their own sources and materials. It is unfortunate but perhaps inevitable that this should have happened. Already in his own time Jung was an extremely controversial figure because he was an outspoken critic on a number of issues relating to Christianity, Judaism, the nature of religious experience, cultural values, Eastern religions, and on the practice of psychotherapy and analysis. His views on these subjects and a number of others have had an enduring quality in our modern times. The continued interest in his life and work has provoked controversy in its own right. Who has the "correct" interpretation of Jung remains an open question. In this chapter I have attempted to describe some of the most important people and organizations that have a stake in how this question is being answered.

Notes

1 This was originally published in *Who Owns Jung?* edited by Ann Casement (published by Karnac Books in 2007), and is reprinted with the kind permission of Karnac Books.
2 This important volume edited by Sonu Shamdasani was published in 2009.

3 *The Jung-White Letters,* ed. Ann Conrad Lammers and Adrian Cunningham, was published by Routledge in 2007; and *Children's Dreams: Notes from the Seminar Given in 1936–1940,* ed. Maria Meyer-Grass and Lorenz Jung, trans. Ernst Falzeder with the collaboration of Tony Woolfson, was published by Princeton University Press in 2010.

References

Freud, S. (1914) *On the History of the Psychoanalytic Movement.* Standard Edition, vol. 14. London: Hogarth Press.

Kirsch, Thomas B. (1995) IAAP and Jungian Identity: A President's Reflections. *Journal of Analytical Psychology* 40(5) (April): 235–48.

Reid, Jane (2001) *Jung, My Mother and I.* Einsiedeln: Daimon Verlag.

Samuels, Andrew (1985) *Jung and the Post Jungians.* London: Routledge, Kegan & Paul.

Time Magazine (1958) Report on First International Congress for Analytical Psychology. Aug. 25: 35.

CHAPTER 13

JOSEPH LEWIS HENDERSON
1903–2007
A Biography

From *Jung Journal: Culture and Psyche* 2(1), 2008[1]

Joe Henderson has been called the "Dean" of American analytical psychologists and is widely known, respected, and loved in the international community of Jungians. The story of his life is closely interwoven with the history of analytical psychology in general and more specifically with its history in the United States. His life, which began in a small Nevada town and included a long stay in Europe and a great many years in San Francisco, makes for a fascinating story. It is hard to imagine a more unlikely beginning for this scholarly writer and analyst than the pioneer American home from which he came.

In order to orient the reader, this biography of the recently deceased co-founder of the C. G. Jung Institute in San Francisco and internationally acclaimed Jungian analyst is divided into seven major sections. The first section, "Origins and early years, 1903–1919," will examine Henderson's family origins and early years in Nevada. The second section, "Student Days, 1919–1928," will examine his life at Lawrenceville Preparatory School and Princeton and the time immediately after graduation from college. The third section, "Analysis and medical training, 1929–1938," will discuss Henderson's analytical experience, marriage, and medical school experience, culminating in 1938 with his graduation from medical school in London. The fourth section, "Transition from Europe to the United States, 1938–1954," will discuss his return to the United States and his beginnings as an analyst. The fifth, "Maturity, 1954–1961," will describe his years amplifying the ideas of Jung. The sixth, "Conclusion of work on initiation, 1961–1967," will describe his major writing projects on initiation. The seventh section, "Continuity, growth, and old age, 1967–2007," will describe the many different interests that occupied him during the last third of his life.

Origins and early years, 1903–1919

Joseph Lewis Henderson was born on August 31, 1903, in Elko, Nevada, a small ranching town in northeastern Nevada. He was the middle child of three children; he had a sister eight years older and a brother nine years younger. Both sides of his family possessed the pioneer spirit of the Old West. On his father's side, his great-grandfather, Lewis Rice Bradley, had left Virginia in 1845 for Missouri, finally ending up in Stockton, California. He became a prominent politician in California

Figure 13.1 Joseph L. Henderson in his San Francisco office, 1996 (photograph: Thomas B. Kirsch, by permission)

but then moved on to Elko where he founded a bank, which was then taken over by Joe's grandfather, Bradley's son-in-law, Jefferson Henderson. John Henderson, Joe's father, became president of the bank upon the death of Jefferson Henderson, and it was John's expectation that Joe would follow in his footsteps. From very early on, however, Joe felt uncomfortable with the expectation that he should go into banking. The family member for whom he was named was his uncle, Joseph Jefferson Henderson, MD, an ophthalmologist in San Francisco.

Joe's mother, Maud Henley Henderson, was born in Red Bluff, California, where her father was a mining engineer. Left an orphan at an early age, she was reared by two maiden aunts. She became a schoolteacher and had her first job in Elko. She met John Henderson and six months later they were married. She was characterized by great warmth and feeling. Like most women of the day, she devoted herself entirely to her family.

One of the most influential experiences in Joe's life happened when he was three months old. He developed an eye infection that threatened to make him totally blind. His uncle, the ophthalmologist after whom he was named, saved the sight in one eye, but the vision in the other was completely lost. As a result, Joe was left without depth perception. In a ranching community, this loss of depth perception hampered his development in normal boyhood activities. On the other hand, as C. G. Jung was later to point out to him, it enhanced his inner vision and his interest in dreams and symbols, and Joe remained closely tuned in to his inner life. Another powerful influence from his childhood was an aunt, Ethel Smith Henderson, who married Joe's uncle, Charles Henderson. She was a woman of considerable

Figure 13.2 Joseph Henderson at his 100th birthday party, 2003 (photograph: Donald Williams, by permission)

intellectual ability, and she urged Joe to go to preparatory school at Lawrenceville, New Jersey. By this time, Joe's father had realized that his son was not cut out to be a banker and released him to go back east to school. At almost the same time, Uncle Charles went to Washington when he was appointed to be the United States Senator from Nevada. The year was 1919 and Joe was now 16 years old. A whole new world was about to open to him.

Student days, 1919–1928

At Lawrenceville, Joe came under the tutelage of Thornton Wilder, a young assistant housemaster who was teaching French. Joe found him an inspired teacher at all levels of culture. He awakened in Joe an interest in literature, the arts, and psychology. Wilder had just spent a year studying in Rome and had come back full of the latest in European culture. Joe was introduced to Proust, Joyce, Freud, and even Jung at that time. However, psychology was not yet ready to emerge as Joe's central interest. Joe was greatly influenced by his reading of Henry Adams. Adams' delicate sensibility and refined taste, amply reflected in *The Education of Henry Adams,* provided a model for his development.

In those days the long trip back to the West Coast was not readily undertaken, so Joe spent his school holidays in Washington, DC, where he stayed with his aunt and uncle. This also provided Joe with a new and stimulating social life. The friendship with Wilder continued at Princeton, where Joe was an undergraduate and Wilder was getting his master's degree. Both received their degrees in French literature in 1927.

With the vague notion of becoming a writer himself, Joe returned to the West Coast after college to live with his parents, who had moved to Oakland, California. His father had suffered from paralysis of the legs, a complication of pernicious anemia, for which there was no treatment at the time. His father remained bedridden until his death in 1933.

Joe began writing book reviews and serving as a drama critic for two San Francisco journals, *The Argonaut* and *The San Franciscan*. At the same time, he became a regular participant at the Salon of Mrs. Elizabeth Ellis. She brought together professors from the English and Philosophy departments at the University of California. Here Joe was introduced to the work of Jung by Dr. Elizabeth Whitney and her husband, Dr. James Whitney. There were several others in this Salon who had been in Zurich for a period of analysis with Jung, including Andrew and Helen Gibb and Henrietta Goodrich Durham. As a young man, unsure about his future vocation, he was urged by these people to go into analysis with Dr. Elizabeth Whitney, the first analyst of any persuasion to practice in the San Francisco area. He began his analysis in the spring of 1928.

Coincidentally, or synchronistically, Dr. H. G. (Peter) Baynes and his wife Cary had come to California for the year and were dividing their time between Berkeley and Carmel, one hundred miles to the south. Dr. Baynes, a familiar name in Jungian circles, was Jung's first assistant, and Cary was an early translator of many of Jung's works into English. Peter Baynes was a warm, extraverted, and generous man who felt strongly that Joe should go to Zurich and work with Jung directly. Joe protested that he did not have the financial means to live in Zurich. He was barely supporting himself with his writing, and he did not like being financially dependent on his family. Baynes showed Joe a reproduction of Jung's painting *Mandala of a Modern Man*,[2] and he also gave him *The Seven Sermons to the Dead*[3] to read. Joe later said, "That absolutely bowled me over; I decided right then and there that, if I possibly could, I would have to go and meet the man who had written this" (Hill 1968, 15).

As fate would have it, in the fall of 1928, he was sent back to New York to review the coming drama season. On a visit to Lawrenceville, which is very close to New York, he was unexpectedly offered a job as assistant housemaster for the coming academic year. Here was the opportunity for him to save the necessary money to go to Zurich in the summer of 1929. Little did he realize then how this journey would change his life.

Analysis and medical training, 1929–1938

On his trip to Europe, he first visited Berlin, spending several weeks with a cousin and seeing firsthand the chaotic conditions in post-World War I Germany. Arriving in Zurich in the fall of 1929, just prior to the beginning of the American Depression, he installed himself in Küsnacht at the Hotel Sonne, where many of Jung's other American analysands were to stay. He began to see Jung three times a week in analysis and attended Jung's English-speaking seminar on dreams. The seminar focused on the dreams of a middle-aged businessman, and Jung divided the seminar into two groups, one doing research on the symbolism of the cross and the other on the symbolism of the crescent. Joe was in the group headed by Esther Harding, researching crescent moon symbolism. This research was the forerunner of Harding's book *Woman's Mysteries* (1971). His own dreams soon revealed a movement toward becoming an analyst himself, for which he felt he would need to become a physician or psychologist. The central theme in his work with Jung was that of initiation, a subject which was to involve him for many years to come.

In a filmed interview with this author, he talked about a particular dream he had at the time:

> I dreamt that Jung was a Protestant clergyman, standing at the pulpit giving a sermon, and we were all in the pews, and when he finished his sermon all the others got up and began to chant, "Mandala, Mandala," the way they might in Christian times have said, "Hosanna," and this represented a worshipful attitude to Jung that was laughable, as you can imagine, and so seemed to me to say, "Well, that's what you really think of this seminar of Jung – he's nothing but a – like a Protestant clergyman, and they are all just sheep following the master." So I thought, I hate to tell Jung this dream, but I did, and he said, "Well, of course you should feel that way. You should have that dream. You're a young man, only 26 or so, and most of these people are in the second half of life, and to you they must look rather ancient and as though they are in a different kind of experience from the one that you are in; and if you feel the way the dream says, you should certainly feel free not to come to the seminar or to make it anything you like." And then I realized that I was absolutely fascinated with this seminar, that it was an experience I wouldn't have missed for anything in the world. I was not at all inhibited by it. To see Jung personally in that situation was absolutely wonderful. It was like sitting at the foot of a great teacher. Something like a kind of Socratic experience and the idea that I should have a dream that he was nothing but a Protestant clergyman struck me as too funny. And then, of course, I saw that the whole thing was a projection – my projection. I was simply projecting my own Protestant background, making Jung a father figure, making the other people into a group which they were not. None of these people had any group feeling whatsoever. They all mistrusted each other. They sat in their little chairs, looking hardly from side to side, and then they immediately got up and left at the end without saying goodbye to anyone. It was a group of very isolated people. And so I saw my projection.
>
> (1977)

Joe saw himself and the others in the dream seminar in a state of transition. He would use the term *liminal* to describe this state. He also noted among those in the seminar differing attitudes toward their expectations of Jung's psychology. Later, he would differentiate these expectations into four cultural attitudes. Again, from the filmed interview, he states:

> Many of them had cultural attitudes that were very different from each other's, and they tended to project into analysis what they expected to find rather than what was actually there. What they expected to find was [*determined by*] whatever cultural patterns they favored.
>
> (1977)

So, in his first year in Zurich, Joe saw the germination of two principal subjects of his life-long research, initiation and culture.

By the summer of 1930, Joe had formulated a clear plan to go to London and study medicine. He did his premedical studies at the University of London and then entered St Bartholomew's Hospital. He liked St Bart's, particularly because it still seemed to connect the spiritual and the physical aspects of healing under the same roof. In London, he was introduced by Cary Baynes to Jo and Jane Wheelwright, as Jo also became a medical student at St Bart's – and thus began a long association that continued until the Wheelwrights retired to their ranch near Santa Barbara in 1989. More will be said about that relationship later on.

Medical school was not easy for Joe's introverted intuitive nature. He had particular problems with surgery, but he graduated in 1938. His analysis with Jung had to be intermittent because he could only get to Zurich during the semester breaks. While in London, he would see Erma Rosenbaum, a German analyst who had come to London to escape the Nazis. The last period of analysis with Jung was in 1938 following his graduation from St Bart's.

One of the main symbols that emerged during Joe's analysis was that of the American Indian. In 1931, while on holiday from his premedical studies, his "second mother," Aunt Ethel Smith Henderson, had invited him and a few others to the Southwest to witness the corn dances of the Zuni and Sia and the snake dances of the Hopis. This trip to Indian country corresponded to what was happening in his inner life. In a filmed interview, he recounts the following:

> The American Indian became a symbol for me that I was surprised to find in Zurich. I had never paid much attention to Indians in my early life. But in Zurich I had dreams of Indians, and the Indian came to symbolize to me my American identity as distinct from my European identity. Living in Europe, I was in danger of becoming too European for my own good, and the Indian kept coming into my dreams to remind me that I was American basically and that the American psyche is really different, and that difference was always carried by the Indian.
>
> (1977)

Joe comments further on his experience in Europe:

> I was so comfortable there, I could easily have stayed. I understand why people – Americans – like to live in Europe. Life in many ways is much easier, much more human, one feels much more connection somehow with one's fellow man. The longer you live in Europe, the more you feel a part of the group, of a circle to which you belong. There are still a good many wide-open spaces in America where people fail to communicate, to relate to each other. The violence in America is everywhere and is present in Europe only in certain pockets where you can avoid it. So it is a great temptation for the American to think that perhaps life would be much nicer there. But I had the feeling that I would never be a European. Whatever I said would always be divided in two by the fact that I was American. And therefore I would lose a certain identity by not coming back and living in my own country. Also perhaps the Indian would be offended.
>
> (1977)

It was during Joe's medical school years that Jung came to London in 1935 and gave his famous Tavistock Lectures to a large group of basically critical psychoanalytically oriented therapists. Joe obtained special permission so that he could attend these crowded lectures. Here, he could see Jung's discomfort in a critical setting, in contrast to the dream seminar in Zurich where everyone adored him. But his respect for Jung increased.

The other important event during his time in England was his meeting Helena Darwin Cornford, who became his wife for almost sixty years. After he had been in London for over two years, he began to feel a sense of isolation from stimulating social contact. Cary Baynes gave him a letter of introduction to the Cornfords in Cambridge. Helena's father, Francis Cornford, was a famous Cambridge philosophy

110 *Joseph Lewis Henderson 1903–2007*

professor who had made definitive translations of Plato's *Republic* and *Timaeus* and was a scholar of Greek philosophy and its origins (1912/1961). Helena's mother, Frances, was a poet of distinction. One brother, John, was a poet who died very young in the Spanish Civil War and has been memorialized in several books. Joe became very close to the whole Cornford family. Joe and Helena were married in a small local church on September 18, 1934, when Joe was 31 and Helena was 21. The Hendersons continued to live in London for the duration of Joe's medical studies. Their only daughter, Elizabeth, was born in May 1936.

The year 1938 was an important one for the Hendersons. Joe had graduated from medical school, the clouds of World War II were on the horizon, and a decision about where to live had to be made. Joe was extremely comfortable in Europe but realized that the American Indian inside was calling him back to America. So, as 1938 came to a close, the Henderson family returned to New York, where the strongest Jungian community in the United States existed. This ended nine extremely important years in Europe, which were to be a foundation for all his later work as an analyst.

Transition from Europe to the United States, 1938–1954

At the time of Joe's arrival in New York in 1938, Drs. Harding, Bertine, and Mann, along with Frances Wickes, had established a Jungian community. As in Zurich, an Analytical Psychology Club made up of analysands had recently been founded. Joe opened an office on the east side of Manhattan and began to see patients. At that time, the New York Jungian community was not connected to the larger psychotherapeutic community, and Joe had some difficulty in finding suitable patients. Jungian analysis was still not well known in those days. Freudians and Jungians hardly spoke to each other. The domination of Harding and Bertine also made it somewhat difficult for a young man trying to find his own way. In addition, Joe and Helena felt that New York was not the best place to raise a child. The atmosphere did not suit Joe's needs, but he was unable to come to a clear realization about where he should finally settle. He was afraid of going back to California because he feared the regressive pull of his family on him and his new family. His dreams were of repeated train trips back and forth across the United States, usually ending somewhere in the Midwest, such as Chicago, or in Princeton. Gradually he came to realize that the issue was not a geographical one but an inner symbolic one. He saw that Princeton meant "prince" town, and "mid-west" meant the centering place of the Self and was not to be taken literally. Gradually, he realized that he belonged in California and returned in 1941.

The time in New York had been an interesting one. Joe renewed old friendships and began his work as an analyst. He published his first paper in 1939 on "Initiation Rites." The subject of initiation was to occupy Joe for the next twenty-five years as a major area of research. He had been opened to the subject by his own experience as an analysand with Jung.

When he arrived in California, he was reunited with Elizabeth Whitney and Jo and Jane Wheelwright. Joe joined the Analytical Psychology Club in San Francisco, founded in 1940 by Elizabeth Whitney, Jo and Jane Wheelwright, and Lucile Elliot. He then joined Jo Wheelwright in downtown San Francisco at the major medical establishment for doctors. Shortly thereafter, Joe's practice was interrupted because he did not have an American medical internship. In an effort to stem the flow of refugee doctors from Europe, a law had been passed that a doctor must have worked for a year in an American hospital. As a result, in 1943, Joe spent a year at the large San Francisco General Hospital. He began as an intern, but when they discovered he was an analyst, the hospital made him the admitting officer for the acute psychiatry service. He obtained invaluable experience in general psychiatry, an area in which he had had relatively little experience previously.

As it was wartime, Joe also worked at the Veterans Rehabilitation Clinic of Mt. Zion Hospital. Psychiatric casualties from the South Pacific were sent here for evaluation. An interesting aspect of the clinic was that the staff included both Jungians and Freudians. Jo Wheelwright and Erik Erikson were also on the staff, which met together weekly. This early contact formed the basis for a mutual respect between the two groups within the San Francisco psychiatric community. This was most unusual as, in most instances, there was hostility between the Jungians and Freudians.

Another outcome of the war situation was that Joe was asked to give the psychiatric lectures at Stanford for the medical students and residents. At the time, Stanford Medical School was in San Francisco, and Joe gave a weekly seminar on dreams. This continued until 1958, at which time the Medical School moved to Palo Alto and Joe was no longer actively involved. Many future analysts first heard about Jungian analysis through those seminars at Stanford Medical School.

In 1943, a decision was reached to form a Medical Society of Analytical Psychology consisting of Henderson, Wheelwright, Whitney, Elliot, and Horace Gray. Wheelwright and Henderson took the leading roles in the formation of this group. They had first met in Zurich in 1932 and had seemed to follow each other to London and then to San Francisco. Two more opposite types of people could not be imagined. Wheelwright was the lone extravert in Jungian circles for so many years, and Joe Henderson was the more typically Jungian introverted intuitive. Despite their vast differences, they maintained a friendship for over fifty-five years. Their differences also allowed both the introverted and extraverted attitudes to live side by side in the San Francisco professional society, and it has helped so far to keep potential splits contained. Both Wheelwright and Henderson held teaching positions at the major psychiatric teaching hospitals in San Francisco, and both had a commitment to being an active part of the larger psychotherapeutic community. Thus, the beginning of the San Francisco Jungian group had a markedly different origin than most other Jungian groups in the world. In 1950, the medical part united with its counterpart group for doctoral psychologists to become the Society of Jungian Analysts of Northern California.

After World War II, Joe Henderson took an office in Wheelwright's building at 2206 Steiner Street in San Francisco, where both were to have their analytic practices for the next thirty years and in which were held the first training seminars of the Society, beginning in 1946.

Contact with Jung had been sparse because of the war, and it was not until 1948 that Joe could see Jung again. By this time, Jung was no longer seeing patients because of his heart attack in 1944, so the relationship was now more social in nature. At the time, Joe did a bit of analytical work with Toni Wolff for the first time. On a subsequent vacation in 1952, both Joe and Helena had another two-week period of seeing Toni Wolff every day in Devon. Miss Wolff had gone to Devon for treatment of her arthritis, and the Hendersons stayed at the same hotel and saw her every morning.

Joe has described the period between 1938 and 1954 as one of transition. There were the geographical moves from England to New York and from New York to San Francisco. There were the various moves within San Francisco. There were the transitions in his career from student to doctor to analyst. By 1954, he had become secure in his identity as an analyst, and within his family, he had made the transition from son to mature adult.

Joseph Lewis Henderson 1903–2007

Maturity, 1954–1961

The year 1954 was pivotal in his life. Medard Boss of the Existential School of Analysis had asked Joe to present a major paper on transference at an International Conference on Psychotherapy in Zurich. This paper, "Resolution of the Transference in the Light of C. G. Jung's Psychology," was the first major statement by a Jungian other than Jung on the nature of transference. In the filmed interview with this author, Henderson describes it in the following manner:

> That Congress was the first time that any of us had talked publicly about Jung's use of the word "Transference." Up to that time, transference had been understood purely in the Freudian sense, the old psychoanalytical sense. A transference is something to live through and break, get rid of, move off of, get back to life again without it. Having done its work it is like a shell that should be cast aside as though it had no further meaning. It seemed to me and to others at that time that Jung's psychology had a rather different viewpoint, and Jung himself acknowledged that the transference in itself has a certain archetypal content that you cannot merely dismiss and feel should be discarded once the initial projections are withdrawn. However, he did consider that it should be ultimately resolved so that it is no longer fixed upon the person of the therapist but it should move on, and it was his understanding that it was the archetypal content of the transference that made this possible. That gives rise to two rather different ideas about the transference. One is that you just live with it, that you don't resolve it, that it just goes on and on and some people believe that that's what a Jungian transference really is. The thing that I did say was that the transference is resolved by the establishment of what I call a symbolic friendship, meaning that when the transference is resolved there is a feeling of friendship rather than a mutual projection, between the therapist and his analysand or patient. But it is not the same as an ordinary friendship. And it can never be the same, quite, as an ordinary friendship, because it started in the analytical situation which was artificial. So it always has something of that quality of its origin but that gives it its symbolic meaning. I felt that the best way to describe that was to say that it feels as if in that personal transference there was something symbolic that carries through, and it makes that relationship especially meaningful and somewhat different from others.
>
> (1977)

During the 1950s, the Hendersons went to Europe every two years. On these trips, Joe would have a formal appointment with Jung, and then afterward they would have a meal together. These meetings were usually dominated by whatever subject Jung was interested in. It was during these visits that Jung encouraged Henderson to continue his own research on initiation and the archetype of culture. In 1960, Jung invited Joe to contribute a paper to *Man and his Symbols,* and Joe recalled that this invitation stimulated his own writing, beyond the miscellaneous papers he had published in the 1940s and 1950s. He wrote a long paper, "Ancient Myths and Modern Man" (1961), where he described the dreams of modern clients and amplified the dreams with anthropological and mythological examples of initiation. In the work, he illustrated his theoretical description with clinical vignettes. He described two basic patterns of initiation. One was the pattern of descent into the earth as exemplified by the myth of Inanna. The second pattern was the magic light upward as demonstrated in shamanism. As Joe was the only

Figure 13.3 Joseph Henderson in Carmel California at the annual meeting of the San Francisco and Los Angeles analysts, 1960s

American and the only non-Swiss author in the book, he received many requests for various Jungian-oriented endeavors based upon his being an author in this book.

Joe traveled to Zurich in 1960 for a planning session for *Man and his Symbols*, but Jung was too weak to attend. When Jung died in 1961, this brought an end to a phase in Joe's life. No longer was the master alive, and now Joe was more on his own as a creative thinker and analyst.

Conclusion of work on initiation, 1961–1967

The next period was a relatively short one. It was a time in which Henderson finished his book on initiation, which had been germinating for thirty years. It also was a time when new directions in his work began to emerge. His first task was an invitation by Alan Watts to write a book with Maud Oakes called *The Wisdom of the Serpent* (1963). The book was to be the first of a series on mythology, which, unfortunately, was never completed. In this volume, Henderson described the serpent as a symbol of the archetype of death and rebirth. For her part, Maud Oakes detailed many myths of the serpent taken from around the world. The book was dedicated to the memory of Jung.

In 1962, Henderson was elected vice-president of the International Association for Analytical Psychology (IAAP), the newly formed professional organization of Jungian analysts. He held that post until 1965, when he was proposed as nominee for the presidency. He gave the matter serious thought but then realized that it would take him too far afield from his research and writing. In the end, he declined the nomination.

In the same year, he gave his first paper on another important area of his research, culture. It was presented at the Second International Congress for Analytical

Psychology and was titled "The Archetype of Culture" (1964). The paper was considered extremely controversial because it outlined a cultural unconscious layer between the personal and collective unconscious. As this area of research was to continue for many years, I shall describe the development of Henderson's ideas in the next phase.

Also in 1962, Joe edited the four-hour film in which Professor Richard Evans had interviewed Jung. This interview had been done in 1957, but Jung was a bit disappointed with the results. The film interview covers a wide range of topics, and in it Jung is extremely engaging.

It was in 1967 that *Thresholds of Initiation* was published and his work on the subject was completed. In this book, Henderson demonstrated the validity of the archetype of initiation. In the foreword, he followed Jung's development of archetypal theory. Henderson emphasized that archetypes are both a primordial image as well as a pattern of behavior. The theory of archetypes became a working hypothesis, and the archetype of initiation needed to be seen in that light. With this background, Henderson described various modal points when initiatory symbolism emerges from the patient's unconscious. In the analysis of these situations, Henderson brought in a range of scholarship to amplify his hypothesis. Dozens of clinical examples from thirty years of practice were used to demonstrate initiation at various times in an individual's life.

Behind the case examples, there was an underlying developmental theory as well as a Jungian model of neurosis. Henderson described those cut off from psychological development as "pre-uninitiated," and he developed his idea of the archetypal basis for the fixation in terms of the *puer aeternus* and *puella aeterna*. Those identifications with the Self presumed that eternal wholeness had already been attained in youth, and that further step-wise growth into maturity was unnecessary. This inflation was a normal pattern in adolescence, helpful in giving a young person a sense of the possibilities of existence and of self-worth, but when the individual had a fear of taking the next step into genuine actualization of the sensed potential, there might be an unhealthy tendency to cling to what was only the archetypal possibility of wholeness and live in fantasy. The *puer-* and *puella-*identified individuals resisted the enormous effort that, in reality, was required to rescue the capacity to be oneself from the barriers set up by the positive or negative expectations from mother, father, peers, and one's own innate inertia. This resistance expressed itself as a false, law-unto-itself individuality that did not represent a real working through of the problem of negotiating with society and instinct to establish a path of one's own into life. If this behavior became fixed into a pattern that more or less dominated the personality, then Henderson saw serious arrested development, sometimes with strong antisocial trends, sometimes with schizoid characteristics.

The irresponsible, power-driven, pleasure-loving attitude toward life that can move into antisocial behavior was described by Henderson in terms of the trickster archetype, a sort of shadow archetype to the *puer aeternus*. For the individual to be released from the grip of the trickster archetype, the archetype of initiation is needed. Henderson postulated that this archetype acted to convert the trickster cycle into a hero cycle. He further postulated that the trickster cycle was under the aegis of the mother archetype and that the hero archetype would be under the influence of the father. Thus, the early developmental step, in both sexes, was from mother to father, with initiation as the means of passing from one stage to another.

Both trickster and hero cycles were, in turn, superseded by the appearance of the stage of the true initiate, which put an end to the self-perpetuating tendency of the first two cycles. The initiate was the one who had submitted fully to the initiation archetype with its rites of vision, trials of strength, and ordeals, and was willing to be remade into an adult man or woman who could take a responsible place in society in an ecological way, as part of a wider whole that she or he did not need to try to avoid or dominate.

According to Henderson, it was through initiation symbolism and experience – which he postulated as a true archetype of initiation – that the life of the individual was transformed into a psychosocial modality. Acceptance of initiation was the beginning of real individuation and the end of false individuality; it meant the search for individual identity within the context of a respectful attitude toward both the collective unconscious and the consciousness of one's social group. Yet he also explored failures of initiation that might stem from limitations in the culture itself.

Many striking clinical examples were used to demonstrate the effectiveness of this theory in elucidating common neurotic problems and the dream material that an analyst would see every day in a clinical practice. Neurosis in young people became failed or blocked initiation that the unconscious, through dreams and symptoms, was urgently seeking to remedy.

This book seemed as if it were the culmination of a life's work, but also, it was a symbolic threshold to the next phase in Joe's life.

Continuity, growth, and old age, 1967–2007

Joe's energy seemed to increase as he entered old age. Beginning in 1966, he began to see patients only three weeks out of each month, and this left him with more time to pursue his research and writing interests. One of the major projects of the past forty years was his continued study of the role of culture in Jung's theories and practice. This culminated in the publication of the book *Cultural Attitudes in Psychological Perspective* (1984). In the filmed interview with this author (1977), Henderson states:

Well, I became less interested in initiation and more interested in problems of general culture, so in recent years all my work has been to try to define what we mean by culture and to try to clear the way for us to understand psychologically how culture arises and what it means and what forms it takes so as not to confuse it with individual psychology, and there's a tendency among Jungians as well as other psychologists to confuse culture patterns with psychological patterns. Psychological patterns are not the same as cultural patterns. [In Zurich] among these people who were there for analysis, many of them had cultural alignments that were very different from each other, and they tended to project into analysis what they expected to find rather than what was actually there, and what they expected to find was whatever cultural pattern they favored. In other words, if they were favoring a religious attitude, they tended to find religion in it, if they favored social betterment or political attitudes, they hoped to find that. If it was aesthetic, they expected to find it as if it were like works of art. If they were philosophical, they tried to make psychology into a philosophy. They are still doing that, by the way. Quite a number of very intelligent and interested students of philosophy are intrigued by psychology and feel that it should be given a place in the philosophical scheme of things. And this is valuable up to a point, but it can also falsify something of the psychology that Jung created.

116 *Joseph Lewis Henderson 1903–2007*

In *Cultural Attitudes in Psychological Perspective,* Henderson developed his ideas further about the four cultural attitudes – religious, social, aesthetic, and philosophic – with the contemporary emergence of a fifth cultural attitude, the psychological attitude. He also discussed culture patterns in relation to archetypes, carefully distinguishing the two. Again, from the film interview:

> Yes, they tend to confuse the term archetype with culture pattern so there's another area in which I try to distinguish between. We simply don't know what an archetype looks like as such. We only know how it looks when it gets into some cultural form, but we move these cultural forms around and talk about them as if they were archetypes. And this is somewhat confusing unless we clearly differentiate between the cultural forms that have real archetypal content and those that are merely stereotypes.
>
> (1977)

When asked to differentiate between stereotype and archetype, Henderson gave the following response:

> If you look through Blake's paintings, you find that some of them give you the impression of the kind of art that we find our patients doing. We speak of them as unconscious drawings. That is, they seem to be so spontaneous that they don't look like anything that we've ever seen before. They are even not too well drawn in some cases. They are rather unstructured in a way. Yet there are others that are very well structured and seem to convey the picture of something that we already know about. The former is archetypal and the latter is stereotypical.
>
> (1977)

A second major project had been Henderson's long-standing interest in art. Through the years, he had written many papers on art and its relationship to the unconscious. He continued to support the Archive for Research in Archetypal Symbolism (ARAS). This project, initially begun by Jung at Eranos, was then taken over by the Jung Foundation in New York. The project entailed the cataloguing and organizing of thousands of pictures of various symbols from all over the world. The New York Foundation expanded the collection, but in 1967, it decided that the costs were too great, and it was about to end the program. Henderson realized that this archive was a unique treasure and volunteered his time and effort to continue it in San Francisco. Eventually, a joint effort between San Francisco and New York made it possible for the archive to expand and have the whole collection copied. A grant was given to ARAS to make it a national archive, which then included Los Angeles as well. The ups and downs of its history are less important to us at this moment than to say that Henderson indirectly helped to guide it to its present existence and growth. It is the *only* place where one can look up a particular symbol and find a psychological amplification that corresponds to the image. Three books on archetypal symbolism have been published using the images of the ARAS collection. For the past ten years, national ARAS has been working on publishing a dictionary of symbols. In addition, the ARAS collection has been completely digitized and so can be accessed anywhere in the world with a paid subscription.

Another area of interest to Henderson had been the area of popular culture. Perhaps this was a continuation of his interest in drama, which was first expressed when he was a drama critic for two San Francisco magazines after college. For over twenty years, he contributed a number of reviews on movies to *Psychological Perspectives.* I think that this was his way of keeping in touch with modern popular culture. His movie reviews included Bergman's *Cries and Whispers, The Magic Flute, Easy Rider, Butch Cassidy and the Sundance Kid, Chariots of Fire,* as well as many others. He also wrote an article on "Psychology and the Roots of Design" about the landscape architect Lawrence Halprin, and a survey of the career of West Coast American visionary artist Morris Graves. Many of these shorter reviews and other papers, along with a seminar on "Shadow and Self," were published as a book titled *Shadow and Self,* published by Chiron in 1990.

Along with his broad intellectual and cultural interests, Henderson found the time to be quite active in the Society of Jungian Analysts of Northern California and the C. G. Jung Institute of San Francisco. He was a founding member of the Society when it was formed. As the Society grew, his participation paralleled its growth. He was President of the Society and Institute in 1967–8 and again in 1972–3. He was the librarian for many years before it became a committee. He was on the Certifying Board from 1967 to 1971. He served gladly on many other committees, too numerous to mention. He attended quarterly Board of Governors meetings until well past age 100. What was so remarkable about him was that he did not seem to be at all power driven. In meetings, he presented his ideas and opinions in a quiet, thoughtful way, but he did not force his point of view on the rest of the group. The younger members were free to find their own way in the Institute without feeling that the "wise old man" was going to tell them what to do. This has been a significant factor in why the San Francisco group functions as well as it does. How this will evolve in the future, only time will tell.

Henderson continued to practice analysis, supervise, and write papers on various subjects related to analytical psychology until he was 102 years old. He gave the first invited lecture of the four United Kingdom groups in 1991, followed the next day by a workshop that was later published in the *Journal of Analytical Psychology* as "C. G. Jung's Psychology: Additions and Extensions" (1991, 429–42). He continued to work on alchemical topics, specifically the *Splendor Solis,* a manuscript that he had first come upon in 1938 in London while studying for his final medical exam. He was specifically interested in how the images of the *Splendor Solis* reflected the analytic process. His seminars on the topic stimulated the interest of Dyane Sherwood. At the time of Henderson's 100th birthday, the two of them published a book that amplified the images, *Transformation of the Psyche: The Symbolic Alchemy of the Splendor Solis* (2003).

Joe continued his involvement as a board member of national ARAS and wrote a history of how the ARAS collection had evolved in the United States over forty years. In his later years, he was not able to attend the meetings, but national ARAS made him an honorary member for life. In connection with the national ARAS, he made a series of interviews for McKenzie Oaks Films in Eugene, Oregon (1997), where he discussed the amplification of imagery, initiation rites, and his own personal history in relationship to Jung and analytical psychology.

Henderson continued to drive and to see patients in his second-floor office in San Francisco until aged 98. Difficulty in walking and problems with balance required him to close the San Francisco office, but he saw people in his home office until his retirement.

A large birthday celebration was held to celebrate his 100th birthday in September 2003. An outpouring of people from all over the country came to honor him on that day. The next year a conference on initiation was held in San Francisco, where analysts influenced by Henderson presented their own research on the archetype of initiation. These presentations were published in 2007 as *Initiation: The Reality of an Archetype,* edited by Tom Kirsch, Virginia Beane Rutter, and Tom Singer.

Figure 13.4 Joseph Henderson with his granddaughter, Julia Eisenman, at his 100th birthday, 2003 (photograph: Donald Williams, by permission)

Figure 13.5 Joe and Helena Henderson, London

As part of the 100th birthday celebration, funds were raised to reprint his classic book on initiation, long out of print, *Thresholds of Initiation*. The new edition with some minor editorial changes was published in 2005 by Chiron. After his 100th birthday celebration, a follow-up interview to the one made for *Matter of Heart* in 1977 was done by this author and Suzanne Wagner. Over three hours of interviews on two separate occasions were made.

On a personal level, Joe's wife of sixty years, Helena, died in 1994 from complications of diabetes, and Elizabeth, their daughter, died in 2001. Dr. Henderson's own health gradually deteriorated over the years. He had greater difficulty in walking and moving around, and for the last three years he was confined to a wheelchair with occasional assisted walking. His memory, which for the first 100 years had been remarkable in its accuracy, began to fade, and his psyche moved between the unconscious and conscious in daily life. This shift in his psyche required that he retire from practice. He continued to see old patients, friends, and family, as these physical and psychological changes gradually took their toll. He had full-time help so that he could continue to stay in his home, which he and Helena had built in 1954, until the very end. The quality of his life continued to lessen, but even three weeks before his death, he went to the 200th anniversary celebration of the founding of his preparatory school, Lawrenceville, in San Francisco, where he received a standing ovation and was taken home by limousine. He died on November 17, 2007, after a brief bout of pneumonia.

It is difficult to sum up the long, complicated, and full life of Joseph Lewis Henderson. He lived through the turmoil of the twentieth century, remembering

Figure 13.6 Joseph Henderson at his 100th birthday party, 2003 (photograph: Donald Williams, by permission)

120 *Joseph Lewis Henderson 1903–2007*

where he was at the time of the sinking of the *Titanic* all the way to the present war in Iraq, which initially he followed closely. He was the singularly most contained and centered individual whom I have ever met in my life. His centeredness had a healing effect on a great number of individuals, and his equanimity and psychological-mindedness influenced many generations of Jungian analysts in San Francisco and beyond. People came to see him from all over. For the past several years, he had been the only person of those who had analysis with Jung during his most active analytical time (1919 to 1939) who was still alive and could talk about it in a clear and objective manner. Besides his enormous professional accomplishments and the wealth and breadth of his experience, he was a wonderful *raconteur,* absolutely charming in a social situation, with a good sense of humor, and he loved to laugh and enjoyed social interactions, especially as he aged. He was a truly unique individual who was a living example of what Jung meant by individuation, and I do not believe that we will see the likes of him again. As one colleague put it, "It's truly the end of an era and it was a great era."

Notes

1 "Joseph Lewis Henderson: A Biography," *Jung Journal: Culture and Psyche* 2(1): 78–97. © 2008 by the Virginia Allan Detloff Library, C. G. Jung Institute of San Francisco. All rights reserved. Reprinted by permission of the C. G. Jung Institute of San Francisco (http://www.sfjung.org).
2 Frontispiece of C. G. Jung, *The Archetypes and the Collective Unconscious.* Collected Works, vol. 9/1. New York: Pantheon Books, 1959.
3 This was not published until appendix 5 as part of *Memories, Dreams, Reflections.* Recorded and edited by Aniela Jaffe. New York: Pantheon Books, 1961, 1962, 1963.

References

Cornford, F. (1912/1961) *From Religion to Philosophy.* Princeton, NJ: Princeton University Press.

Harding, M. E. (1971/2001) *Women's Mysteries: Ancient and Modern.* Boston, MA: Shambhala.

Henderson, J. L. (1939) Initiation Rites. *Bulletin of the Analytical Psychology Club.* New York, 3.

Henderson, J. L. (1954) Resolution of the Transference in the Light of C. G. Jung's Psychology. *Acta Psychotherapeutica* 2(3–4): 267–83.

Henderson, J. L. (1961/1964) "Ancient Myths and Modern Man." In C. G. Jung (ed.), *Man and his Symbols.* Garden City, NY: Doubleday & Co., pp. 104–57

Henderson, J. L. (1964) "The Archetype of Culture." In A. Guggenbuhl-Craig (ed.), *Proceedings of the Second International Congress for Analytical Psychology.* Basel/New York: S Karger, pp. 3–14.

Henderson, J. L. (1977) Interview of Joseph L. Henderson by Thomas Kirsch. Executive Producer, Suzanne Wagner. Los Angeles, CA: C. G. Jung Institute of Los Angeles.

Henderson, J. L. (1984) *Cultural Attitudes in Psychological Perspective.* Toronto: Inner City Books.

Henderson, J. L. (1990) *Shadow and Self: Selected Papers in Analytical Psychology.* Wilmette, IL: Chiron Publications.

Henderson, J. L. (1991) C. G. Jung's Psychology: Additions and Extensions. *Journal of Analytical Psychology* 36(4): 429–42.

Henderson, J. L. (1997) Filmed interviews sponsored by ARAS. Eugene, OR: Mckenzie Oaks Films. Available online at: www.mckenzieoaks.com.

Henderson, J. L. (1967/2005) *Thresholds of Initiation.* Wilmette, IL: Chiron. (Originally published Middletown, CT: Wesleyan University Press, 1967.)

Henderson, J. L., and Oakes, M. (1963) *The Wisdom of the Serpent: The Myths of Death, Rebirth, and Resurrection.* Princeton, NJ: Princeton University Press.

Henderson, J. L., and Sherwood, D. N. (2003) *Transformation of the Psyche: The Symbolic Alchemy of the Splendor Solis.* Hove and New York: Brunner-Routledge.

Hill, G. (1968) "J. L. H.: His Life and Work." In *The Shaman from Elko.* San Francisco, CA: C. G. Jung Institute of San Francisco.

Kirsch, T. B., Rutter, V. B., and Singer, T. (eds) (2007) *Initiation: The Living Reality of an Archetype.* Hove and New York: Routledge.

CHAPTER 14

A VISIT TO HILDEMARIE STREICH

From *Jung Journal: Culture and Psyche* 3(2), 2009, coauthored with Jean Kirsch[1]

Our visit to Hildemarie Streich on July 9, 2008, in Berlin, was arranged by Jörg Rasche, who has studied with Ms. Streich for many years; he considers her a close friend and a respected colleague. The visit was the highlight of the general tour he gave us of sites of historical and personal interest in Berlin. Jörg drove us to her apartment, which lies in a nondescript, modern neighborhood of small, gray concrete buildings, and joined us for our interview. She greeted us at the door wearing a long housecoat of pale blue print, buttoned to the neck over a bright blue silk scarf, loosely tied and pouffed above the collar. Hildemarie[2] is a tiny, frail, and upright woman. She wore her gray hair pulled back to the nape of her neck. A marked strabismus of her right eye made her instantly trustworthy and familiar because the right eye of the late Joseph Henderson, our beloved analyst, teacher, and friend, was also inactive as a result of a childhood illness.

Although the building and neighborhood in which she lived were of that universal, post-war modernist style typical of any nation, within, her home was quintessentially European. Clearly, this was the home of a musician and scholar, crowded with books and musical instruments and mementos of the past. As we entered the main room, the first thing we saw was a circle of four chairs and a miniature harpsichord clustered around four tightly wedged music stands. Many wooden wind instruments stood close to the chairs, one of them a majestic instrument of deeply burnished red lacquer standing almost six feet tall, which may have been a bass or subbass recorder. A small organ filled the back wall of the main room and a concert-sized harpsichord dominated the central space. Along a side wall several dozen recorders of varying sizes were neatly mounted. The room seemed to be holding itself in dusty readiness for the return of musicians long gone, as though their spirits hovered lovingly in the gloomy air. Hildemarie gave us a few moments to absorb the room's ambience and then led us into her consulting room, where she showed the three of us to a sofa and seated herself at her desk, facing us. She spoke softly and breathily, but very distinctly, in English and chose her words carefully.

Tom had known of Hildemarie Streich because his parents mentioned her frequently. She had met James and Hilde Kirsch in 1975 in Ascona, Switzerland, at an Eranos conference. The threesome became fast friends. The Kirsches subsequently visited her in Berlin, and in 1978, they invited her to Los Angeles to a Panarion conference, an annual Jungian conference held just months before Hilde Kirsch's death in December 1978. "Hilde Kirsch was like a sister; her heart was very German and Jewish. She was always filled with grief for the events of Nazi

Figure 14.1 Thomas Kirsch, Hildemarie Streich, and Jörg Rasche (left to right). Berlin, July 9, 2008 (photograph: Jean Kirsch)

Germany." "James always wanted to know what was going on in Berlin. He came to visit me after Hilde's death with his third wife, Sandra." Hildemarie showed us pictures of herself with her husband and James. She told us that she had heard of a saying in the 1920s: "If you have problems with your eyes, go to R [She gave the name of a respected German ophthalmologist]; if you have problems with your head, go to Kirsch."

Unfortunately, Hildemarie is not a widely known analyst, for she is not a member of the dominant Berlin Jungian group. She told us that this circumstance arose because of a conflict between her first Jungian analyst Kaethe Bügler and Hans Dieckmann, who was the leader of the fledgling institute that combined with Freudian psychoanalysts early in the 1950s. He gained Jung's support and the society became known as the C. G. Jung Institut Berlin (now part of the German national group, Deutsche Gesellschaft für Analytische Psychologie). Kaethe Bügler, on the other hand, wanted a Jungian-only training society and when she applied to her former analyst, Jung, for support, he withheld it, advising her to join the group that was already in existence. Thus, Hildemarie Streich, a loyal analysand, was never accepted into the combined Jungian training group. "Kaethe Bügler did not agree with the mixed institute of Dieckmann, which had Jung's blessing; she tried to start another only Jungian group, but Jung did not support her."

Hildemarie did not begin as a Jungian. She had been educated in Heidelberg as a psycho-diagnostician and music therapist. She was an educated musician who primarily played the recorder. Early on, she decided to become a psychoanalyst, so she began a training analysis with a female Freudian analyst. She told us this female analyst had many psychological problems and turned to her young analysand for help. Finding that she was not getting the analysis she desired, Hildemarie terminated the treatment but did not abandon her desire to become an analyst. In the 1950s, after she had married her musician/scholar husband and moved to Berlin

124 *A visit to Hildemarie Streich*

from Heidelberg, she sought out a Jungian: "I had heard of Jung as a schoolgirl from a friend of my parents and decided to go that direction. I did not want another analyst who would become my patient!" She was recommended to Kaethe Bügler, "the only analyst of high esteem." Hildemarie said that the year was 1963 and she was 42 years old. For her second analysis, she told us that she saw Gustav Heyer, although she said that she was warned by dreams, one in which she saw a swastika and another that warned her not to mix him up with her father. "I got a lot from him, but there was no father transference."[3]

She then told us about her father, "A great scholar!" who had studied and meditated upon the *Zohar* throughout World War II, although he was not Jewish. His interest was unusual and in direct violation of Nazi policy, an action that might have generated a visit by the SS if widely known. "When I met Gershon Scholem[4] and heard him speak about the *Zohar,* I was very disappointed because he was not meditative like my father."

Our visit was reminiscent of many we have made over the years, generated by Tom's wish to call upon any elderly European Jungian who is familiar with Jung, his parents, and/or the history that has become the subject of his Jungian studies. Inevitably, the interviews are full of gossip and recollections of the many friendships and rivalries among Jung's wide circle of analysands, students, and followers. Hildemarie had prepared for our visit, spreading out several articles and photos on the desk before her. One of them is the article "Music in Dreams," which she told us she had delivered at the 2nd World Congress for Psychotherapy, on July 5, 1999, in Vienna, Austria. The paper interested us, and we thought it might also be of interest to others. When we asked if we might give it to the editor of *Jung Journal* to consider for republication, she assented.[5]

Notes

1 "A Visit to Hildemarie Streich," *Jung Journal: Culture & Psyche,* Volume 3, Number 2, pp. 59–62. © 2009 Virginia Allan Detloff Library, C.G. Jung Institute of San Francisco. All rights reserved. Reprinted by permission of the C. G. Jung Institute of San Francisco (http://www.sfjung.org).

2 A comment on the use of first names: I was introduced to the Jungian tradition of using first names by my mother-in-law when I hesitated, at our first meeting, at the point of needing to address her by a name. "I am Hilde and that is what you should call me; you should call him [pointing to Tom's father] James!" Instant clarification! This was my introduction to what I believe is a widespread Jungian practice.

3 We do not know why she terminated her analysis with Kaethe Bügler and transferred to Richard Gustav Heyer. Dr. Heyer had been a close associate of Jung before World War II, writing two Jungian books and acting as Jung's honorary secretary for the first year of Jung's presidency of the International Association for Medical Psychotherapy. Later Heyer joined the Nazi Party and became a leading member of the Göring Institute, the main training institute for the Nazis. He had a close relationship to Kaethe Bügler and managed to protect her during the war. After the war, Jung would no longer have any contact with Heyer, although some Jungians continued to see him in analysis. He retired to the forest outside of Munich where he continued to practice. His former wife, Lucy Heyer, was an early exponent of body movement and therapy and taught many famous body therapists; we know of two who practiced in the Bay Area, Hildegard Elsberg and Marion Rosen. She was also asked to write the first biography on Jung, but her attempt was unsuccessful.

4 Gershom Scholem (December 5, 1897 to February 21, 1982) was a Jewish philosopher and historian raised in Germany. He is widely regarded as the founder of the modern academic study of Kabbalah, becoming the first Professor of Jewish Mysticism at the

Hebrew University of Jerusalem. Scholem is best known for his collection of lectures *Major Trends in Jewish Mysticism* (1941) and for his biography *Sabbatai Zevi, the Mystical Messiah* (1973).

5 "Music in Dreams" by Dr. Hildemarie Streich was published in *Jung Journal* 3(2) (2009): 63–73. DOI: 10.1525/jung.2009.3.2.63.

CHAPTER 15

REFLECTIONS ON THE WORD "JUNGIAN"

From *Cultures and Identities in Transition: Jungian Perspectives*, edited by
Murray Stein and Raya A. Jones, Routledge 2010[1]

The word "Jungian" is bandied about freely, as if it communicates something
that as Jungians we immediately understand. For instance, we might say that a
particular movie or book is Jungian. I was told some time ago, for example, that
Saul Bellow's (1998) novel, *The Dean's December*, had an alchemical subtext and
therefore would be of interest to me as a Jungian. I read this novel about a Chicago
college dean who was critical of Chicago politics and who at the time was visiting
his dying mother-in-law in Bucharest. It was a wonderful story with remarkable
parallels between the corruption in Chicago and communist Bucharest. However,
it was, for me, a real stretch to say that this novel was either alchemical or Jungian.
So what do we mean when we use the term "Jungian"? This has been a life-long
question for me, and it features in the title of my book, *The Jungians* (2000).

Jungian communities

The meanings of the word "Jungian" have expanded as Jung was read by a
wider, rather than purely clinical and insider, audience. Jung had many facets
to his nature, which has made it extremely difficult to pinpoint what is meant
when one says the word "Jungian". Let me briefly outline several of them. As a
student at the University of Basel, his interest in philosophy and religion was quite
evident although he was enrolled in the medical faculty. He then moved away
from these fields and into natural science and eventually became a psychiatrist
and a psychoanalyst. As a psychiatrist, however, he could maintain his interest
in many other fields such as archaeology, anthropology, philosophy, and religion.
After almost a decade of clinical practice at the Burghölzli Psychiatric Hospital
in Zurich, he gravitated towards the fields of mythology, anthropology, and
comparative religion to help him understand the imagery of dreams and psychosis.
After the break with Freud in 1914 and his "confrontation with the unconscious",
his interests moved towards Eastern religions, early Christianity, Gnosticism, and
philosophy, which eventually led also to alchemy. As he grew older, his interests
shifted away from clinical matters toward medieval alchemy and related fields. All
his major works in the last two decades of his life were based on medieval alchemy.
He thought that no single individual would be able to write a biography of him,
because no biographer would have sufficient knowledge; and, indeed, there are
now close to forty biographical studies on different aspects of Jung's life.

I present this brief biographical sketch to show how difficult it is to say what it
means to be Jungian based purely on the biography and published writings of Jung

himself. Are we Jungian if we use Jungian methods in the consulting room, or are we Jungian if we use Jung's theories of the collective unconscious, archetypes, and synchronicity to analyze a piece of literature, art, music, or some aspect of modern society? Are we Jungian if we simply find his ideas compatible with our own ideas about ourselves, culture, and society?

Jung was not interested in formally organizing and training the analysts who used his methods to treat patients. His foray into organizations did not go well. His experiences with the two most significant organizations that he had been president of – the International Psychoanalytic Association and the International Medical Association for Psychotherapy – had been disastrous for him personally. From the former he became ostracized permanently as a psychoanalyst and from the latter he gained the reputation of being a Nazi. Beyond those particulars, moreover, Jung felt that organizations generally tended to limit individuality and to promote a collectivity that deadened the spirit. However, a professional analytical psychology organization was formed in 1955 by some of Jung's closest followers – the International Association for Analytical Psychology – and this did gratify him. He attended parts of the first IAAP Congress in 1958 in Zurich. From an initial membership of a little over 100 analysts, it has grown to its present size of close to 3,000. Part of its history will be described later in this chapter.

On the other hand, there have always been individuals who have used Jung's theories in academia, in business, and in other domains. However, it has been extremely difficult to teach Jung and Jungian ideas in academic circles. For most of the twentieth century, to espouse Jung meant that one would not advance professionally. A "Jungian" of any ilk was relegated to the periphery, if not the outback, of any mainline professional group. One was thought to be "woolly" or a "mystic." Many well-known individuals in the arts and culture, however, were deeply attracted to Jung's ideas and to his views of the unconscious, so that his popularity derived from non-academic sources. But in the academic world, any interest in Jung had to be kept private or it would negatively influence the progress of one's career. There was the occasional course on Jung, but rarely was this encouraged in most academic settings. This has slowly changed as societies worldwide have become more open to the non-rational aspects of the psyche. Jung's works have become ever more popular since the 1960s and 1970s, and this shift has allowed some individuals interested in analytical psychology to obtain teaching positions. They no longer have to hide their interest in Jung. We now see a professorship in analytical psychology at the Centre for Psychoanalytic Studies at the University of Essex in England, a professorship in analytical psychology at Texas A&M University, and other professorships becoming available to Jungian-oriented academics. The fact that there are too many people to single out in this regard nowadays demonstrates just how much the situation has changed in academia. These individuals are generally known as "Jungians", and they accept this designation readily. This does not mean that they teach or write about Jung uncritically. As academics, they are, in fact, likely to read Jung critically and to question the relevance of his ideas in present-day society. These academics are unlike Jungian analysts in that there is no requirement for them to have undergone a personal analysis, although many have done so. Furthermore, there is quite often the expectation that they will not conduct a clinical practice, although teaching Jungian subjects often raises personal issues for students, which they bring to the professor.

In recent years, a separate Jungian organization called the International Association for Jungian Studies (IAJS), supported by IAAP analysts, has formed around those in academia who teach Jung in their various disciplines. IAJS includes members from all over the world and now holds regular congresses paralleling the IAAP congresses. Most members of this organization would also call themselves Jungian. Here we find people from many different academic fields using Jung's work to interpret culture, film, literature, art, theatre, history, religious studies, etc. and they refer to themselves as Jungian or Jungian-oriented. They form a group that is quite distinct from the clinical field. Their email discussion list is extremely active, and many intellectual subjects related to Jung's psychology are discussed there. Anyone can join the organization, so the level of discussion varies.

Then there are the people who have taken their inspiration from Jung's important book *Psychological Types*, published in 1921. The psychologists Myers and Briggs developed a psychological test based on Jung's type theory. While several other similar psychological tests have also been developed over time, the Myers-Briggs Type Inventory (MBTI) has been the most successful by far and is widely used in business and academia. For the most part, this community of practitioners has lost its connection to Jung except for a few Jungians such as the Wheelwrights, John Beebe, and John Giannini, who have strongly maintained an affiliation. The MBTI organization has only the slimmest thread of connection to Jung, and most of its members would not consider themselves Jungian even though, in a sense, they are.

Personal experiences

I would like to speak a bit about my own experience growing up in a household where both my parents were well-known Jungians. They each had their primary analysis with Jung himself. In our household, almost every life experience was looked at from a Jungian perspective. Jung's name came up frequently in conversation, and as children we recognized early on the reverence with which he was regarded in the family. We realized that criticism of Jung was not allowed. Only much later did I realize that both my parents were caught in a powerful transference to him and that is why it was so difficult even to tease about him. My early years were during World War II, at a time when they were completely cut off from any contact with Jung. As a result, he became larger-than-life, and everyone we knew was categorized as either adequately Jungian or not Jungian enough. In the late 1940s and early 1950s in Los Angeles and in a few other places in the United States, the Jungian movement was beginning to get underway. In the United States, particularly in Los Angeles and New York, Jung's reputation was questionable, to say the least. In the immediate post-war environment, when the world was assimilating the Holocaust, Jung came under severe attack for his having had contact with Nazis prior to the Second World War. As a Swiss neutral, he was free to interact with Germans of any ideology, including Nazis. This contact with Nazis in the 1930s and some statements written at that time have been used against him up until the present. In Los Angeles and New York where large Jewish psychoanalytic populations lived, to be both Jewish and Jungian was to be marginalized by the larger Freudian Jewish psychotherapeutic community. In those days, one was either totally Jungian or not Jungian at all. There was little room in between for those who had an interest in Jung along with other pursuits. Even some Jungian analysts were considered not Jungian enough, which meant that they did not spend enough time with their inner imagery through active imagination and dreams, and/or were too interested in their adaptation to the collective.

I went to college and medical school with the vague notion of becoming a Jungian analyst. It was terribly important to me that I went to the "right" schools and received the proper accreditation. I did not want to have happen to me what had happened to my parents in Los Angeles. My father's medical degree from Heidelberg was not accepted in California, and my mother had no education past high school. As a result, they had to practice as Jungian analysts at first without licenses and then later were "grandfathered" in as psychologists; they were always marginal in the larger community and were treated as undesirables by the then dominant psychoanalytic community.

It was from this upbringing and background that I began in psychiatry and entered into a Jungian analysis in 1962 in the San Francisco Bay Area. It is important to point out that in the early 1960s those in psychoanalysis generally called it "Freudian analysis." Moreover, in the United States and particularly in Los Angeles and New York, Jungians and Freudians rarely spoke to one another. The direct descendants of Jung and Freud were very much in the picture, and many carried on the personal conflict between Freud and Jung. Freudian psychoanalysis was at the peak of its influence, and by becoming a Jungian analyst one ran the risk of not being able to earn a living. This was a difficult choice for many young people just starting out in their professional careers. I talked with many people who were quite fascinated with Jung's ideas, but they could not risk what it would do to their careers if they chose to become Jungian analysts. I was told that I had a promising career in academic psychiatry but that going into Jungian analysis would have a negative effect on those opportunities. Given my background, however, I was able to withstand the loss of prestige in not having an academic career, and I did go into Jungian analysis and eventually into Jungian training to become an analyst.

What Jungian meant at that time was to be a part of a family or community. Almost every one of the first generation of Jungians lived and breathed Jung from morning until night. It was not a profession that one kept separate from personal life. It was a true vocation that enveloped every aspect of life. We children of that first generation heard all the Jungian terms bandied about at the dinner table, and different individuals, sometimes even patients, were portrayed in Jungian terms. We had very little understanding of what these terms really meant, but that did not prevent us from using them. The social life of the family also centered on doing things with patients. For instance, the person who taught me to swim was a patient of my mother's. My three half-siblings had difficulty with this and generally kept more distance from this type of interaction. My way of handling this intense Jungian professional and social mixture was to work hard at an American adaptation at school. I did not react negatively to Jung, but I did react negatively to everything European. Of course, I regret that now. I could have easily been bilingual in German and English. Since my parents worked at home, bringing friends home from school was sometimes a bit awkward, especially if a patient was waiting in the dining room.

Some of my early dreams in analysis featured Jung. It gradually emerged that the Jung in my dreams was not primarily Jung the actual man. I began to understand that the Jung in my dreams represented a central image in my unconscious and that he symbolized an individuating factor. The Jung in my dreams also did not appear as he actually was, but often as a young American man with short hair. This was my subjective Jung, not the objective Jung. I had met Jung when he was in his 80s, and these images of Jung as a young man appeared only a few years after my having met him. As I began to assimilate the image and meaning of Jung in my dreams, what was said about Jung the man became less emotionally charged. Jung became a symbol, albeit a powerful one, as he has for many of us. The mention of Jung continues to constellate strong reactions, both positive and negative.

130 *Reflections on the word "Jungian"*

Jung and the field of analytical psychology

When Jung broke with Freud, he termed his own new depth psychology "analytical psychology" to differentiate it from psychoanalysis. The name "analytical psychology" has not caught on strongly in many quarters. Although there are analysts who call themselves analytical psychologists, the majority prefer to identify themselves with the word "Jungian" in the title, such as "Jungian psychoanalyst", or more commonly in the United States "Jungian analyst".

Why do we continue to identify ourselves as "Jungian" so many years after Jung's death and after many other authors have made important contributions to the field? My hypothesis is that as a profession we have not yet been able to integrate the work of Jung, and until we do that we shall unconsciously still be "Jungian analysts" and not analytical psychologists. When I entered psychiatry, the term "Freudian analysis" was much more common than it is today, with these analysts now generally called "psychoanalysts". In the 1960s, ego psychology was the dominant influence in psychoanalysis in the United States. The big point of differentiation for psychoanalysis in those days was the relevance of instinct theory versus the Sullivanian interpersonal school. Since that time psychoanalysis has developed many different branches – such as object relations, self psychology, and the interpersonal school to name some of the dominant theoretical orientations.

Analytical psychology has also seen its theory and practice evolve into distinct patterns. Andrew Samuels' (1985) classic study, *Jung and the Post-Jungians,* was the first publication formally to define qualities upon which this categorization could be made. He based his classification on the emphasis that different analysts placed on the theory of archetypes, the Self, transference, and the role of developmental issues in analysis. Without going into detail, the classical analysts placed greater attention on the emergence of archetypal themes, especially the Self, in their analysands. Transference phenomena were not emphasized, and early development issues played a lesser role. On the other hand, the so-called "developmental" group placed greater emphasis on early development, relied heavily on transference interpretations, and used the terms "archetype" and "symbol" in a much different manner from the classical analysts. Developmental theory also modified the use of the term "self" to include a primal self in the first half of life. Developmental Jungian analysts were heavily influenced by psychoanalysis, especially object-relations theory as developed by Klein, Bion, Winnicott, and others.

When one listened to clinical material presented by analysts from the two groups, one wondered where the common thread of being Jungian resided. The classical analysts presented dreams with amplifications and placed a great emphasis on the images and symbols as essential to healing. The developmental analysts presented images and fantasies from early childhood with special reference to the body, including many references to the body of the analyst. Transference and its interpretation were of primary importance.

When these divergent clinical views were first presented at international Jungian meetings, the tension in the air was palpable. Since the 1960s there has been a softening on both sides with respect to their respective positions. Developmental Jungian analysts have become gradually more interested in Jung's symbolic approach to the unconscious, and many of the classical analysts have seen the need to understand and explore developmental issues with their analysands. There has been a settling into two distinct camps but also with many overlaps.

It still leaves us with the question of what it means to be Jungian today? I was wrestling with this question when I came upon a helpful paper by Adolf

Guggenbühl-Craig delivered to the Swiss Society for Analytical Psychology in June 1996. I outline his arguments next.

Originally we all start with Jung. We may have read something by him, or perhaps were positively influenced by a Jungian to the extent of choosing a career as a Jungian psychotherapist. Initially we developed a strong adherence to a Jungian model, even if later we may have developed a critical attitude towards Jung's writings. Thus, Guggenbühl-Craig says, we all have our original "historical identity" as Jungians. We also have an analysis and personal analyst who were in some way related to the Jungian tradition. We are either grandchildren or by now great-grandchildren of Jung. Just like any extended family, we may have little in common except our ancestry. It is kinship libido that brings the extended family together. However, this is insufficient to hold us together as a professional group. Hence, we see the many splits within the professional family that still want to remain part of the tradition.

We also share a kind of ideological identity. Guggenbühl-Craig characterizes this as a "transcendental attitude." By this, he does not mean Jung's transcendent function, but rather that all Jungians believe that behind psychological concepts and theories there exists another dimension of reality. Logical positivism as a philosophical attitude holds little value in the Jungian worldview. A large majority of Jungians have an affinity towards the twilight areas of the psyche and have some notion of individuation, which implies a broader view of the psyche than a purely rational one.

Guggenbühl-Craig's third point is more complex to explain. He describes three different archetypal patterns that influenced Jung's thinking. They are the priest/theologian, the physician, and the shaman. One can easily see the priest/theologian and the physician in Jung's writings. Shamanism, which values the ecstatic, is a path to transpersonal experience for the individual, especially in primitive cultures. We need to be cautious about how shamanic experience is seen in analytical psychology. It has been used as a shortcut to bypass personal complexes, and then the individual is subject to psychic inflation and identification with the so-called mana personality. On the other hand, ecstatic experience, or the numinous, can be the most healing experience in analysis. Jung says in an often-quoted letter (dated August 20, 1945) to P. W. Martin: "But the fact is that the approach to the numinous is the real therapy, and inasmuch as you attain to the numinous experiences you are released from the curse of pathology" (Jung, 1973: 377).

What is "Jungian"?

Guggenbühl-Craig's (1996) paper helps explain how our divergent attitudes and practices as Jungian analysts can all be contained under the rubric of "Jungians." This still does not adequately answer the more general question, however, of why some things are considered "Jungian" and some not. There is about this term an elusive and subtle quality that involves the unconscious, which Jung spent his entire professional career attempting to elucidate. Jung's approach to the unconscious was influenced from as far back as the pre-Socratic philosophers Heraclitus and Anaximander, through Plato and Aristotle, and in the last three hundred years by Leibnitz, Kant, Schopenhauer, and a host of others. We can think of Plato's ideal forms and Kant's noumenal and phenomenal worlds as the philosophical forerunners to understanding this level of the psyche. When we attempt to pin it down, however, we can easily lose its essence. That unknowable quality of the symbol gets lost. When we sense that our own deeper unconscious has been tapped by a particular image or object, we intuitively feel that this particular work, be it a book, music, or art, is Jungian.

132 *Reflections on the word "Jungian"*

It is interesting to look back and see how in my own lifetime the meaning of the word "Jungian" has changed. I belong to the dying group of people who actually had some personal contact with Jung, and it was important for me to have my analysis and other contacts with first-generation Jungians. It is also clearly marked in my memory how others treated me when they found out I was Jungian. Both in college and medical school it was generally negative. It would be the occasional person who would respond positively to the fact that I was Jungian, and then I was often eagerly sought out.

From the beginning of my training as a psychiatrist until now, I have been identified as Jungian. As part of my nature, I have wanted to represent myself as Jungian within the broader psychoanalytic and psychiatric framework. I have put myself into many psychiatric situations where my Jungian identity has stood out. Most of the time it has worked out, but I have also received some extremely hostile responses as well. Because I am Jewish and have refugee immigrant parents, I often present a puzzle to those anti-Jungians who think that all Jungians are conservative and right-wing and do not want to talk about sex and aggression.

Conclusion

In today's world the term "Jungian" does not generally stir up the strong emotions that were still present when I was a young psychiatrist and Jungian analyst. As we have moved away from Jung the person and more to his ideas and intellectual legacy, we can discuss them with more dispassionate objectivity. However, there is still an older generation of Freudian psychoanalysts who blame Jung for not doing more to prevent what happened in Germany, and who somewhere believe that Jung was anti-Semitic and a Nazi. That does not go away.

What will it mean to be a Jungian in the future? I look at some of the clinical Jungian training programs around the world, and they tend to have less and less of Jung and more of whomever is fashionable at the time. On the other hand, I find that the interests of the academics in the IAJS hark back to basic notions of Jung.

I would like to conclude this chapter by stating that the term "Jungian" cannot be completely grasped and understood. What I have attempted to do is to circumambulate the symbol "Jungian" and to share with the reader some of my experiences as a Jungian.

Note

1 "Reflections on the Word 'Jungian,'" in Murray Stein and Raya A. Jones (eds), *Cultures and Identities in Transition: Jungian Perspectives*, pp. 190–8. Hove, UK: Routledge, 2010. Reprinted with the permission of the publisher.

References

Bellow, S. (1998) *The Dean's December*. New York: Penguin Classics.
Guggenbühl-Craig, A. (1996) What Makes one a Jungian? Paper presented at the annual meeting of the Swiss Society for Analytical Psychology (SGFAP), June 2.
Jung, C. G. (1963) *Memories, Dreams, Reflections*, ed. A. Jaffé. New York: Vintage.
Jung, C. G. (1973) *Collected Letters*, vol. 1, *1906–1950*, ed. G. Adler and A. Jaffé. Princeton, NJ: Princeton University Press.
Kirsch, T. (2000) *The Jungians: A Comparative and Historical Perspective*. London: Routledge.
Samuels, A. (1985) *Jung and the Post-Jungians*. London: Routledge & Kegan Paul.

CHAPTER 16

C.G. JUNG
Fifty years after his death

From the *International Journal of Jungian Studies* 3(2), September 2011[1]

It has been fifty years since the death of C. G. Jung and it is a good occasion to see how the image of Jung has changed during this period. As someone who was already identified as a Jungian prior to Jung's death, going back over these fifty plus years has been a complex inner process. Through my parents' influence, first-generation Jungian analysts who had had their primary analyses with Jung, I had seen how they had both idealized Jung and suffered when he was criticized. In his lifetime after Freud, Jung was the most famous depth psychologist of the twentieth century, but at the same time to be a Jungian meant that one was professionally marginalized. When I began my psychiatric residency in 1962, one year after Jung's death, labeled as a Jungian, one of my professors quietly told me that I was throwing away a promising career in psychiatry by going into Jungian training. Others in my psychiatric residency were also drawn to Jung's ideas, but they feared that they would not be able to financially survive and took more conventional paths. I saw that both my parents had successful practices and that was not a big concern. Plus, I was in a Jungian analysis that was really finally helping me mature. I was not about to give that up. This gives one a sense of the atmosphere that surrounded Jung around the time of his death in the United States. To be Jungian meant that one would most likely be marginalized, one might have difficulty earning a living, and if one were a psychiatrist, one would definitely not be readily accepted in general psychiatric circles. In England and continental Europe to be Jungian was somewhat easier, but there was still a big stigma to be seen as a Jungian.

Jung died on June 6, 1961, after a brief final illness in his 86th year. The funeral was held three days later on June 9, at the Reformed Protestant Church in Küsnacht, the local church for the Jung family, and he was buried in the family plot. The pastor, Hans Schaer, a personal friend of Jung's, called him a "heretic" in his eulogy. Jung's strong interest in Gnosticism and medieval alchemy had prompted Pastor Schaer to label Jung as such. Still, Jung wanted to have a conventional funeral and to be buried with his family. I mention this because rumors initiated by Richard Noll suggest that Jung had formed a cult and the ceremony around his death had been part of a cult ritual.

Freudian psychoanalysis was at the peak of its influence, and the Cold War between the United States and its allies versus Russia was at its height. The threat of a nuclear catastrophe was on everyone's mind, and the Berlin Wall had just been erected to separate East and West. Jung's *Collected Works* were in the process of being translated into English under the auspices of the Bollingen Foundation, and the C. G. Jung Institute in Zurich had opened its doors in 1948 with approximately thirty students from around the world studying there. In London the Society of Analytical Psychology (SAP) had formed, and there were three small Jungian training centers in the United States: New York, San Francisco, and Los Angeles. There were individual Jungian analysts in a number of other countries, including Israel, Italy, France, Germany, Australia, and New Zealand. The International Association for Analytical Psychology (IAAP) had been founded in 1955, and the first international Congress had taken place in Zurich in August 1958. Jung himself had attended the opening session and the final banquet. Jung's focus on the collective unconscious and the religious dimension of the psyche had attracted a number of artists, theologians, doctors, psychologists, and writers to his work. However, his ideas were not accepted in academic circles and it was rare to find Jung taught at the university level. He was considered a "woolly mystic, questionable anti-Semite, and a womanizer," and the Freudian establishment, especially in the United States, saw to it that his reputation remained doubtful. To be Jungian meant that one was marginal, and as in my case, being Jewish just added to the complexity. How could I as a Jew be Jungian? I defended myself by saying that my parents had been in analysis during the 1930s when Jung was supposed to be anti-Semitic and they did not experience it. In fact, my mother felt that her connection to being Jewish was deepened by her analysis with Jung. This particular issue has been part of my professional legacy from that time until the present. Many new data have been discovered on this important topic, and I have learned that Jung had extremely complex reactions toward Jews and the Jewish religion. To go further into this subject here would require a whole other paper.

My parents as refugees from Germany ended up in Los Angeles, founding a Jungian group. As if being Jungian was not bad enough, a further complication was that neither of my parents had the proper credentials to practice in California. My father had received his medical and psychiatric training in Germany, which was not recognized in California. My mother had no education beyond high school and was a true lay analyst; this was a significant factor in their marginalization. From a very young age the expectation was that I would become a Jungian analyst and that I would obtain the proper credentials. In other words, I was to live their unlived lives. To become a Jungian analyst worked for me, and I have been practicing for forty-three years.

Through the intervention of my parents I met Jung on three occasions between 1955 and 1958 – the last time I had an individual hour with him. Jung the man made a deep impression upon me with his warmth and directness, and it solidified my intention to become a Jungian analyst. Another pivotal meeting occurred in 1958, when my parents and I attended a dinner in Zurich with Marie Louise von Franz and Barbara Hannah. They were discussing the just completed first International Congress and were complaining that Jung was too accepting of Fordham's emphasis on early child development and transference. Why was Jung not more dismissive of Fordham? My interpretation of this conversation fifty years later is that Jung always had the grand design of his psychology including all of psychology, wherein Fordham's point of view was an important one, and it was essential that it was included.

When it came time to enter a psychiatric training, I chose the San Francisco Bay Area because it had the only Jungian training program in the United States at the time where the senior Jungian analysts were integrated into general psychiatric training and where the Jungian analysts were on collegial terms with the majority Freudian psychoanalysts. It was extremely important for me not to continue the pattern of marginalization that many Jungian analysts, including my parents, seemed to need. By then I had experienced taking classes at the Jung Institute in Zurich, had

had Jungian analysis in New York, and had seen my parents begin a Jungian group in Los Angeles. In all these places I experienced how the Jungian community both saw itself above, i.e., superior to the collective, and at the same time feeling inferior, wanting to be accepted by the collective. Jo Wheelwright and Joe Henderson who as highly respected doctors were accepted by the largely Freudian psychoanalytic collective led the Jungians in San Francisco. To be part of the collective was a new experience but other Jungian groups often criticized the San Francisco Jungians as having "sold out" in order to belong.

While I was in psychiatric training in the early 1960s, two important books by Jung were published, and I read them as they were published. *Memories, Dreams, Reflections* (Jung, 1963) came out first in English in 1963 and caused a bit of a sensation in the collective world. Erich Fromm in his review in *Scientific American* stated that Jung was an "opportunist," and D. W. Winnicott stated in his 1964 review in the *International Journal of Psychoanalysis* that Jung had suffered from a childhood psychosis but had recovered. *Man and his Symbols* (Jung *et al.*, 1964) was published as a book in 1964, and Jung's introductory article there was meant for the general public. It was Jung's last piece of writing and the beautifully illustrated edition became a popular coffee-table book.

The reader may wonder why I am going into detail about my entrance into Jungian training. I want to demonstrate the state of Jung's psychology in the United States and Switzerland around the time of Jung's death. There were two rather esoteric training programs in New York and Los Angeles and the other training program in San Francisco was considered too influenced by the medical model. What one needs to remember is that at that time psychoanalysis was almost entirely dominated by medical psychoanalysts and all other practitioners were considered inferior. The San Francisco Jungians were dominated by medical doctors, although they had allowed psychologists to train and so looked much more like a typical Freudian psychoanalytic institute of its day. This positioning meant that the San Francisco analysts were much more "professional" in their interactions with their analysands, and there was much less mixing of professional and personal relationships. The pattern up to then in Jungian circles had been to mix completely professional and personal relationships. This professionalism was completely new to me, but over time it has become second nature.

The year 1962 was pivotal for analytical psychology. Jung had died the previous year and the second International Congress had once again been held in Zurich. The long smoldering dispute, which I had witnessed in Zurich in 1958 between the London-based analysts who were heavily influenced by Melanie Klein's object-relations, and the Zurich analysts who were deeply immersed into amplification of archetypal symbols, irrupted at the 1962 Congress. Murray Jackson, representing the London developmental point of view, presented his version of the use of symbols and his discussant, Esther Harding, rebuked him for his lack of understanding of the meaning of archetypes. Murray Jackson left the Jungian Professional Group, the SAP, shortly thereafter, and for the rest of his professional career became a Kleinian analyst. The tension between these two points of view dominated the International Congresses for the next two decades. The Jerusalem Congress of 1983, "Symbolic versus the Clinical," was supposed to bring some clarity to this discussion. The changes both within analytical psychology, as well as those which were taking place within psychoanalysis, made this discussion less emotional. Kohut's "self-psychology" and "Interrelational Psychoanalysis" were of interest to Jungians and represented points of view closer to Jung's. Many Jungians besides the London developmental group were interested in what was going on in psychoanalysis. The

136   *C. G. Jung*

tension between the classical and the developmental became less emotional. The two strands are still separate but now there is dialogue between the two points of view. There could be more.

James Hillman who had trained at the Jung Institute in Zurich and then had become director of studies developed a third stream of analytical psychology. Hillman based his theories on the archetypal image. He defined his psychology as "Archetypal Psychology," and he developed a following among those who focused on the image in culture. Hillman was not interested in psychodynamics and in early childhood development. He was more interested in the existential questions. Archetypal psychology has never become a clinical discipline of its own. Hillman is a brilliant writer and continues to influence analytical psychology with his views on the nature of "soul" and culture.

Jung's writings became fashionable at the time of the psychedelic revolution in the late 1960s and early 1970s. Looking for parallels to their own experience with LSD and similar substances, many people found in Jung's writings a way to understand their experiences. This identification led to a major resurgence of interest in people wanting to become Jungian analysts, as well as his books becoming popular. For the first time it was not considered marginal to be Jungian. His time of popularity in the United States lasted about twenty years, but even when he was no longer considered fashionable, his books remained popular. His so-called autobiography *Memories, Dreams, Reflections* has been a constant seller since its publication in 1963; the *I Ching* with its introduction by Jung (1950) has been a constant seller for Princeton University Press, while Joseph Campbell's series on myth for both television and books has increased the popularity of Jung and widened his influence on the general public.

The professional organization of Jungian analysts, the International Association for Analytical Psychology (IAAP), has grown from a little over 100 members in 1955 to around 3,000 members worldwide in 2011. In the early days the C. G. Jung Institute in Zurich was the mecca for all those who wished to become Jungian analysts; the ability to be in analysis with one of Jung's close associates was an attraction. Obviously, not many people could afford to train in Zurich so at the same time local institutes developed. Most of the early national institutes developed in Europe, and in many instances splits occurred so that there were two and sometimes three or four institutes in a particular country. In most countries there was a central national group with satellite institutes in various cities of the country. Often these splits were related to theoretical differences, but just as often they were related to personality conflicts between the leaders of different factions. The one significant exception to national groups has been the United States where there is no organized national group but there are a number of independent local institutes. The various groups come together for an informal meeting every year, but there is no national central authority. Each local institute is vetted directly by the IAAP.

For twenty years after Jung's death, the center of Jungian thought was in Zurich. The first generation of analysts who had been in analysis with Jung contributed the most to the literature on analytical psychology, mainly with amplification of particular archetypal images. A good example would be Marie Louise von Franz's study of the *Puer Aeternus* archetype, which became a popular book in Jungian training programs (von Franz, 1970/2000). In this study, von Franz outlines the clinical characteristics of an individual who is stuck in the archetype of the *puer*. She describes the person caught in the "provisional life syndrome" who cannot make a commitment. She illustrates this pattern through the interpretation of the writings of Antoine Saint-Exupery's *The Little Prince*.

The central energy of Jung's psychology gradually shifted to the UK where the emphasis on early childhood development, transference, and countertransference were given the core value in the analytic process. Acting out of the transference had been a problematic issue in the early generation of Jungian analysts. Although transference and countertransference were acknowledged by Zurich-trained analysts, the concepts had never been given the prominence that they have had by most practicing analysts in the UK. Furthermore, greater significance was given to diagnosis and treatment in analysis. The British Jungian analysts had been heavily influenced by object-relations psychoanalysis and their theories and practices had been incorporated into Jungian analysis. The use of the couch, frequency of sessions, the description of regressive states, and the analysis of childhood are hallmarks of the developmental approach to Jungian analysis. At first there was resistance from the rest of the Jungian world to accepting these ideas, but over time they have been acknowledged as important factors in analysis.

Until 1989 professional Jungian psychology had primarily a continental European, United Kingdom, and North American axis, although there were groups in Brazil, Venezuela, Israel, Australia, and New Zealand. When the Berlin Wall came down with the fall of Communism in Eastern Europe and the Soviet Union, the IAAP heard from individuals who had been secretly studying Jung. Over the past twenty years study groups have formed in the former Czechoslovakia, Hungary, Bulgaria, Serbia, Ukraine, Poland, and in different cities in Russia, including St Petersburg and Moscow. A group of analysts from the UK, organized by Jan Wiener and Catherine Crowder, have been visiting Russia on a regular basis to conduct analysis, supervision, and seminars. In 2007 enough people had gone through the training that an official Russian institute for analytical psychology recognized by the IAAP could be formed.

In addition to the foray into Eastern Europe and Russia, other geographical areas opened up. In Asia professional societies now exist in Japan and South Korea. Chinese culture has four centers of Jungian activity: Shanghai, Guangzhou, Hong Kong, and Taipei. Most of the South American countries now have a Jung society of mixed professional and lay interest. In addition, there are professional groups in Brazil and Venezuela.

The academic community has begun to recognize Jung as an important and serious thinker, and it is now acceptable to write books and papers from a Jungian perspective. Andrew Samuels and Renos Papadopoulos hold a joint professorship at the University of Essex in the UK, and David Rosen has an endowed professorship at Texas A&M. Samuels and Papadopoulos were instrumental in forming the International Academic Jungian Studies (IAJS) in 2001, which allows the growing number of academicians interested in Jung to gather and exchange ideas. The IAJS is open to analysts as well. Starting as a small enterprise the IAJS has become a forum for the exchange of Jungian ideas through its list-serve, journal, and many conferences.

An unexpected event happened with the publication on October 7, 2009, of Jung's *The Red Book* (Jung, 2009), which compiles his dialogues and drawings from 1913–14 when Jung was undergoing his "Confrontation with the Unconscious." This expensive book with fifty-three full-page paintings caught the imagination of the American reading public and in spite of its high cost is now in its seventh printing in the United States. It will soon be published in many other languages, including Japanese, French, and Spanish. It was published simultaneously in German last year. It has not been as popular in continental Europe and the UK as in the US, but it still has sold many more copies than was originally anticipated. This whole

138 *C. G. Jung*

phenomenon has come as a complete surprise to the publishing houses, but it shows how strong an interest there is in Jung's psychology.

At present there is no single focus for Jung's analytical psychology. Zurich and London are still vibrant centers of Jungian thought, but Jung's influence spreads all over the world. There are regular large conferences in China on Chinese culture and Jungian psychology, conferences in Eastern Europe, large conferences on analytical psychology in South America, and many conferences and workshops in the United States and Canada. There is no shortage of conferences. The IAAP continues to have/hold its conference every three years in different cities around the world, and this is one way to keep up with the latest ideas in Jungian psychology. The *Journal of Analytical Psychology* has regional conferences on a variety of subjects related to analytical psychology. So far these regional conferences have either been in Europe, Mexico, or the United States. In May of 2011, they will host a conference on ancestors in St Petersburg, Russia. The IAJS was formed in 2001 and continues to have an active list-serve, its own journal, and regular conferences that attract academicians from cinema, literature, the arts, philosophy, anthropology, history, and religion. There are over twenty journals specifically devoted to analytical psychology in many languages, which appear to be thriving. Jung is no longer marginal.

Today one can speak about Jung's psychology as a clinical discipline worldwide and also as a way of speaking about society, culture, and religion. There is a definite clinical field of Jungian analysis where analysts run the spectrum from archetypal to developmental. Analysis of the unconscious and the dialectic nature of the analytical relationship are core concepts in this practice. Depth psychology as a field no longer has the pre-eminence which it once had. For many, Freud is considered an historical figure and nothing more. Freudian-five-times-a-week psychoanalysis as a treatment modality is becoming rare. Today many people are looking for quick answers through medication and short-term therapies that do not take into account the unconscious. Jungian analysis is both lumped together with psychoanalysis and, at the same time, it is a separate discipline. The net result is that now there are fewer people wanting to do the long-term work of Jungian analysis. On the other hand, Jung's research into the unconscious and to the religious dimension of the psyche has attracted many new people to his ideas. As an example take the collective response to *The Red Book*. Some writers have even declared the twenty-first century as Jung's century. Jung the man is still a controversial figure in many quarters, but fifty years after his death his ideas have increasing relevance to the dis-ease and malaise of modern society.

Note

1 *International Journal of Jungian Studies* 3(2) (Sept. 2011): 103–9. Reprinted with the permission of Taylor & Francis Group for the *International Journal of Analytical Psychology*. © 2011 Taylor & Francis, http://dx.doi.org/10.1080/19409052.2011.5927 17, http://www.tandfonline.com.

References

I Ching or Book of Changes (1950) Trans. R. Wilhelm, foreword by C. G. Jung. Bollingen Foundation, reissued Princeton, NJ: Princeton University Press.
Jung, C. G. (1963) *Memories, Dreams, Reflections*, ed. A. Jaffe. New York: Pantheon Books.
Jung, C. G. (2009) *The Red Book of C. G. Jung*, ed. S. Shamdasani. New York: Norton.
Jung, C. G., von Franz, M. L., Henderson, J. L., Jacobi, J., and Jaffe, A. (1964) *Man and his Symbols*. London: Aldus.
von Franz, M. L. (1970/2000) *The Problem of the Puer Aeternus*. Toronto: Inner City Press.

CHAPTER 17

PREFACE TO *THE JUNG–KIRSCH LETTERS*

From *The Jung–Kirsch Letters: The Correspondence of C. G. Jung and James Kirsch*, edited by Ann Conrad Lammers, Routledge 2011[1]

Figure 17.1 James Kirsch with grandson, 1967 (photo © 1967, Thomas B. Kirsch, courtesy Thomas B. Kirsch)

It has been twenty-one years since my father died and almost fifty years since the death of C. G. Jung. I had known about the letters from Jung to my father for many years, and I knew that he valued them highly. About ten years ago I received a telephone call from Sasha Rosen, an American Jung-oriented sandplay therapist who had moved to southern England. She was doing research on the life of Margaret Lowenfeld,

140 *Preface to* The Jung–Kirsch Letters

the original founder of sandplay therapy, at the ETH (Eidgenössische Technische Hochschule) in Zurich, and she had come upon the complete correspondence of my father to Jung. This meant that both sides of the correspondence existed. In my father's archive I had already found forty-four letters from Jung to my father. Yvonne Voegeli, responsible archivist of the C. G. Jung Papers Collection at the ETH-Bibliothek (the ETH Library), sent me copies of my father's letters in August 2004. I was eager to have the entire correspondence translated into English, so that I could have a deeper understanding of the relationship between the two. Initially there was little consideration to publishing the correspondence, but in studying it I realized there were some important themes that Jung discussed with my father which might have relevance for a larger audience.

The next question was, did I want to edit the letters myself? I did not. I felt that I had spent enough time and energy on my father, both in real life and in analysis, and that at this stage of my life I did not want to devote myself to the absorbing task of editing the correspondence. However, I also did not want to completely let go of the correspondence and wanted to participate in some meaningful way. I looked for persons familiar with Jung who at the same time had established themselves as scholars. Ann Lammers seemed a perfect fit, because she was just finishing the Jung–White correspondence, so she was familiar with the problems of editing a correspondence, knew Jung's oeuvre, and had worked with the Jung heirs. And she was open to the project. As the careful researcher that she is, she found many other letters that Jung wrote to my father, both in my father's archive and in the Jung archive in Zurich. She also spent several weeks at our house going over my father's correspondence of sixty years, where she found much relevant information, which has been incorporated into the footnotes. In addition, she found a delightful Christmas card that Jung and others at the Psychological Club sent to my parents in 1958. Thus the correspondence became much larger and richer than had been originally planned.

The correspondence published here represents all the letters known to exist between the two men. No letters have been withheld, and no material from within any of the letters has been withheld (except as required to protect third-party confidentiality), so one sees both the positive side and the shadow of the two men in this correspondence. The three most consistent themes are the Jewish/Christian issue, my father's relationship to his anima and to his women patients, and the hypothesis of synchronicity. Other topics mentioned are relationships to other Jungians, the development of the Jung Institute in Los Angeles, and the promotion of Jung's ideas to the larger collective. Let me elaborate further on each of these themes:

1 The discussion of the Jewish/Christian question occurred during a time when European Jewry was being systematically stamped out. Jung was being labeled as an anti-Semite and a Nazi, and my father, writing from Tel Aviv, was questioning these rumors about Jung's anti-Jewish activities. After receiving Jung's reply, my father vigorously defended Jung, and enlisted other Jewish Jungians to defend him, especially in Zionist and psychological publications.

2 My father's relationship to his anima was a lifelong struggle. He had a tendency to become over-involved with his women patients, which led to sexual entanglements that should not have occurred. Although such boundary violations were common in those days, the extent to which my father got involved was unusual. I am sure his underlying insecurity with the anima was one of the issues that brought my father into analysis in the first place. From

his earliest letters, Jung warned my father that he faced a serious challenge in confronting the anima, and that unconsciousness in this area could have dire consequences. In writing to Jung, my father presented his projections onto women patients in rather abstract terms. In one of his last letters to Jung he referred to his projections of the "Anthropos," the primordial God figure in the form of universal man. Jung, replying in kind, used archetypal language to defuse the intensity of some of these projections. My father also saw Toni Wolff in analysis and consulted with her about his cases. She was a strong critic of my father's behavior towards his own anima and his women patients.

3   Synchronicity and other theoretical topics: Jung discussed with my father many of his psychological ideas, including alchemy, synchronicity, flying saucers, and other psychological and parapsychological phenomena.

What also becomes clear from this correspondence is the special place in Jung's heart occupied by my father, and one senses the care with which Jung dealt with him. So when my father appealed to this personal connection and called on Jung as an authority, Jung met him in a serious and concerned therapeutic manner. The problem that I (and many others) had with my father was that he identified with Jung and saw himself as expressing the wisdom of Jung when he spoke to us. It would have been so much easier for my father, with his colleagues and his family, if he had been more secure in his own authority and leaned less on Jung's. As I was growing up, having Jung in the forefront of family life made us all uncomfortable, so my father's children pushed Jung into the background as much as possible. Even as a child, though, I responded positively to Jung, though ambivalently. I attribute my attraction to Jung to the positive and loving influence of my mother, whose sensitivity I attributed to her relationship to Jung.

Going through these letters later in my own life, I have come to realize that my father actually had an extremely close relationship to Jung, and furthermore (for reasons that are not completely clear to me even today), my father was an important colleague to Jung. For instance, in his introduction to *The Red Book,* Sonu Shamdasani (2009, 215) notes that my father was one of very few outside Jung's immediate family to have seen the original text. Jung apparently showed him the *Red Book* in 1929, when my father first came to him for analysis. I think that Jung valued my father because he saw not only my father's troubled psyche, but also his sensitivity to the workings of the unconscious. Jung also sought understanding of Jewish culture and history, based on my father's vast knowledge of Judaism.

I would like to step back at this point to present the historical context from which my father sought analysis with Jung. My father came from an Orthodox Eastern European Jewish family who one generation previously had moved to Berlin from Poland. His father then did what many German Jewish men did at the time, which was to travel to the Americas and open a business, usually a general store. My father's father opened a button business in Guatemala City, Guatemala. As a result my father and his three older sisters and one younger brother were born in Guatemala City. James Kirsch was born on July 21, 1901. Realizing that his children would not get a proper education in Guatemala, his father sent them all back to Berlin in 1907, visiting them every two years. My father was an excellent student. Against his family's wishes, he decided to study medicine at the University of Heidelberg. Meanwhile, my grandfather remained in Guatemala. The fact of World War I meant that he did not visit his family in Germany for nine years, between 1912 and 1921. According to my father, my grandfather may have had a second, Indian family in Guatemala. No members of a second family have ever surfaced.

142 *Preface to* The Jung–Kirsch Letters

At the University of Heidelberg my father became a Zionist and joined the Blau-Weiss, one of many Zionist organizations that were developing all over Europe to promote Palestine as the homeland for the Jews. My father made two life-long friends through the Blau-Weiss Society: Erich Fromm, the psychoanalyst, and Ernst Simon, a close associate of Martin Buber. Fromm was in analysis with Frieda Reichmann, during which time they fell in love and married. The marriage did not last, but my father saw at close hand what could happen in an analytic relationship.

My father returned to Berlin after his medical studies and began working in a psychiatric hospital. He began a Freudian analysis, but was dissatisfied and ended it after two years. He then read Jung's *Psychological Types* and entered analysis with the Jungian lay analyst Toni Sussmann.[2] In late 1928 he wrote to Jung asking to schedule appointments in Zurich. Jung wrote back, saying that it would be possible to meet the following May, and that exchange initiated a series of sixty analytical hours. My father's analysis with Jung also constituted his most important professional training as a Jungian analyst. In today's terms sixty hours doesn't seem like very much, but in those days sixty hours was considered a lengthy analysis. These hours were not consecutive, but my father would visit Zurich periodically, and he would also meet Jung for a chance hour or two when they were both attending a conference. In later life, when my father added up all his professional training, he listed his hours not only with Jung but also with Toni Sussmann, Toni Wolff, Liliane Frey-Rohn, and C. A. Meier.

It is important to locate Jung in his career trajectory at this time. After his "confrontation with the unconscious," the period lasting from 1913 to 1918, Jung's ideas had matured, and the psychology that he developed offered a completely different vision of the psyche than Freud's. Between the end of the First World War and the beginning of the Second World War in 1939, students from all over the world sought him out for analysis and analytic training. That was the time when Jung gave ongoing seminars in English at the Psychological Club, on dreams, visions, and Nietzsche's *Zarathustra*. He also gave lectures in German at the ETH, including his lectures on the Exercises of St Ignatius of Loyola. And he gave seminars on children's dreams. Thus, individuals who came to Jung had the opportunity to attend seminars with him, in addition to having an individual analysis. They also would often see a second analyst, usually a woman, and that often turned out to be Toni Wolff. This was the training of most first-generation Jungian analysts.

Practically every member of the German Jewish group in Berlin whom my father had befriended (Erich Neumann, Gerhard Adler, Ernst Bernhard, Werner Engel, Heinz Westmann, and others) eventually ended up in analysis with Jung. With the rise of the Nazis, these new Jungian analysts spread to various corners of the globe. Given his earlier Zionist leanings, my father first emigrated to Palestine. My mother, who was a patient of my father's at the time, was in deep mourning for her late husband, who had died in 1933. He had suffered fulminating multiple sclerosis and had committed suicide. Her transference to my father was intense, and she followed him to Palestine with her two young sons, even though he was married and had two small children of his own. They all ended up in Tel Aviv, where two years later my father divorced his first wife, Eva, who then returned to practice as a therapist in Berlin. In 1938 he helped Eva leave Berlin to settle in England.

During this time my father wrote to Jung about the rumors he had heard that Jung was anti-Semitic and even a Nazi. Their correspondence thus offers primary documentation about this thorny issue, which continues to haunt students of Jung to this day. I personally believe that this is the most important part of the lengthy correspondence, since Jung goes to great lengths to explain his views on Jews,

Preface to The Jung–Kirsch Letters   143

Judaism and Jewish mysticism. Hopefully, it will open some eyes to the complexity of Jung's relationship to Judaism.

In one of these letters, September 29, 1934, where he gives his views on Judaism, Jung switches in the last paragraph to offer a clinical consultation to my father. He describes the analytic process when the unconscious of both the patient and the analyst are activated, and interprets the patient's dream as the product of their unconscious relationship. It seems to me that Jung was exactly describing the position of what later has become the Relational School of Psychoanalysis, where the unconscious manifestation is always the product of what happens between the two psyches.

In 1935 my mother and father, now together, moved from Tel Aviv to London. They experienced the early Zionists as more fanatical than they were comfortable with. Living conditions in Palestine were also considered too primitive for those who were used to the modern conveniences of European life.

The family began anew in London, where my father again opened his analytic practice and where I was born. It was in London that my mother became an analyst as well. Jung sent to her a physician-analysand whom he could not see. This doctor had chosen my mother, a choice he checked out with Jung, who thought it was a good idea. That is the informal way that my mother became an analyst, even though she did not have a complete education, nor had she completed many hours of personal analysis with Jung and had had no supervision except from my father. Meanwhile, my father continued his correspondence with Jung from his new home in England.

When it appeared that the German war machine was ready to overrun the UK, my parents hurriedly made contact with relatives in San Francisco and got on the first boat which would take them to the United States. It was the good ship *Samaria* that carried us across the Atlantic in October 1940, accompanied by a destroyer convoy and air cover. Many such crossings were not as lucky as ours, and the *Samaria* was sunk two months later while attempting another crossing. My family settled in Los Angeles as the first Jungians, and they helped to build up a Jungian community there over the next forty-five years. Although my parents wrote to Jung in 1944, there were no wartime letters from Jung to my parents between 1941 and 1945. The correspondence picked up after the war and continued until 1960. The topics they discussed were the religious and psychological differences between Christianity and Judaism, Jung's theory of synchronicity, further questions about my father's relationships with his women patients, and the political complications arising within the growing Jungian community in Los Angeles.

My father's continuing difficulties with his women patients were of great concern to Jung, and many of their letters allude to this problem. This was still a time when there were no legal ramifications for sexual contact with a patient. From Jung's responses one can tell that he was aware of the depth of the problem for my father. Jung continued to voice his concern about my father's behavior with women patients but seemed to realize that my father was painfully helpless in the face of it. He was not completely open with Jung about his behavior, and it was only in his last letters to Jung that the psychological roots of the problem were revealed. Rather than discuss the problem in more depth here, I shall leave the reader to explore the development of this issue throughout the correspondence.

Meanwhile my mother and father, James and Hilde, along with Max Zeller, were working hard to build the Jungian community in Los Angeles. Most of the first members were German Jewish doctors and therapists (wartime refugees) who did not have the proper credentials to practice in California. In spite of this drawback, more and more people became interested in Jungian psychology. Starting in 1942

Figure 17.2   James and Hilde Kirsch, Israel, 1972 (photographer unknown, courtesy Thomas B. Kirsch)

my father gave weekly seminars on Jung and Jungian material, continuing until 1988, one year before his death. Both analysts and patients attended the weekly seminar, and while my mother was alive she prepared cookies, cake, coffee, and tea for the participants. There are literally hundreds of tapes of all the seminars and lectures that my father gave to various groups in Los Angeles. The Jung Institute in Los Angeles named the lecture room after him, and he was honored at the time. In addition to the weekly seminars, he wrote two books, *Shakespeare's Royal Self* (1966) and *The Reluctant Prophet* (1973), a story of the late nineteenth-century Rabbi Hile Wechsler, who dreamed that he and his flock should leave Germany and emigrate to Palestine. My father must have felt a strong affinity with Rabbi Wechsler when he was advising all his patients, friends, and family to leave Germany in 1933.

My mother and father continued to visit Jung until 1960 and continued to visit Zurich on an almost yearly basis up until their respective deaths in 1978 and 1989. Through them I had three occasions to meet with Jung, and these encounters strengthened my desire to become a Jungian analyst myself.

Unfortunately, because of his boundary violations with various woman patients and his arrogant attitude towards those who did not know Jung's psychology well enough to satisfy his high standards, James Kirsch has left a mixed legacy in Los Angeles.

This correspondence, translated from German into English by Ursula Egli and Ann Lammers and edited by Ann Lammers, should help to elucidate the long and complicated relationship between Jung and my father. I would also like to thank the Stiftung der Werke von C. G. Jung (formerly the Erbengemeinschaft C. G. Jung), especially Ulrich Hoerni and Peter Jung, for their permission to publish Jung's side of this important correspondence.

Note

1 *The Jung–Kirsch Letters: The Correspondence of C. G. Jung and James Kirsch,* edited by Ann Conrad Lammers, trans. Ann Conrad Lammers and Ursula Egli, pp. ix–xvi. Hove, UK: Routledge, 2011. Reprinted with the permission of the publisher.

2 Jungian lay analyst and trainer of analysts, then working in Berlin, who had analyzed and trained with Jung. A Jewish convert to Catholicism, Sussmann fled Germany in 1938 and established herself in Oxford. Her determination to combine Indian theosophy with Jungian psychology raised concerns for Jung (cf. Jung, Aug. 19, 1929, p. 6 and note, and Jan. 28, 1933, p. 34) and led him in the 1940s to distance himself from her work (cf. Jung and White, 2007, pp. 41–48, 77, 79).

References

Jung, C. G., and White, V. (2007) *The Jung–White Letters,* ed. Ann Conrad Lammers and Adrian Cunningham. New York and London: Routledge.

Kirsch, James (1966) *Shakespeare's Royal Self.* Zurich: Daimon Verlag; and New York: C. G. Jung Foundation of New York.

Kirsch, James (1973) *The Reluctant Prophet: An Exploration of Prophecy and Dreams.* Los Angeles: Sherbourne Press, Inc.

Shamdasani, Sonu (2009) Introduction. In C. G. Jung, *The Red Book: Liber Novus,* ed. Sonu Shamdasani, trans. Mark Kyburz, John Peck, and Sonu Shamdasani. Philemon Series/ Foundation of the Works of C. G. Jung, New York: W. W. Norton & Co.

CHAPTER 18

INTRODUCTION TO FIRST REFLECTIONS

Initial responses to C. G. Jung's *Red Book* (*Liber Novus*), based on essays presented in San Francisco, 4–6 June 2010

From *The Red Book: Reflections on C. G. Jung's Liber Novus,*
edited by Thomas B. Kirsch and George Hogenson, Routledge, 2013[1]

The *Red Book,* Jung's personal diary of his confrontation with the unconscious, has now been published, ninety-five years after it was written. Beginning in the autumn of 1913 and essentially finishing by April 1914, he wrote his visions, fantasies, and dreams in a series of black books. Later, he transferred his writings to a large leather-bound Red Book and added medieval-style calligraphy and a series of mandala paintings. Those in the Jungian community have been aware of the existence of this Red Book, but very few outside the family had actually seen it. Now, after over a decade of editorial work by Sonu Shamdasani, and with the cooperation of the Jung estate, we have this beautifully illustrated, magnificent *Red Book*. Jung himself was unsure whether to publish it out of concern for his scientific reputation. In today's world, however, it has been fabulously received.

The *Red Book* gives us a picture of the raw material from which Jung developed most of his mature writings. Reading it is not an easy task. I myself could only stay with the material for a short period of time before I needed a break. I have heard from many others whose experience of reading the *Red Book* has been similar. It came out on October 7, 2009, and many of us are dipping into it a little bit at a time. I find it to be like my first encounter with Jung's writings on alchemy, which made little sense to me initially. Over these many years I have come to appreciate and understand why he used alchemical language to describe the modern unconscious process. I am hoping that over time I will have the same experience with the *Red Book*.

There is no question that the *Red Book* is an important first step toward Jung's own individuation and rediscovery of his soul. Let me give you the context in which Jung began to have spontaneous visions in the autumn of 1913. In January of that year he and Freud had broken off their personal relationship. They had seen one another in September 1913 in Munich at the International Psychoanalytic Congress, but they did not speak to each other. Jung was president of the International Psychoanalytic Association, editor of the *Jahrbuch*, and still considered himself a psychoanalyst. It was a time of transition in many senses, both personally and intellectually for Jung and collectively for the world. He mourned the loss of his relationship to Freud and, as he recounts in *Memories, Dreams,*

Reflections, "Toward the autumn of 1913 the pressure which I had felt was in *me* seemed to be moving outward, as if there were something in the air" (1963, 175). The winds of World War I were in the air.

The visions began on a short train ride to visit his wife's family, and although they occurred over a relatively short period of time, he was to work over these fantasies through inner dialogue, painting, and medieval calligraphy until 1928 when he lay aside the project. What enabled him to stop working on the *Red Book* was a synchronous event. He had painted a mandala with a castle in the center, and it felt to him as though it were distinctively Chinese. He writes in *Memories, Dreams, Reflections* (1963), "In 1928, when I was painting this picture, showing the golden, well-fortified castle, Richard Wilhelm in Frankfurt sent me the thousand-year-old Chinese text on the yellow castle, the germ of the immortal body." It was *The Secret of the Golden Flower*, a Chinese alchemical Taoist work, in which he found images and texts quite like the ones that he had been working with in his own *Red Book*. This relieved him of his isolation. In the 1950s, he attempted to return to the *Red Book*, but he stopped in midsentence and never picked it up again.

The essays in this book are initial attempts at an interpretation from important scholars in the field of analytical psychology, although I suspect that a definitive interpretation of the *Red Book* may never be possible. They were presented at a conference in San Francisco, California, on June 4–6, 2010. The conference was sponsored by the Extended Education Committee of the C. G. Jung Institute of San Francisco to celebrate the publication of the *Red Book*. Each author is deeply involved in Jung studies, and together they present a wide variety of viewpoints.

Ulrich Hoerni, one of Jung's grandsons and the member of the Jung family most responsible for the publication of the *Red Book*, started us out on the first full day of talks. Hoerni is the head of the Jung family's foundation, which was set up to oversee publication of Jung's unpublished works, and he has studied Jung's works deeply. Here, he relates the history and development of the *Red Book* project.

The keynote speaker was Paul Bishop, professor of German at the University of Glasgow and a well-known Jungian scholar and author. His essay discusses the relationship of Goethe, Schiller, and German Romanticism to reading the *Red Book*, revealing how Jung's language is amazingly similar to Goethe's in his epic *Faust*.

He was followed by Joseph Cambray, president of the IAAP and a much-published author in the Jungian world. His essay is a fascinating amplification of Jung's paintings from a dream of the radiolarian, a form of jelly fish, in relationship to the biological illustrations of Ernst Haeckel from the turn of the twentieth century. There is an amazing similarity between the Haeckel images of the radiolarian and Jung's mandala paintings from his dream.

The third lecture of the morning was delivered by Bou-Young Rhi, professor of psychiatry at Seoul National University, a Jungian analyst, and founder of the Jung Study Group in Korea. His essay discusses Korean shamanism and its relationship to the mandala symbolism in Jung.

In the afternoon, our first lecturer was Susan Thackrey, a former art gallery owner, historian, poet, and now a Jungian analyst in San Francisco. Her essay discusses and interprets much of the art that Jung painted for his *Red Book*. There are fifty-three full-page mandalas reproduced in the published *Red Book*.

The next speaker of the afternoon was Christine Maillard, professor of medieval philosophy in Strasbourg, France, and the translator of the *Red Book* into French. She is a leading expert on Jung and Gnosticism, and in her essay she speaks about Jung's *Seven Sermons to the Dead*, which had previously been published separately as an appendix to *Memories, Dreams, Reflections*.

148   *Introduction to first reflections*

The following morning the conference concluded with two presentations. George Hogenson, co-editor of these essays, presented imagery and literature from Western medieval philosophy, relating it to modern science. Hogenson has a PhD in philosophy and is a Jungian analyst in Chicago. His essay is complex, brilliantly written, and introduces the reader to many unfamiliar and esoteric names in Western philosophy.

The final speaker of the conference was John Beebe, a well-known Jungian analyst from San Francisco, who in his essay invokes the trickster archetype, comparing Jung's inner journey in the *Red Book* to Cervantes' famous figure of Don Quixote.

The conference was a truly memorable event with an overflow audience. All the participants have been waiting for over two years to read these papers. We hope this volume will reach an equally enthusiastic reading audience.

Note

1   "Introduction to First Reflections: Initial Responses to C. G. Jung's *Red Book (Liber Novus)*, Based on Essays Presented in San Francisco, 4–6 June 2010." In Thomas Kirsch and George Hogenson (eds), *The Red Book: Reflections on C.G. Jung's Liber Novus*, pp. 1–3. London: Routledge, 2013. Reprinted with the permission of the publisher.

Reference

Jung, C. G. (1963) *Memories, Dreams, Reflections*, recorded and ed. Aniela Jaffe. New York: Random House.

CHAPTER 19

A LIFELONG READING OF JUNG

From *How and Why We Still Read Jung: Personal and Professional Reflections*, edited by Jean Kirsch and Murray Stein, Routledge, 2013[1]

From the vantage point of age, Tom Kirsch shares his experience of first coming to and reading Jung, beginning in his late teens and then extending through the years of his early development as a Jungian analyst to the present, some fifty years later. His essay includes an impressive meeting with Jung himself as well as an account of his early encounters with some of Jung's written works. Just as, at the start of a personal analysis, the powerful images and affects of an initial dream may continue to reverberate for decades and become a living symbol in the psyche of the dreamer (a symbol that is never fully unpacked), so Kirsch's initial experience of reading Jung as a young man seems to go on living vividly within his psyche. [J. K.]

All my life I have been attracted to the study of Jung, yet have felt an equally strong resistance. I began reading him when I was 17 and have continued to do so for nearly sixty years. Growing up with two Jungian analysts, whose primary analyses were with Jung, he loomed as a larger than life figure in our household. My father, who had been educated in the classical European manner along with the Jewish tradition of study, spent many hours every day studying Jung's texts. My mother lacked a formal education beyond high school, but she, too, studied Jung intensely and respected the Jewish tradition of scholarship. Both parents expected that I would become a Jungian scholar and follow in my father's footsteps. While I could sense the importance of Jung for my parents and even for myself, their desire put me in conflict with my desire to belong in our Jewish neighbourhood of post-war Los Angeles and to become part of the American culture of the 1950s – a powerful lure for my extraverted, social, and athletic temperament. My father, especially, was distressed and disappointed by my interest in tennis and Hollywood musicals instead of opera and serious studies. I vividly remember driving along Sunset Boulevard through Beverly Hills with my dad in his 1949 silver Chrysler. I was 15 and not terribly interested in what he had to say. I still remember what he said on that ride: "You'll see! People will read Jung and appreciate him more fifty years from now!" Though I passed it off with "Yeah, Dad," his words have come back to me many times over the years.

My father read Jung avidly and asked Jung for copies of everything he wrote as soon as it was published; sometimes, and always with Jung's approval, he translated them from German in order to pass along the latest essay to his growing number of students in Los Angeles. The most significant example was his translation of "Answer to Job" (Jung, 1952/1958). Although he knew that the Bollingen Foundation had arranged for a translation of *The Collected Works* by R. F. C. Hull, he also knew about the time lag for Jung's other books to appear in English, and he considered

150   *A lifelong reading of Jung*

"Answer to Job" crucial at that moment, so he made a translation. Subsequently, there was some discussion about what should be done with it. Finally, the publisher decided to use Hull's translation for the sake of uniformity, with acknowledgement that my father's translation had been consulted. Actually, Hull and my father met for several days in Ascona, Switzerland, to go over the translation word by word. Still, my father was disappointed that he never got the recognition that he rightly deserved, but to his credit he did not make a fuss.

As *The Collected Works* were published in English, my father gave weekly seminars on all of Jung's alchemical texts. They were all recorded, with the expectation that one day I would transcribe, edit, and eventually publish the tapes. Alchemy was my father's love, not mine; studying and writing about alchemy is not a natural thing for me. So, for my own individuation I felt that I needed to put those tapes aside for someone else to attend to.

It was my mother who facilitated my first reading of Jung; in fact, she was the pivot for a major turning point in my life. In June 1953, I turned 17 and had just graduated from the American public school system. She had gone to Zurich in the early spring to analyse with C. A. Meier, not realizing the importance of those final months for an American teenager. Alone with my father and an older cousin, I had to face the anxieties of a high school senior without her guidance, and I became ill. She pushed me to return to Europe after graduation, to the place of my birth and to the spiritual center of my parents' psyches – Zurich, Switzerland. That summer I left Los Angeles with my father, mainly wanting to be united with her, not to see Europe. We travelled via New York, where we stopped to see my father's old friend Werner Engel, and thence to London, where we visited my mother's brother and his family. Then we travelled by train and boat from London to Paris, where we scoured the city on foot, eight hours a day, for a week. My father was indefatigable in his hunger for culture and desire to influence me! When at long last we arrived in Zurich, I found the warmth I had been missing desperately, especially after seeing war-torn London, where its population was still digging its way out of the rubble and where food was still in short supply. I was enormously relieved to be with my mother after five months with my father, who was not the most related of characters, for all his intellect and his caring for me. I took in the beauty of the Swiss landscape, along with her presence; ever since Switzerland has been a second home for me. The contrast with Los Angeles in the 1950s, with its glamour and reliance on the automobile, was striking. I appreciated the public transport system in Switzerland. More directly, I experienced a desire to immerse myself in European culture, which I had so strongly resisted, and I suddenly wanted to study the French and German languages. In this context, my mother gave me a book she thought would be a basic introduction to Jung: *Introduction to Jung's Psychology* by Frieda Fordham (1953). It was easy to read, and I still have the book, although nothing about it stands out in my mind. A week of travel south through war-torn Italy with my mother and my cousin Peter completed my introduction to the world of Jung and my parents' origins – or as close to their homeland, Germany, as they dared go emotionally or physically. Switzerland and Jung had become their homeland. After that trip, I was prepared for college and ready to read Jung seriously.

Shortly after returning to Los Angeles, I bought the first paperback edition of *Modern Man in Search of a Soul* (1933), which I carried to Reed College to read during my freshman year. In the dawning era of paperbacks, that was the one book of Jung's available in paperback for the cost of $1.35. I still have that book, too. What struck me about this reading was Jung's common sense, which appealed to me deeply. I knew that I wanted to study more of Jung from reading *Modern Man*. I hate to admit it, but at college I was a naïve and callow youth and had been puffed up by life in proximity to the movie industry. My father was the analyst of many well-known movie stars and studio executives, and it had been more than gratifying when my friends were blown away by the sight of one of them sitting in the dining room, which served as the waiting area for my parents' home offices. I was swept up by the importance of our lives in Los Angeles, and when I went to Reed College I had classmates who were from rural parts of the country. As a consequence, I bragged about my parents' connections and became known as a superficial, Southern California, Jewish smart-ass. Though it was painful, my classmates' reaction shocked me into a new level of self-realization. Ever since that painful college experience, I have been much more modest, inhibiting myself from speaking candidly, being specific, and elaborating my observations and reflections. I neither wanted to suffer more rejection, nor did I want to make my parents look bad.

The next important experience for me in reading Jung came three years later between my junior and senior years at Reed. Again, my parents were making their annual pilgrimage to Switzerland, but this time I went with them. In 1956, Scandinavian Airlines had opened their polar route from Los Angeles to Copenhagen, with stops in Winnipeg and Greenland. It was a twenty-four-hour journey. By this time, *Two Essays on Analytical Psychology* had been published in paperback (Jung, 1956). Throughout that night and day, to the constant drone of the plane's four engines, I read this seminal work. Jung's comprehensive view of the psyche, relating his own psychology to that of Freud and Adler, and also tracing his psychology back to the roots of psychoanalysis, made eminent sense to me. We travelled to Salzburg, Austria, where we attended five operas in five days, with chamber concerts in between. I heard Mozart and appreciated his music as never before. Later that summer, I had the opportunity to visit Jung with my father, who wanted to pay a call to express his condolences, for Emma Jung had died the previous winter. We sat in the garden beside the lake. Jung was subdued and in mourning.

One of Jung's statements in *Two Essays* was that "all knowledge was relative" (Jung, 1956). In my sophomoric way, I questioned Jung about that statement, asking him if that was not an absolute statement. I cannot remember his answer, but I do recall that I did not feel shamed or made to feel uncomfortable by his response. The curious thing is that in two recent readings that I have given this book in preparation for teaching I have not been able to find this statement. That idea itself does not mean too much to me now; I only look upon it as symbolic of my immaturity. In fact, talking to Jung and experiencing his quiet wisdom had a profound effect, especially having just read his work. Jung's depth of perspective, which for me was more a matter of his feeling for life than what he thought about it, made a deep impression on me and has shaped both my personal and professional development.

When I returned to Reed for my senior year, I was crammed with undigested experience, which I unloaded on my unsuspecting roommate, Bob Hertzberg, who to this day thanks me for opening his "Los Angeles frame of mind" to a world he has since explored for himself. I think that my entire life has centred around the assimilation and recapitulation of my experiences that summer in Europe. Reading Jung is my touchstone in that process.

Two years later, I was between my first year at Albert Einstein Medical School and about to transfer to Yale, where I ultimately graduated. That summer in 1958 I had an individual hour with Jung. My father was teaching at the Jung Institute in Zurich during the hour Jung had made available, and I was allowed to go in his stead. I was prepped by my Zurich analyst, C. A. Meier, about what would interest

152   *A lifelong reading of Jung*

Jung, who was then 83 years old. The growing circle of Jungian students and analysands in Zurich, well aware of Jung's importance to the world, felt it was their responsibility and privilege to assist his research by contributing material. At the time, Jung was working on his monograph on *Flying Saucers* (Jung, 1958/1968), and Meier helped me select dreams that might interest him. Jung cut through that veneer by announcing as we sat down, "So you want to see the old man before he dies!" I was totally taken aback by his directness, but over the years I have come to appreciate it.

Six years later I began my psychiatric residency and also began working with a Jungian analyst whom I chose, not one my parents had chosen. In the course of this analysis, it gradually became clear that I am an extraverted intuitive feeling type. I had grown up with the belief and expectation that my typology was introverted thinking intuitive, like Jung's. This realization came with a tremendous feeling of relief. I no longer had to be a Jungian scholar, which meant that I did not have to read everything in the Jungian literature. Since this time, reading Jung has been deeply embedded in my psyche, and even though I have never been able to judge how "deep" my reading is, I believe that I took Jung in from my inferior and profoundly unconscious side, that is, through my introverted thinking and sensation functions. My Jung lives inside me like a dark, swift underground river, accessible at any point of contact in time and place in the form in which I originally took it in. Reading Jung feels like an authentic part of my being. The result has been that I am often described, somewhat accusingly, as being a true-blue Jungian.

At the time of Jung's death in 1961, his alchemical writings had been translated and published by the Bollingen Foundation as his *Collected Works*. Many Jungians at that time did not read the alchemical texts but focused on his earlier work on psychotherapy and psychological types. Maybe, like me, they had not caught up with Jung's late-life developments and were still trying to absorb his earlier material. Maybe, again like me, they were caught up in collective movements of the era and needed also to become conversant in the dominant psychoanalytic theory and method if they were to gain legitimacy as psychotherapists or psychiatrists.

Apart from *The Collected Works*, two of Jung's books were published posthumously in the early 1960s, both of which proved to be popular and widely read. *Memories, Dreams, Reflections* (MDR), Jung's so-called autobiography, traced his inner life as related to Aniela Jaffé (Jung, 1961). The second book, *Man and his Symbols*, was a project initiated by John Freeman of the BBC, who had interviewed Jung in March 1959 for the television programme *Face to Face* (Jung and von Franz, 1964). The book, written by various authors, was assembled in order to meet the growing need for a general introduction to Jungian thought. Jung wrote an introductory chapter; the man who became my personal analyst, Dr. Joseph Henderson, also contributed a chapter. Both texts were especially meaningful to me and continue to hold their wider value. Jung's respect for and emphasis on the inner world in the face of increasingly extraverted societal norms has provided validation and a path to follow for those who seek to build a deeper and more meaningful way of life than is ordinarily modelled for us.

Of the many chapters in *Memories, Dreams, Reflections* that were personally meaningful, several stand out. In the first chapter, "Early Years," Jung recounts his earliest dream from age 4 in which he experiences the underground Phallus. That dream made a lifelong impression on me. The dream phallus was to Jung the underground god-not-to-be-named, and it was an affect/image that strongly influenced his development; he called it the source of his creativity. Reflecting on its impact on my developing relationship to the unconscious, I wonder whether

A lifelong reading of Jung   153

I had made a partial identification with Jung. His dream included the enigmatic statement by his mother, "Yes, just look at him. That is the man-eater!" (Jung, 1961, 12). At the age of 4, I, too, had had an encounter with the powerful forces of the unconscious as they were laid out before my young eyes. We lived near Hampstead Heath in London, where the sight of a downed fighter airplane or an unexploded bomb was not uncommon; air-raid sirens sounded at night, sending us to the basement of a local school, where I learned to sleep in a chair beside my mother, who always managed to make me feel safe there. My mother had mediated my experience of the war – an archetypal phenomenon, *par excellence* – and the impetus to study Jung and to become a Jungian analyst primarily came through her.

The chapters in *MDR* that Jung devotes to his choice of psychiatry as a profession and his relationship to Freud were especially significant to me. In the mid-1960s, when I first read it, I was just beginning my own career in psychiatry. The question that loomed for me was how was I going to find my place in contemporary psychiatry as a Jungian? Jung's work had been marginalized, and at that time there were few psychological or psychiatric training programs where Jung was considered worth teaching. To choose a Jungian training meant that, in many respects, I, too, would be marginalized, although people were also attracted to me because of my Jungian ideas. During my psychiatric residency at Stanford University Medical Center, I was specifically told by my professors that a Jungian identity would definitely limit the academic positions to which I might aspire. Since my primary identity up to then had been as a successful and academically competitive student, it was a source of great anxiety. Yet, after having accepted an important academic position at the National Institute of Mental Health, I finally turned it down to continue my personal analysis and pursue Jungian analytic training. That decision changed my life. Making the choice to become a clinical Jungian analyst meant, as it had for Jung, sacrificing all academic ambition. This had tremendous ramifications for my personal life as well, for my wife at the time, who was also a physician, did end up pursuing an academic career, which in many ways divided us.

An important chapter for me in *MDR* was Jung's account of the visionary experience in which he realized himself as a rabbi (Jung, 1961, 288–99). Jung had broken his leg in 1944 and subsequently had a heart attack and nearly died. His central vision, during this period of near death, of the Mystic Marriage in the Garden as it appears in the Kabbalistic tradition transformed him and seems to have erased any ambivalence he felt toward Jews in the aftermath of his relationship to Freud, whom he had seen as unwilling or incapable of realizing the mystery of numinous phenomena, which was central to his vision of spirituality. Although I was unable to understand the dimensions of meaning to which Jung pointed, I was able to grasp the significance of the event intuitively. It also fully satisfied my need, as a Jew, to make Jung acceptable. I had felt accepted as a Jew by Jung through my parents' feelings of his acceptance.

In 1963, after my first year of residency in psychiatry at Stanford, I began analytic training at the C. G. Jung Institute of San Francisco; reading Jung now was a requirement. My personal analyst Dr. Joseph Henderson gave the first seminar, and he chose to base it on a lecture that Jung had given in January 1934 at the Eidgenössische Technische Hochschule (ETH), the premier engineering university in Switzerland. Between 1933 and 1941, Jung gave lectures on psychology to engineering students; shorthand notes were made of the lectures, which were translated into English, privately printed, and distributed with Jung's approval among his English-speaking students.[2] In the lecture that Henderson discussed, Jung used a diagram to show and validate both sides of the psyche, the extraverted

154   *A lifelong reading of Jung*

and the introverted (Jung, 1959, 47). For me, this diagram and lecture affirmed my psychological type in a way that no other writing of Jung's had done, for I had always received the message that only the introverted life was worth living! There were very few extroverts in the Jungian world, and generally we were judged to be superficial and not really "Jungian".

When I was both a psychiatry resident and a candidate in analytic training, I read and reread *Two Essays on Analytical Psychology*. Even though it had been published as volume 7 of *The Collected Works* (Jung, 1953), I studied the paperback edition published in 1956. The text was discussed in an analytic training seminar offered by Dr. Mel Kettner, whose own life had been changed by the book. Mel reports that in 1953, on his way to a year of postgraduate work in a cardiology lab in Geneva, Switzerland, he accompanied a travelling companion on a visit to the Manhattan apartment of John Farrar, head of the publishing company, Farrar, Straus, & Young, Inc. Mr. Farrar began telling him about a most interesting book he had just read by a Swiss psychologist named Carl Jung, who thought that spiritual needs were as instinctual as the sexual. When Dr. Kettner showed interest and said he would buy a copy before he sailed, Mr. Farrar gave him the book, saying it was not yet available for sale since it was an advance copy. The book was *Two Essays on Analytical Psychology*, the second volume of Jung's writing to be published for the Bollingen Foundation by Pantheon Books (which then became volume 7 of *The Collected Works* when published by Princeton University Press). Reading this book during his Atlantic crossing struck a resonant chord and changed the course of his professional life and personal identity, for a year later he enrolled as a student in Zurich at the Jung Institute.[3]

Two Essays is a complex text and somewhat confusing. It is a book in four parts, with two main chapters – the essays – and two lengthy appendices. To read the appendices first and then the two essays makes great sense, for in that order one can see most clearly how Jung built his psychology. The first appendix, "New Paths in Psychology," was written in 1912 in German for a yearbook of Swiss art and culture and was later revised to become the first of the two essays. Here, one finds Jung most under the influence of Freud, explaining, by way of clinical examples, Freud's 1895 text *Studies in Hysteria*, written with Josef Breuer, in which they set forth their original trauma theory of neurosis. They later discarded this theory and followed it with the sexual theory of the origins of the symptoms. This, Jung proclaims, is real knowledge of the human soul required of the medical doctor who is called on to treat the psychological ills of his suffering patients. The second appendix, "The Structure of the Unconscious," is dramatically different in tone and content. It was written in German and translated into French for publication in *Archives de Psychologie* 16 (1916); since the original manuscript was no longer available, the English edition was translated from the French. During the period in which it was written, we know that Jung was still deeply engaged in making sense of his profound psychological experiences of 1913–14, which he described so compellingly in *Memories, Dreams, Reflections* in the chapter called "Confrontation with the Unconscious" (Jung, 1961, 170–99). Publication of Jung's *Red Book* (2009) has given us a wider perspective on this period of Jung's life. Here, we see Jung becoming Jung, making a clear distinction between the personal and the impersonal unconscious, elaborating the phenomena one may observe in the person who begins to connect with and assimilate material from the impersonal unconscious, introducing his hypothesis about the opposition and tension between the two levels of unconsciousness, describing the persona and its function, citing the negative effects of ways in which one may attempt to deal with an upsurge of

A lifelong reading of Jung 155

image and affect-laden material from the collective (impersonal) level of the psyche, and outlining his form of treatment, so that a synthetic solution may be found to one's internal conflict. Here, Jung is setting out to make his unique and powerful impact on the development of depth psychology.

The *Two Essays* proper are the result of several revisions of the originals, which Jung subsequently made; for a full understanding, reading the prefaces he wrote to each revision, also published in volume 7 of his *Collected Works* is worthwhile. The first essay, which he calls "The Psychology of the Unconscious", was most extensively revised in 1916, 1918, 1926, and 1942. In the first part of the essay, Jung adds a description of Adler's theory of the will to power and Freud's sexual theory. He then reflects upon the similarities and differences he sees between the two theories, or hypotheses, as he prefers to call them; in this essay, one may see the formulations that led to his later work on typology. In the last three sections of the first essay, he expands on his own hypotheses and methods.

The second essay, "The Relations Between the Ego and the Unconscious", is a 1934 revision of the original 1916 paper included in the appendices. He tells us in his preface that in its present form it represents an

> expression of a long-standing endeavour to grasp and – at least in its essential feature – to depict the strange character and course of ... the transformation process of the unconscious psyche. This idea of the independence of the unconscious, which distinguishes my views so radically from those of Freud, came to me as far back as 1902, when I was studying the psychic history of a young girl somnambulist.
>
> (Jung, 1956, p. 133)

This essay was an important aid to me in defining my own Jungian and psychiatric identity. It was an era when psychoanalytic theory and methods were the dominant influence in both the collective and the psychiatric worlds. I needed to be able to relate to my psychiatric colleagues and be conversant with their thinking, yet to do so from a Jungian perspective. Because these clinical languages were so different, I had, in a sense, to become bilingual. Through reading, I could see the value of other approaches and treat them respectfully. Also, I could recognize in Jung a man of independent thought, able and willing to assert his own vision in the face of strong cultural countercurrents.

Two Essays also is one of the few places in which Jung gives us a clear view of how he actually worked. In "The Synthetic or Constructive Method", section VI of the first essay, he describes his method, relates the patient's dream of a crab and her associations and gives us the causal-reductive interpretation that he does not give to the patient. He tells us why he did not offer his interpretation to her; he then demonstrates his own synthetic-constructive interpretation (Jung, 1956). In the next section, "Archetypes of the Collective Unconscious", he further amplifies the dream image and illustrates his way of drawing out and relating to his female patient's transference fantasies. This level of detail is rare for Jung, who seldom revealed so much of his analysand's personal history. I think this is because he simply was not interested in writing about that level of analytic work. His mission was to explore the archetypal psyche. My mission was to explore my own unconscious through my dreams and my work with my personal analyst. Reading Jung amplified my understanding of what I was discovering within.

One Sunday during my residency training, I sat down and spent the entire day reading "General Aspects of Dream Psychology" (Jung, 1960). At that time,

156 *A lifelong reading of Jung*

Freud's *Interpretation of Dreams*, first published in 1899, still dictated the standard interpretive treatment of dreams, which were basically seen as wish-fulfilments, with the unconscious operations of disguise and condensation producing the manifest content, the analysis of which invariably led to a reductive interpretation, designating an early infantile origin for the dream's latent content. Things were about to change in the San Francisco Bay Area, which was transformation central for a revolutionary new movement toward a humanistic approach to the psyche. Harry Wilmer (later to become a Jungian analyst) had brought a new model of treatment for mental disorders, which he had been introduced to by Maxwell Jones in the UK, to the therapeutic community at Oak Knoll Naval Hospital in Oakland. The National Institute of Mental Health had given a huge grant to nearby San Mateo County Hospital's psychiatry department to develop a model program for community mental health. The newly opened and beautifully designed Stanford Hospital and medical school, planted among the oak forests and golden hillsides of a vast ranch that had become Leland Stanford Junior University, was setting its sights on becoming one of the nation's leading research centers. Teaming with the San Mateo Hospital and the Palo Alto Veterans Hospital as training sites for its medical students and resident physicians, Stanford instituted the forward-thinking, democratic model of the therapeutic community in its mental health programmes. William Dement, whose pioneering work in EEG studies of sleep at the University of Chicago led to the discovery of the rapid-eye movement phase associated with dreaming, had joined its faculty. Timothy Leary and Richard Alpert, later to take the name Ram Dass, were doing their research on LSD in Stanford's psychology department. Ken Kesey was living at the edge of the Stanford campus, working at the Palo Alto Veterans Hospital, one of Stanford's sites for educating medical students and resident physicians, and writing his novel *One Flew over the Cuckoo's Nest*. Many of the psychiatry residents were experimenting with LSD and dipping into the wild affect-imagery of the collective unconscious without the benefit of any form of psychological guidance.

I discovered my own way of approaching the same material through my dreams and personal analysis, and this path was affirmed most dramatically the weekend when I read Jung's "General Aspects of Dream Psychology." That weekend my wife was on-call, which meant that she spent from Friday afternoon through Sunday evening at the hospital. I was serving on Stanford Hospital's small in-patient unit but was not on-call that weekend, and its staff, dedicated to the concept of the therapeutic community, had organized a party at someone's home that Saturday evening. I attended to join the group spirit that animated the unit and found myself becoming too intimate with one of the young nurses. I was probably slightly drunk when I left the party, feeling guilty. Maybe my decision to read Jung all the next day was my penance. I do remember having a lot of energy for the reading! I have no recollection of what dictated my choice of texts. Perhaps I chose it out of curiosity and the need to understand what was happening between me and my analyst, whose fearless and wide-ranging treatment of my dreams was so impressive and helpful. Having an analyst not chosen by my parents from among their intimate colleagues was a relief; I felt I was just getting started. I had been seeing him twice weekly for several months and wanted to see what Jung had to say about dreams. Perhaps it was synchronicity at work, guiding my hand to the one volume that would strike me most solidly at that moment, for soon I was personally and profoundly engaged and felt as though Jung were speaking directly to me. Imagine my shock when Jung began to analyse a dream that reflected in its imagery and affect the inner situation of a young man who was guilt-filled over an illicit erotic encounter! Jung analysed it by Freud's causal method of interpretation and introduced his own additional (but not to be substituted for the causal) final method, which asks us to consider to what purpose the dreamer produces a dream.

> All psychological phenomena have some such sense of purpose inherent in them, even merely reactive phenomena like emotional reactions. Anger over an insult has its purpose in revenge; the purpose of ostentatious mourning is to arouse the sympathy of others, and so on.
>
> (Jung, 1960, para 456)

And the purpose of being drawn by Eros? I was edified by Jung's lengthy elaboration of my inner status. The apropos nature of this text impressed its content and meaning indelibly on my mind. I *knew* now what Jung meant by the symbol and the compensatory function of the dream. I *knew* what he meant when he said that the dream contains the subliminal material of a given moment and grasped his formulation of its purposive impulse. Intuitively, I *knew* what Jung meant when he said that the whole situation of the dreamer needs to be taken into account to make an adequate interpretation. I *understood* what it meant to differentiate the conscious realization of a psychological fact from its fully conscious integration through direct personal experience.

As Jung wound toward the conclusion of his essay on dreams he reflected on the criticism that he had received for venturing into material that he was told was not the purview of the psychologist, but belonged to the philosopher or theologian. He responded:

> If the patient's view of the world becomes a psychological problem, we have to treat it regardless of whether philosophy pertains to psychology or not. Similarly, religious questions are primarily psychological questions so far as we are concerned.
>
> (Jung, 1960, para 526)

Jung went on to say that medical doctors were least apt to understand his psychology, for they were trained to act, not think, and would not understand his ideas or his methods. True as this was for most doctors, at the time I first read this I had the opposite problem. From childhood, I was on intimate terms with Jung's psychology, so I had no trouble with his basic ideas, which had been a subtle part of what shaped my mind; rather, I had struggled to adapt to the expectations of my medical education and often wondered whether it was worth my while to learn all that I had to learn, when I knew, more or less from the beginning, that I wanted to become a Jungian analyst. So, although what Jung said struck me as true of the medical profession, I saw promising signs in the kind of psychiatry I was being taught in the liberal era of the 1960s and 1970s. However, the direction in which psychiatry was headed abruptly shifted in the political climate of the late 1970s and 1980s and, subsequently, with the development of powerful psychoactive medications and the phenomenal rise of the psychopharmacology industry. What Jung observed of psychiatry (what he called *medical psychology*) in 1948, the date of his most recent revision of this essay, is even more true today, when any form of psychotherapy is eschewed in favor of a prescription.

In retrospect, though, I am grateful for two aspects of my medical education that set me apart from my nonmedical Jungian colleagues and gave me a solid foundation from which I still approach each patient in every encounter. First, I developed a

158 *A lifelong reading of Jung*

clinical attitude. This is a subtle attribute and not easy to describe. Through learning the patterns in which the doctor approaches his or her patient, carefully listening and observing during the process of obtaining a history of the presenting problem "as if" a physical exam were to be the culmination of the encounter, I developed habits of appraising the whole person and the presenting problem that I believe are unique to the physician. Recently, I had occasion to be examined by a senior physician in one of the medical specialties, who had a young medical student at his side; I smiled inwardly as I listened to his careful explanation of my physical condition as revealed by a CT scan, illuminated on the computer monitor before all three of us, as he pressed his stethoscope to my body and urged her to listen here, compared to there, preparing her to recognize by physical examination alone what was visible on the screen. He was inculcating in her a particular attitude, a stance toward the human organism, which will become so deeply integrated into her personality that she will, over time, be transformed into a doctor. It is this imperceptible function for which I am grateful, this way of apprehending and perceiving, with which I appraise the patient's well-being or non-well-being. Quietly, it was integrated into me and became second nature to my being.

The second is the ability to look at death. A medical student's first patient is a cadaver to be dissected over the course of the first year of medical training. The memory of that single individual who surrendered his or her body for my education is indelible, and it was the first of many opportunities to know the reality of death and dying, to observe the way in which people died and the reactions of those around them, to listen carefully to the ways in which my teachers related to the dying person and the family members, and to participate, assuming some of the responsibilities attending the event on my own. I could easily recognize those among my teachers whose abilities I wanted to emulate and make part of my own character, and I am grateful for their capacity to allow me to align myself with them and thus acquire those attributes for myself. This familiarity with death lends gravitas to the serious business of inviting the approach of other human beings for my participation in their intimate emotional lives.

Of course, the personally directed meanings that filled me on that Sunday afternoon were submerged in the course of time, but not before setting me straight, outwardly as well as psychologically, along the Jungian path. I felt I neither needed LSD to explore the unconscious, nor required further sexual experimentation to know that side of my shadow. (I also knew I did not want to be like my dad, whose protracted self-discovery through Eros had been the source of so much pain in my family.) I did, however, become an enthusiast for the inner way of self-realization. I began to proselytize for Jung like crazy and got myself into trouble. Stanford was aimed at medical science and research and here were all these students and psychiatry residents taking LSD and clamouring instead for Jungian analysis! Little did any of us know that our education was coincident with the first stirrings of a cultural revolution. The early 1960s was a very interesting time to be in the Bay Area. My whole situation fitted together like two halves of a seed that weekend, my outer experience of partying on Saturday and then drawing back from outer enactment to read all day on Sunday, paired with my inner experience of temptation/guilt and my conscious realization of the power of the unconscious. Subsequently, I have taught Jung's essay "General Aspects of Dream Psychology" in many venues and still believe that it retains its freshness for every reading. It is one of Jung's clearest, most straightforward and least equivocal texts.

Reading Jung deeply and why we do so are the primary questions raised by the editors of this book. The short answer is a resounding yes – we do need to read

Jung deeply now because his message is more relevant today than when he was writing in the first half of the twentieth century. What my father told me when I was a teenager about his importance has proved true. My father was a difficult man to be around because he followed his own wishes without much consideration for the rest of his family. In the 1950s, Freud and psychoanalysis were at the peak of their influence, and many believed that through psychoanalysis the world's problems would be solved. Jung's concepts of complex, archetypes, collective unconscious, individuation, and synchronicity were poorly understood, whereas his psychological type theory had taken hold and introvert and extrovert had become part of everyday language. Generally, Jung was seen as a "woolly mystic" and more or less a kind of guru figure, a description that, from personal experience, I knew that he rejected!

Over the past half century many of the issues that Jung raised have become much more relevant. His interest in the religious experience, the numinous, and transcendence as it was expressed in different cultures led him on broad explorations. He was the first modern psychologist to study Oriental philosophies, having been invited in 1928 by the German sinologist, Richard Wilhelm, to comment on his translation of *The Secret of the Golden Flower*, an ancient Chinese alchemical text (Jung, 1967). The publication of Wilhelm's translation of the *I Ching or Book of Changes*, a 3,000-year-old Taoist philosophical treatise, by the Bollingen Foundation in 1950, with a lengthy introduction written by Jung, was a landmark that allowed this ancient text of wisdom to have an increasing influence in the West.

Modern man is *still* in search of soul food, as I am reminded daily in my clinical work. It is increasingly the task of individuals buffeted by the world of technology and our contemporary culture of instant communication, with its sense of *anomie*, a term borrowed from anthropology and sociology that describes our growing sense of alienation. Our traditional religions no longer contain the spiritual urges that are a natural part of the human psyche, and we are tempted by the media to substitute its opposite, materialism, whose value is fleeting and always demanding of greater novelty and excess. But it cannot last. Our search for meaning will always find a voice and Jung's psychology, developed out of his own courageous exploration into the depths of his psyche, can help us in our quest for a deeper understanding and wisdom. This is why I think his oeuvre has become essential for us to read and assimilate. I offer my own early experience with the hope that another beginner might find that following in my footsteps provides him or her with assistance into some of Jung's most accessible work.

Notes

1 "A Lifelong Reading of Jung." In Jean Kirsch and Murray Stein (eds), *How and Why We Still Read Jung: Personal and Professional Reflections,* pp. 195–209. Hove, UK: Routledge, 2013. Reprinted with the permission of the publisher.
2 These lectures will be republished by the Philemon Foundation.
3 I am indebted to my friend and colleague, Mel, for sharing the details of his story, which will appear in the memoir he is preparing for publication.

References

Fordham, Frieda (1953) *Introduction to Jung's Psychology.* London: Pelican Books.
Freud, Sigmund (1899/1961) *The Interpretation of Dreams.* Standard Edition of the Complete Psychological Works of Sigmund Freud, trans. James Strachey. London: Hogarth Press.

160 *A lifelong reading of Jung*

Freud, Sigmund and Breuer, Josef (1895) *Studies in Hysteria.* Standard Edition of the Complete Psychological Works of Sigmund Freud, vol. 2. London: Hogarth Press.

Jung, C. G. (1933) *Modern Man in Search of a Soul.* New York: Harcourt, Brace.

Jung, C. J. (1952/1958) Answer to Job. In *Psychology and Religion: West and East.* Collected Works, vol. 11. Princeton, NJ: Princeton University Press, pp. 355–470.

Jung, C. G. (1953) *Two Essays on Analytical Psychology.* Collected Works, vol. 7. New York: Pantheon Books for the Bollingen Foundation.

Jung, C. G. (1956) *Two Essays on Analytical Psychology.* New York: Meridian Books.

Jung, C. G. (1958/1968) Flying Saucers: A Modern Myth of Things Seen in the Skies. In *Civilization in Transition.* Collected Works, vol. 10, trans. R. F. C. Hull. Princeton, NJ: Princeton University Press.

Jung, C. G. (1959) Notes on Lectures Given at the Eidgenössische Technische Hochschule, Zurich, by Prof. Dr C. G. Jung, October 1933 to July 1935. In *Modern Psychology*, vols. 1 and 2. 2nd ed. Zurich: C. G. Jung Institute, p. 47.

Jung, C. G. (1960) General Aspects of Dream Psychology. In *The Structure and Dynamics of the Psyche.* Collected Works, vol. 8. New York: Pantheon Books for Bollingen Foundation, pp. 237–81.

Jung, C. G. (1961) *Memories, Dreams, Reflections*, recorded and ed. Aniela Jaffé, trans. Richard and Clara Winston. New York: Pantheon Books.

Jung, C. G. (1967) Commentary on the *Secret of the Golden Flower.* In *Alchemical Studies.* Collected Works, vol. 13. Princeton, NJ: Princeton University Press, pp. 1–56.

Jung, C. G. (2009) *The Red Book: Liber Novus*, ed. Sonu Shamdasani, New York: W. W. Norton & Co.

Jung, C. G., and von Franz, M.-L. (eds) (1964) *Man and his Symbols.* Garden City, NJ: Doubleday.

Kesey, Ken (1962) *One Flew over the Cuckoo's Nest.* New York, Viking Press.

Wilhelm, Richard (1950) *I Ching or Book of Changes*, with an Introduction by C. G. Jung, Princeton, NJ: Princeton University Press for the Bollingen Foundation.

CHAPTER 20

JUNG'S RELATIONSHIP WITH JEWS AND JUDAISM

From *Analysis and Activism: Political Contributions of Jungian Psychology,*
edited by Emilija Kiehl, Mark Saban, and Andrew Samuels, Routledge, 2016[1]

This chapter is about Jung and his relationship to Jews and Judaism. This topic has stuck to me like glue from childhood through the present, and I am now 80 years old. Basically I have had to defend Jung on too many occasions to remember, and at the same time my views on Jung's relationship to Jews has evolved over these many years.

My father was one of the first Jews to consult Jung after the breakup between Freud and Jung in 1913. James Kirsch, a psychiatrist practicing in Berlin, came from an Orthodox and entirely materialistic Jewish family, and he was looking for something meaningful and spiritual to enrich his life. He also had personal neuroses that demanded attention. After two years of Freudian analysis and a Jungian analysis in Berlin, he sought out Jung in 1928. He began his analysis with Jung in May 1929 when he went to Zurich for two months. In 1930, he gave a lecture at the Jung club in Zurich on the dream symbols of his Jewish patients (Jung and Kirsch, 2016). Many of his patients already had dream images of Nazi thugs. His lecture was so popular that it was given twice, and both Jung and his wife Emma attended. My father decided to leave Germany in 1933, advising his family and all his Jewish patients to leave, because he believed what Hitler had written in *Mein Kampf* (2013),[2] which was that he wanted to kill all German Jews. He emigrated to Tel Aviv, where he was living when he read *The State of Psychotherapy Today*, in which Jung outlined the differences between Jewish psychology and Aryan psychology (Jung, 1934). Jung's description of Jews needing a "host culture" to thrive was similar to Nazi propaganda about the Jews being parasitic and needing a "host culture." These statements by Jung gave credence to what Freud had already written in 1914 in *The History of the Psychoanalytic Movement* – that Jung had temporarily given up his anti-Semitic prejudices to join the psychoanalysis movement, but that he had reverted to his anti-Semitic feelings after leaving it. Ever since, Jung has been labelled "anti-Semitic" by many critics (e.g. Kuriloff, 2013). This has especially been true in America, where Jung has been reviled in psychoanalytic institutes. A psychoanalytic friend reports that in her training she was taught to consider Jung's name as poison, and until we became friends and colleagues she, like so many other psychoanalysts, had never considered actually reading Jung. One of my colleagues arranged for her to meet with Joe Henderson, a leading Jungian analyst in the United States, and she found the meeting meaningful.

After my father's death in 1989, I discovered his extensive correspondence with Jung, in which my father questioned Jung's relationship to Jews and was aghast when he read what Jung had said about the Jews needing a "host culture." He also questioned Jung about his affiliation with the Nazis and asked whether he had become a Nazi. Jung answered him strongly to say that all those rumors were untrue, for in fact he was trying to save German psychotherapy from the Nazi regime and to ensure that Jews would be allowed to participate in the renamed "International General Medical Psychotherapy Association" as individual members. I think the fact that Jung had even deigned to work with the Nazis during the 1930s was enough to label him a Nazi! Jung's stance was a very Swiss kind of action. The Swiss idea is to work with the enemy in order to find a compromise. It is why Switzerland has a reputation for neutrality and so many international meetings take place there. Jung answered my father fully to state that he was definitely not anti-Semitic, and that he got along well with the Jewish colleagues who had been drawn to him. This satisfied my father at the time, but upon reading Jung's answer today, it would not satisfy most people. Jung's answer would be seen as racist. He did go on to say that Jews were too sensitive, however, and that any personal criticism was too easily and quickly generalized as an anti-Jewish statement. Jung ended by saying:

> In general, you really ought to know me well enough not to attribute to me uncritically a non-individual stupidity like anti-Semitism. You know well enough to what extent I approach each person as a personality, whom I endeavor to lift out of the collective conditioning and make into an individual.
>
> (Jung and Kirsch, 2011, p. 47)

At the end of the letter he becomes a little defensive, saying that if necessary he will provide letters from sworn witnesses who will attest to the truth of his statements.

My mother, who came from an assimilated professional Jewish family in Berlin and had not known much about her Jewish roots, began her analysis with Jung in 1935. For the rest of her life she often said that Jung had helped her to connect with her Jewish origins and to her Jewish soul.

My parents ended up in Los Angeles at the end of 1940 after their circuitous journey leaving Nazi Germany, with intermediate stops in Tel Aviv and London. They began the Jungian community in Los Angeles. In the 1940s, relations between the Freudians and Jungians were ice cold. When my father gave a talk in public at a well-known hospital, the Freudians in the audience left the room. My father had no love for the Freudians either, so my first experience of the Freud/Jung debate and Jung's anti-Semitism was seen through the eyes of my parents. I sided with them and shared their idealized view of Jung. For years, I continued to share their view of Jung and rejected completely the notion that Jung was anti-Semitic. Only later was I able to differentiate my thinking from theirs, but I continued to defend Jung because the attacks on him were often so fantastical and based on very little fact. I attempted to bring facts about Jung into the picture.

This idealization of Jung continued through my college and medical school years and was reinforced by three meetings with Jung when I was in my early twenties. The first was in 1955 at his 80th birthday celebration when I was introduced to him and experienced the warmth of his handshake. For many years, I thought that my reaction to the handshake was pure transference, but then at the Red Book Conference at the Library of Congress in Washington, DC in 2010, I heard that one of Jung's grandsons had a similar reaction to a handshake with his grandfather. Yes, there was transference, but there was also something special about Jung's handshake. In 1956, after the death of Jung's wife, Emma, my father and I went to his home in Küsnacht, where we sat in the garden to have tea. By then I had read *Two Essays on Analytical Psychology* (Jung, 1953a) and questioned him about some matters written in those pieces. In retrospect, I was sophomoric but he was non-defensive and straightforward. I asked him about his statement that "all knowledge was relative"; but I thought that was an absolute statement. I cannot remember how he answered me. What is interesting is that I have never been able to find that statement in *Two Essays!* He made a tremendously positive impression on me. Then in 1958 I had an individual hour with him, which was even more powerful. His opening remark to me was "So you want to see the old man before he dies!" I was completely taken aback, but of course it was true. He was direct, personal, and absolutely friendly. This encounter solidified my desire to become a Jungian analyst. I mention these encounters with Jung because they had a huge impact on me and eventually settled the issue for me to become a Jungian analyst. It was perhaps the most significant vocational experience of my life and so it has been difficult for me to hear some of the criticism that has been thrown about. It does not coincide with my own personal experience. I might add that I have had similar warm experiences with Jung's son and grandsons. His grandson Andreas and his wife, Vreni Jung, are exceptional people, and we have developed a real friendship.

Even though my own attitudes toward Jung remained positive, I heard persistent comments that Jung was a Nazi and an anti-Semite. I defended Jung by stating that my Jewish parents were in analysis with Jung during the time that Jung was supposedly most anti-Semitic, and they never felt a trace of it, and I knew many other Jewish patients of Jung who had similar feelings; this silenced some of his detractors but did not satisfy most.

The first person within the Jungian community to do research with regard to the anti-Semitic question was Andrew Samuels. He demonstrated Jung's shadowy relationship to the Nazis and found statements that could be read as anti-Semitic. Samuels (1993) has researched the history of writings on racial differences and has shown that Jung's writing style and phraseology is similar to some of the early racist writers in Germany (pp. 283–312). Whether these connections were conscious, or what we might today recognize as an implicit influence, is a question that cannot be answered at this moment. It is unlikely that this question will ever be resolved definitely. The important thing is that Samuels' research opened up the question of Jung's anti-Semitism to the larger Jungian community. It was no longer coming solely from the Freudian camp, but from within our own community. Jungians then began to research this question, and now we have many interpretations of Jung's behavior from the 1930s. No one has found a "smoking gun," so to speak, and it has become quite difficult to pinpoint Jung's position on this most sensitive subject, which has influenced his acceptance in many places, especially the United States, where over the last several years Jungian scholars and analysts have undertaken to enlarge upon this subject. For example, there is Jay Sherry, who in his book *Carl Gustav Jung: Avant-Garde Conservative* (2010) claims to have the definitive word on Jung's relationship to Jews! Sherry has much interesting new information about Jung, but in my opinion, it is in no way definitive. New material on the subject has come out since his book, which gives a different picture, including the Jung–James Kirsch correspondence and, more recently, the Jung–Neumann correspondence. The Italian scholar Giovanni Sorge's yet-unpublished thesis on Jung in the 1930s includes what Jung did to help individual Jews get out of Nazi Europe. Sorge's material is more up to date and shows a more sympathetic side of Jung's attitude towards Jews. In his doctoral thesis, he has cited many letters Jung wrote on behalf of individual Jews to aid their escape from Nazi threats in the 1930s; for instance, he wrote a letter of recommendation for my father, which enabled him to enter the United Kingdom and practice as a Jungian analyst.

164 *Jung's relationship with Jews and Judaism*

Jung was fascinated by what was going on in Germany in the early 1930s. Initially, he had great hopes that Germany would recover from the awful economic inflation and social chaos that decimated German society after World War I. But, by 1935, Jung had definitely diagnosed Germany's collective psychosis. In Lecture V of the Tavistock Lectures, he speaks about the power of the collective unconscious to infect the psyche and how he himself, when he went to Germany, was similarly infected:

> It gets you below the belt and not in your mind, your brain counts for nothing, your sympathetic system is gripped ... And because it is an archetype, it has historical aspects, and we cannot understand the events without knowing history.

(Jung, 1935, para 372)

He states that there is no way to reason with people gripped by this phenomenon. One just has to accept the collective explosion. In light of our greater awareness today of the destructive power of such collective phenomena, I disagree with Jung's conclusion. We cannot just accept the collective explosion.

In 1962 I began my psychiatric residency. I was immediately identified as a Jungian, and although I was personally respected and generally liked, my being a Jungian held me back from receiving recognition in my training program. So often I have been asked how could I be Jewish and a Jungian – as if the two were incompatible. Jung is still generally not accepted in the psychiatric and psychological field, and Jung's statements about "Jewish psychology" in the 1930s still play a large part in his non-acceptance. The professional stance toward Jung has gradually changed and become more positive as his views on the role of religious experience and spirituality have become more acceptable. At the same time Freud's influence has waned as the neuroscientific study of the brain has gained in prominence. I like Jung's approach to the psyche, and personally, he was most gracious to me. I know that there are many interpretations of Jung's behavior in the 1930s, and I do believe that he made a grave mistake in writing about Jews needing a "host culture." He realized that after World War II, and privately he apologized to his Jewish colleagues about his writings on Jewish psychology in the 1930s. He never made a public statement on the subject, which many of his Jewish followers wanted him to do. He thought that it would be seen as defensive. Instead, he let his Jewish students do the speaking for him. I also recognize that, in 1934, when my father was living in Palestine and wrote about the changes he witnessed there, Jung wrote back optimistically about the opportunity for Jews to develop their own culture. So even in the 1930s Jung was open to Jewish psychology being grounded in new roots and removed from its 2000-year history in Europe.

Another place where Jung speaks about his relationship to Jews and Judaism is in an interview that he did with the psychoanalyst Kurt Eissler on August 29, 1953 (Jung, 1953b). Eissler wanted to know about Jung's relationship to Freud. He had never agreed before to speak about Freud, but at age 78, he was candid about Freud and also about Jewish psychology. One interesting observation was about Martha Bernays, Freud's wife, as having been "extinguished, without an ego." Both he and Emma, according to the interview, found that Martha Bernays had no idea what Freud was up to with the creation of psychoanalysis. Her role was attending to the children and the household. Jung thought this role was common for women in general, but especially for Jewish women of that era. In order to compensate for that lack of ego "many of them are so loud, aren't they ... but please do not think that this is anti-Semitism!" Eissler agrees with Jung that this is not anti-Semitism and adds "the position of women in Judaism is very unique, and they really come up short." Jung responds, "I have treated a great many of them, very many Jewish women – in all these women there is a loss of individuality, either too much or too little. But the compensation is always for the lack. That is to say ... not the right attitude." Jung states that Jewish men have always been the brides of Yahweh, which means that the women are obsolete. Therefore, Freud was only occupied with the father. Jung never developed this line of thinking about Jews further, but it is an interesting and controversial statement about Jewish psychology. I am sure many people would see this as anti-Semitic, but Jung saw it as a clinical observation. As Jung said, he had many Jewish patients, including my mother and father, so this was not just a throwaway comment.

Jung's most profound experience of Judaism came in 1944 after he broke his foot and then had a heart attack. He lived between life and death for several weeks and had the following vision, which he describes in *Memories, Dreams, Reflections* (Jung, 1961). His nurse became an old Jewish woman who was preparing kosher dishes for him. Jung himself was in the *Pardes Rimmonium*, the garden of pomegranates, and the wedding of Tifereth and Malchuth was taking place. Jung was Rabbi Simon Ben Yochai, whose wedding in the afterlife was being celebrated. It was the mystic marriage as it appears in the Kabbalistic tradition. Other marriages followed, including the Marriage of the Lamb and then the marriage of Zeus and Hera as described in *The Iliad*. Jung had a prolonged recovery from this illness and basically retired from his clinical practice. He did see old patients from time to time, but spent most of his final fifteen years writing. In his writings, he now referred to Jewish mystical sources with great frequency as he had experienced the mystical tradition in his 1944 vision. So a profound change had occurred in Jung's psyche toward Judaism.

Notes

1 "Jung's Relationship to Jews and Judaism," in *Analysis and Activism: Political Contributions of Jungian Psychology,* edited by Emilija Kiehl, Mark Saban, and Andrew Samuels, London: Routledge: 2016. Reprinted with the permission of the publisher.
2 The British edition of *Mein Kampf* was published in 1939.

References

Hitler, A. (2013) *Mein Kampf,* trans. J. Murphy. Camarillo, CA: Elite Minds, Inc.
Jung, C. G. (1934) *The State of Psychotherapy Today.* Collected Works, vol. 10. Princeton, NJ: Princeton University Press.
Jung, C. G. (1935) *The Tavistock Lectures.* Collected Works, vol. 18. Princeton, NJ: Princeton University Press.
Jung, C. G. (1953a) *Two Essays on Analytical Psychology.* Collected Works, vol. 7. Princeton, NJ: Princeton University Press.
Jung, C. G. (1953b) Interview by Kurt Eissler with Jung on Freud, Aug. 29. Washington, DC: Library of Congress.
Jung, C. G. (1961) *Memories, Dreams, Reflections.* New York: Random House.
Jung, C. G., and Kirsch, James (ed.) (2011) *The Jung–Kirsch Letters: The Correspondence of C. G. Jung and James Kirsch,* ed. A. C. Lammers, trans. U. Egli and A. C. Lammers. London: Routledge.

166 *Jung's relationship with Jews and Judaism*

Jung, C. G., and Kirsch, James (ed.) (2016) *The Jung–Kirsch Letters: The Correspondence of C. G. Jung and James Kirsch*, ed. A. C. Lammers, revised edn, trans. U. Egli and A. C. Lammers. London: Routledge.

Kuriloff, E. (2013) *Contemporary Psychoanalysis and the Legacy of the Third Reich*. New York: Routledge.

Samuels, A. (1993) *The Political Psyche*. London: Routledge.

Sherry, J. (2010) *Carl Gustav Jung: Avant-Garde Conservative*. New York: Palgrave Macmillan.

INDEX

academia, application of Jung's theories 127
accreditation 52; *see also* training; training
   analysis
Adams, H. 106
Adler, G. 11, 14, 15, 36, 37, 61
ages, of analyst and clients 17
alchemy 49, 95, 126, 146–7, 150
Alexander, F.G. 83
Alpert, R. 156
analysis: length of 97; reactions to 71
analytic neutrality 85
analytic-reductive view 13
analytical psychology: use of term 96; *see
   also* history of analytical psychology
Analytical Psychology Club, Los Angeles
   59, 96
Analytical Psychology Club, New York 55,
   75, 96, 110
Analytical Psychology Club, San Francisco
   57, 96, 110
Analytical Psychology Club, UK 61, 96
Analytical Psychology Club, Zurich 41–2,
   50, 96
Analytical Psychology Clubs, importance of
   96–7
"Ancient Myths and Modern Man"
   (Henderson) 112–13
anima/animus 7–8; Wolff-Kirsch
   correspondence 43
anti-Semitism 29–30, 64, 81–3, 84–6,
   142–3, 161–2; research into 163; *see
   also* Jews; Judaism
archetypal images 88
archetypal psychology 136
archetype of initiation 23
archetypes 79; and culture 116; Henderson,
   J.L. on 114–15; meaning of 1–2
"Archetypes of the Collective Unconscious"
   155
archisleep 3

Archive for Research in Archetypal
   Symbolism (ARAS) 56, 116, 117
Association for Analytical Psychology 50
Association of Analytical Clinical
   Psychologists 57
Association of Graduate Analytical
   Psychologists of the C.G. Jung Institute of
   Zurich 98
Association of Jungian Analysts (AJA) 61, 62
Aumüller, A. 72

Baynes, C. 107
Baynes, H.G. 33, 60, 61, 107
Beebe, J. 95, 148
being a Jungian 66–7
Bernays, M. 164–5
Bernhard, E. 36, 65
Bertine, E. 55, 71
Binswanger, L. 48
Bishop, P. 147
Bitter, W. 64
Bleuler, E. 47
Bollingen Foundation 29, 55–6
Bollingen Tower 48
Boss, M. 112–13
Bou-Young, R. 147
boundary issues 90–1, 144
Breuer, J. 80, 154
British Association for Psychotherapy (BAP)
   61–2
British Confederation of Psychotherapists 62
Buber, M. 44
Bugler, K. 63, 64, 123, 124
Burghölzli Clinic 47, 48, 50

Cambray, J. 147
Campbell, J. 136
Canada 60
candidate evaluation 91
candidate quality 78

168   Index

Carl Gustav Jung: Avant-Garde Conservative (Sherry) 163
Casement, A. 94
cat studies, REM research 3, 4
catharsis 13
C.G. Jung Foundation 56–7, 72, 75
C.G. Jung Institute, San Francisco 58–9, 117
C.G. Jung Institute, Stuttgart 64
C.G. Jung Institute, Zurich 49, 51–4, 89, 96, 97–9, 133–4, 136
C.G. Jung Society, Berlin 63
C.G. Jung Society, San Francisco 57
children 2, 4; *see also* neonates
Christianity 57–8
classical model 34, 90, 130, 136
Clinic and Research Center for Jungian Psychology, dream research 4
clinical boundaries 53
clinical examples 9–11
Cold War 133
collective psychosis, Germany 164
collective responsibility, and individuality 23–4
collective unconscious 2, 88
complex, use of term 79
confession 13
"Confrontation with the Unconscious" 96
context, assumption of 79
control analysts 26
Council of American Societies of Jungian Analysts (CASJA) 60
Council of North American Societies of Jungian Analysts (CNASJA) 60
counterprojection 15
countertransference 15; Freud-Jung relationship 30; Jungian analysis 32; training analysis 24–5, 27, 89
Crowther, C. 66
cultural, use of term 79
Cultural Attitudes in Psychological Perspective (Henderson) 115–16
cultural complexes: anti-Semitism 81–3, 84–6; author's history 83–7; as contaminants 83; context and overview 79–80; denial 83–4; developments in Freudian and Jungian schools 81–2; effects of 83–7; emotional reactivity 84; Freud-Jung schism 81; initial relationship between Jung and Freud 81; International Association for the History of Psychanalysis, conference 2000 85–6; Jung's critique of Freud 85; modes of expression 83–4; origins of 83; role of unconscious 86–7; *see also* Freud-Jung relationship
cultural shift 85

death 158
Dement, W. 1, 3–4, 156
developmental model 98–9, 130, 135, 136
dialectical method 7, 13–14; training analysis 90
diaspora: context and overview 36; major figures 37–9
Dieckmann, H. 123
disillusionment 71
dream deprivation 3
dreams: children 2, 4; effect of drugs 3; quality of 4; study of images 96; training analysis 89; *see also* REM research
drugs, effect on dreaming 3

ecstatic experience 131
Edinger, E. 59; interview 69–78; photo **69**
education 13–14
ego-consciousness, in dreams 4–5
ego psychology 130
Eidgenosse Technische Hochschule (ETH) 51, 89, 100–1, 153–4
Eissler, K. 164–5
Ellenberger, H. 31
Ellis, E. 107
elucidation 13
endings 17–18; training analysis 27
England 33–4
Eranos conferences 95–6
Erbengemeinschaft C.G. Jung 100
estate trust 100
Europe, training guidelines 90
extraversion, energy flow 8

Family Matters paper: author background 29; changes 34–5; context and overview 29; England 33–4; Freud-Jung relationship 30–2; Jungian analysis compared to Freudian model 32–3; post-World War I 32; professional associations 34; United States 34
fascism 37
feeling 8
Fenichel, O. 38–9
Ferenczi, S. 85
50th anniversary: 1962 as pivotal year 135; author's history 133–5; context and overview 133; Jung as fashionable 136; locations and spread 137–8; reactions to Jung's work 134–5; summary and conclusions 138
Flying Saucers 152
Fordham, M. 22, 24, 25, 27, 32, 33–4, 37, 51, 61–2, 92, 98, 134
France, history of analytical psychology 66
Freeman, J. 30, 152

Freud-Jung relationship 30–3; beginnings 48; break-up 48–9; England 33–4; nature of differences 54–5; understanding 47; *see also* cultural complexes

Freud-Jung schism 29–30, 81, 146–7

Freud, S. 154, 161; archaic remnants 1, 3; background 30, 80; criticism of 85; denunciation of Jung 50; extent of influence 133; infantile psyche 14; influences 47; Jung's critique 85; meeting Jung 48; ownership of psychoanalysis 94; unconscious 2; visit to US 54–5

Freudian analysis, compared to Jungian 32–3

Froebe-Kapteyn, O. 56

Fromm, E. 135

function types 8

furniture, use of 15

"General Aspects of Dream Psychology" 155–7

General Medical Society for Psychotherapy, Germany 63–4

German Association of Jungian Analysts 64

German Medical Society for Psychotherapy 81–2

Germany: collective psychosis 164; history of analytical psychology 49, 63–4

Goering Institute 64

Goering, M. 64, 82

Group for the Advancement of Psychiatry (GAP) 33

Guggenbühl-Craig, A. 53, 131

Guild for Psychological Studies 57–8

Hannah, B. 134

Harding, E. 55, 56, 61, 70, 71, 72, 98–9, 107, 135

health 49

Heidegger, M. 86

Henderson, E. 119

Henderson, E.S. 105–6, 109

Henderson, H. (née Cornford) 109–10, 119

Henderson, J.J. 105

Henderson, J.L. 10, 15, 16, 57, 71, 79, 153–4; 100th birthday 117, 119; analysis and medical training 107–10; and ARAS 116, 117; on archetypes 114–15; beginning practice 110; contact with Jung 111; context and overview 104; declining health 119; extended working life 117; eye infection 105; family business 104–5; interest in art 116; interest in popular culture

116–17; interviews 119; introduction to Jung's work 107; later life 115–19; later meetings with Jung 112–13; later writings 117; marriage and family 109–10; maturity 112–13; in New York 110; origins and early years 104–6; parents 105–6; photos **105, 106, 118, 119**; reactions to Europe 109; return to US 110–11; in San Francisco 110–11; Society of Jungian Analysts of Southern California 117; as student 106–7; summary and conclusions 119–20; visit to Berlin 107; work on culture 115–16; work on initiation 112–15; working with Jung 107–8; as writer 107; writings 112–13; in Zurich 107–8

Henderson, John 105, 106, 107

Henley, E. 71

Hertzberg, B. 151

Heyer, R.G. 63, 64, 124

Hillman, J. 99, 136

Hinkle, B. 54–5

historical material, accuracy 31

history of analytical psychology: Archive for Research in Archetypal Symbolism (ARAS) 56; C.G. Jung Foundation 56–7; C.G. Jung Institute 51–4; context and overview 47; current status 66; development trajectories 50; divisions 61–2; France 66; Freud-Jung relationship 48–9; Germany 49, 63–4; Israel 65; Italy 65; Jung biography 47–8; Jung meets Freud 48; Jung's developing reputation 49, 50–1; later developments in US 60; Los Angeles 59; New York 54–6; professional and lay groups 50; proliferation 66; Research and Training Centre in Depth Psychology 53–4; San Francisco 57–9; Switzerland 50–4; terminology 49; theoretical reformulations 50; United Kingdom 60–3; United States 54–60

Hitler, A. 161

Hoerni, U. 100, 147

Hogenson, G. 148

Howes, E. 57–8

Hull, R.F.C. 149–50

Humbert, E. 66

Husserl, E. 86

I Ching 136, 159

idealization of Jung 162

identity 94

ideological identity 131

Iliad 74

Independent Group of Analytical

170 *Index*

Psychologists (IGAP) 61, 62
individuality: of analysis 7; and responsibility 23–4
individuation 14, 32
infantile psyche 13, 14
influence, extent of 94–5
initiation, Henderson's work 112–15
Initiation: The Reality of and Archetype (ed Hirsch *et al*) 117
instincts 2
intellectualism 15–16
Inter-Regional Society of Jungian Analysts (IRSJA) 60
International Association for Analytical Psychology (IAAP) 49, 52, 65, 89, 97, 98–9, 100, 113, 134, 136
International Association for Jungian Studies (IAJS) 127–8, 137
International Association for the History of Psychanalysis, conference 2000 85–6
International Conference of Medical Women 55
International General Medical Society for Psychotherapy 49, 64, 82, 96
International Medical Association for Psychotherapy 127
International Psychoanalytical Association (IPA) 96, 127
Interpretation of Dreams (Freud) 156
Introduction to Jung's Psychology (Fordham) 150
introversion: energy flow 8; Jung, C.G. 88
intuition 8
Israel, history of analytical psychology 65
Italy, history of analytical psychology 65

Jackson, M. 98–9, 135
Jaffe, A. 31, 37
JAP conferences 29
Jerusalem Congress, 1963 135
Jews 161; as Jungians 164; Jung's apology 164; research into Jung's attitude 163; *see also* Judaism
Journal of Analytical Psychology 49, 61, 99
Jouvet, M. 3
Judaism 142–3; author's history 161ff; context and overview 161; Eissler-Jung interview 164–5; Jung-Kirsch letters 161–2; Jung's vision 165; meetings with Jung and his family 162–3; *see also* anti-Semitism; Jews
Jung, A. 100, 163
Jung and the Post-Jungians (Samuels) 99, 130
Jung-bashing 77
Jung, C.G.: on aims of analysis 17–18;

on archetypes 1–2; autobiography 31, 47; background 30, 80–1; biographical background 47–8; funeral 133; health 49; honors 49; on instincts 2; introversion 88; meeting Freud 48; on the numinous 131; and organizations 65, 127; period of disorientation 96; publications 49–50; range of interests 126; on role of analyst 7; on Semitic psychology 82; *see also* Jews; Judaism; as symbol 94; Tavistock Lectures 109; on training analysis 20; on transference 10; visits to UK 60–1; visits to US 54
Jung, E. (née Rauschenbach) 47–8
Jung-Freud relationship *see* Freud-Jung relationship
Jung-Kirsch letters 161–2, 163; choice of editor 140; context and overview 139–40; context of James Kirsch's analysis 141–3; Jung-Kirsch relationship 141; Kirsch family relationships 141; themes 140–1, 143
Jung-Neumann letters 163
Jung, P. 100
Jung, V. 163
Jungian, being 66–7
"Jungian" – reflections on word: in academic context 127–8; analytical psychology 130–1; author's history 128–9; changing meaning 131–2; context and overview 126; divergence 130; expansion of meanings 126–7; ideological identity 131; Jungian communities 126–8; as preferred term 130; summary and conclusions 132
Jungian analysis: age of analyst and clients 17; aims 17–18; compared to Freudian model 32–3; context and overview 13; countertransference 15; development of relationship 15; dialectical method 13–14; distinct features 18–19; endings 18; final stage 16; growth of 133–4; as intellectual 15–16; locations and spread 137–8; process 32; as risky profession 129, 133, 153; the spiral 16–17; transference 14–16; transference-countertransference 32; as vocation 129

Kerr, J. 31
Kesey, K. 156
Kettner, M. 154
Kimbles, S. 79, 87
Kirsch, E. 142
Kirsch-Edinger interview 69–78
Kirsch family: in London 143; in Palestine 142–3; relationship with Jung 144; in

US 143–4
Kirsch, H. 59, 83, 97; photo **144**; reading Jung 149, 150
Kirsch, J. 36, 37, 38–9, 41, 59, 83, 161; clientele 151; in Los Angeles 143–4; photos **139, 144**; reading Jung 149–50; *see also* Jung-Kirsch letters; Wolff-Kirsch correspondence
Kirsch. T. *see* reading Jung
Klein, M. 33, 135
Klinik am Zurichberg 53
Klopfer, B. 44
Kretschmer, E. 63–4, 82
Kristine Mann Library 55, 75

Lammers, A. 140
Langley Porter Neuropsychiatric Institute 57
Lawrenceville 106, 107
leakage 26
Leary, T. 156
legacy: context and overview 94; extent of influence 95, 99–100; factions 99; focus of chapter 96; Jung as symbol 94; Philemon Foundation 101–2; spread of practice 99–100; summary and conclusions 102
libido, definitions of 54–5
life events and processes 15
logical positivism 131
London developmental school 61
Long, C. 33, 55
Los Angeles 59, 143–4
Lowenfeld, M. 139–40

Maeder, A. 50
Maillard, C. 147
Man and his Symbols 135, 152
mandalas 2
Mann, K. 55
marriage and family 47–8
Martin, S. 102
Medical Society for Analytical Psychology, New York 56
Medical Society for Analytical Psychology, San Francisco 57, 111
medieval alchemy 95
Meier, C.A. 4, 75–6, 151–2
Mellon, M. 55
Mellon, P. 55, 56
Memories, Dreams, Reflections 88, 96, 135, 136, 146–7, 152–3, 154
mental disorder, treatment model 156
Miss M. 42
Modern Man in Search of a Soul 70, 150
Moon, S. 57–8

motifs 2
multiple analyses 89; advantages and disadvantages 17; advantages of 7–8; clinical examples 9–10; communication 8–9; context and overview 7; criticism of 51; as norm 97; personality types 8; training analysis 25–6, 91; transference 10–12; varying attitudes to 11
"Music in Dreams" (Streich) 124
Myers-Briggs Type Inventory (MBTI) 95, 128
Mystic Marriage in the Garden 153

Nazism 36, 49, 63–4, 82–3, 128, 142–3, 162
neonates: REM research 3–4; *see also* children
Neumann, E. 36, 37–8, 65
Neumann, J. 65
Neumann, M. 37
New York 74–5; training 71
New York Association of Analytical Psychology 71–2
New York Jung Foundation 56
North-South Conference 58, 59
Norther Californian Society of Jungian Analysts 57
numinous 131

Oakes, M. 113
object-relation theorists 22
object-relations theory 130, 135
On the History of the Psychoanalytic Movement (Freud) 50, 81
organizations, Jung's attitude to 49, 65, 127
Ostrowski, Frau 44–5
ownership: family's position 96, 100–1; of Jung 94, 99; of psychoanalysis 94; *see also* legacy

Papadopoulos, R. 63, 137
pathological nexus 27
personal analysis, limits of 92
personal equation 7, 14
personal unconscious 2
personality types 8, 14; *see also* psychological types
Philemon Foundation 101–2
Pound, E. 29
Pratt, J. 56
primordial images 88
Princeton 106
professional associations 34, 50, 53; Jung's attitude to 96; *see also* individual organizations
psyche, infantile 13, 14
psychic energy, flow of 8
psychoanalysis: changes to 85; review and

172 *Index*

changes 34–5
"psychoanalyst," use of title 94
psychological types 49; recognition of 19; training analysis 89; *see also* personality types
Psychological Types 49, 95, 97, 128
Psychology and Alchemy 17–18
Psychology of the Unconscious 49, 97
publications 55–6; translations 100; *see also* writings
puer aeternus/puella aeterna 114, 136

quoting from Jung 94–5

racial unconscious 29–30
Rasche, J. 122
reading Jung: analysis 152; analytic training 153–4; at college 151; context and overview 149; early experience of unconscious 153; family background 149–50; making a start 150–1; at medical school 151–2; and medical training 157–8; meetings with Jung 151–2, 162–3; necessity of 158–9; personal meaning and significance 152–3; psychiatric residency 152–3; relevance 159; at Stanford Hospital 156; in Zurich 150; *see also* individual titles
Red Book Conference 162
Relational School 143
relationship, development of 15
religion 37, 72, 126
REM research: and analytical psychology 2–4; cat studies 3, 4; experimental approach 4–5; and Jung's theory of dreams 1–2; neonates 3–4; REM deprivation 3; summary and conclusions 5; variations in REM 5; *see also* dreams
Research and Training Centre in Depth Psychology 53–4
"Resolution of the Transference in the Light of C.G. Jung's Psychology" (Henderson) 112
responsibility, and individuality 23–4
Rickman, J. 63
Roffwarg, H. 3
Rosen, D. 137

Samuels, A. 62, 63, 99, 130, 137, 163
Scholem, G. 124
schools of thought 61, 74–5
Schultz-Henke, H. 64
Selesnick, S.T. 83
Self, archetype and symbols 10–11
seminars 51, 88–9
sensation 8

Seven Sermons to the Dead 31–2
shamanic initiation 23
shamanism 131
Shamdasani, S. 50, 100, 102, 146
Sherman, J. 75
Sherry, J. 163
Sherwood, D. 117
Silber, H. 38
Singer, T. 79, 87
Society of Analytical Psychology (SAP) 33, 34, 61, 62, 96, 98–9, 134
Society of Jungian Analysts of Southern California 59, 117
Sorge, G. 163
soul food, search for 159
Spielrein, S. 36, 48
spiral 16–17
stereotypes 116
Streich, H. 122–4; photo **123**
Studies in Hysteria (Freud and Breuer) 80, 154
Stuttgart 64
supervision 26
Sussmann, T. 142
Switzerland, history of analytical psychology 50–4
symbolic amplification 15–16
symbolic friendship 15
symbolic vs. developmental divide, training analysis 90
symbols 16–17
symptoms, nature of 18
synthetic-hermeneutic view 13

Tavistock Lectures 109
Taylor, C. 75
termination, temporary 17–18
terminology, variations in usage 32, 49
Thackrey, S. 147
"The Archetype of Culture" (Henderson) 79, 114
The Collected Works 37, 149–50, 152
The History of the Psychoanalytic Movement (Freud) 161
The Red Book 31, 96, 100, 137–8, 146–8, 154–5
The Secret of the Golden Flower 147
The State of Psychotherapy Today 161
"The Synthetic or Constructive Method" 155
The Wisdom of the Serpent (Henderson and Oakes) 113
theories, applications of 127
theory of dreams 1–2
theory of psychological types 8, 49
therapeutic communities 156

Thibaudier, V. 32
thinking 8
Thresholds of Initiation (Henderson) 114, 119
training: accreditation 52; C.G. Jung Institute, Zurich 97–8; changes in 52; early haphazardness 97; elements of 52–3; as erratic 51; formalization 89; Jung's attitude to 127; New York 58, 71; San Francisco 58; schools of 51; variations in 135
training analysis 14; age and maturation 24; boundary issues 90–1; candidate background and suitability 21; candidate evaluation 22–3; centrality of 21–2; context and overview 20, 88; core concepts 89–90; definition of 21; dialectical method 90; dreams 89; ego demands 23; endings 27; historical introduction 88–9; importance of 20; institutionalization 21; Jung's practice 88–9; limits of 92; multiple analyses 25–6, 51, 91; nature of 91–2; pre-training 22; psychological issues 25; psychological types 89; requirements 22, 91–2; rivalry 25; role of control analyst 26; summary and conclusions 27; supervision 26; symbolic vs. developmental divide 90; training issues 90–1; transference-countertransference 24–5, 27, 89; US and European guidelines 90
training analysts 21, 90
transference: clinical examples 10–11; exploration of 13; Freud-Jung relationship 30; Jungian analysis 14–16, 32; multiple analyses 10–12; quoting from Jung 94–5; training analysis 24–5, 27, 89
transference neurosis 15
transformation 14
translations 100
travel, difficulties of 97
Trüb, H. 44
trust 19
Tucci, G. 37
Two Essays on Analytical Psychology 151, 154–5, 162–3

unconscious: collective 88; and cultural complexes 86–7; personal and collective 2; racial 29–30; reality of 18
United Kingdom: history of analytical psychology 60–3; as key location 137
United Kingdom Council for Psychotherapy (UKCP) 62

United States 34; history of analytical psychology 54–60; training guidelines 90
University of Essex, Centre for Psychoanalytic Studies 63

Vienna 80
visions 146–7, 153, 165
Voegeli, Y. 140
Von Franz group 53–4
Von Franz, M.L. 23, 53, 98, 134, 136

wall decoration from Tiryns 17
Watts, A. 113
Weiss, E. 36–7
Weltanschauung 14
Wheelright, Jane 57, 108–9
Wheelright, Jo 33, 57, 108–9, 111
Whitmont, C. 56, 72
Whitney, C. 57
Whitney, E. 107
Whitney, J. Sr 57, 107
Wickes, F. 55
Wiener, J. 66
Wilder, T. 106
Wilhelm, R. 49, 159
Wilmer, H. 156
Winnicott, D.W. 33, 135
wise old woman 11
Wolff-Kirsch correspondence: Analytical Psychology Club 41–2; anima/animus 43; arthritis 45; biographical background 40–1; context and overview 40; evaluation of 45; Frau Ostrowski 44–5; Goethe lecture 42; Klopfer, B. 44; Los Angeles 43, 44–5; origins of 41; redwood 44; screenwriter 43–4; Trüb, H. 44; Wolff-Jung relationship 43–4
Wolff, T. 36, 37, 40–1, 47–8, 89, 97, 111
word association test 79
world view 14
writings 95; *see also* publications; individual titles
Wyles, S. 75

Zabriskie, P. 75
Zeller, L. 59
Zeller, M. 43, 59
Zentrum 98
Zofingia lectures 31
Zurich: as center 136; *see also* C.G. Jung Institute, Zurich
Zurich classical school 61
Zurich Psychoanalytical Association 50

Taylor & Francis eBooks

Helping you to choose the right eBooks for your Library

Add Routledge titles to your library's digital collection today. Taylor and Francis ebooks contains over 50,000 titles in the Humanities, Social Sciences, Behavioural Sciences, Built Environment and Law.

Choose from a range of subject packages or create your own!

Benefits for you
- Free MARC records
- COUNTER-compliant usage statistics
- Flexible purchase and pricing options
- All titles DRM-free.

Benefits for your user
- Off-site, anytime access via Athens or referring URL
- Print or copy pages or chapters
- Full content search
- Bookmark, highlight and annotate text
- Access to thousands of pages of quality research at the click of a button.

REQUEST YOUR FREE INSTITUTIONAL TRIAL TODAY

Free Trials Available
We offer free trials to qualifying academic, corporate and government customers.

eCollections – Choose from over 30 subject eCollections, including:

Archaeology	Language Learning
Architecture	Law
Asian Studies	Literature
Business & Management	Media & Communication
Classical Studies	Middle East Studies
Construction	Music
Creative & Media Arts	Philosophy
Criminology & Criminal Justice	Planning
Economics	Politics
Education	Psychology & Mental Health
Energy	Religion
Engineering	Security
English Language & Linguistics	Social Work
Environment & Sustainability	Sociology
Geography	Sport
Health Studies	Theatre & Performance
History	Tourism, Hospitality & Events

For more information, pricing enquiries or to order a free trial, please contact your local sales team:
www.tandfebooks.com/page/sales

 Routledge | The home of
Taylor & Francis Group | Routledge books

www.tandfebooks.com